"*Chrysalis Crisis* provides a treasure tr[...] s
gleaned from several decades of enl[...]
apy by a leading clinical psychologis[...] 1
instructive life experiences, Frank Pasciuti deftly weaves a tapestry of
sage analysis in sharing and integrating deep lessons through stories of
people coming into the true purpose of their lives, many driven by the
challenges of hardship—the engine that strengthens us most as human
beings. Brilliant work!"

—Eben Alexander, MD, Neurosurgeon and author of
Proof of Heaven and *Living in a Mindful Universe*

"In *Chrysalis Crisis*, psychotherapist Frank Pasciuti provides a majestic
analysis of how life's challenges can lead to psychological and spiritual
transformation. This is a remarkable, inspiring book by an imminently
wise, compassionate expert. I can think of no one who will not benefit
from it. Highly recommended!"

—Larry Dossey, MD, Author of *Healing Words: The Power of Prayer and
the Practice of Medicine*, and *One Mind: How Our Individual Mind is Part of
a Greater Consciousness and Why It Matters*

"When a psychological crisis intrudes into the domain of the so-called
"paranormal," the conventional reaction in healthcare usually involves
alarm bells, orderlies in white coats, and heavy duty medication. But
sometimes other treatments are far more effective. Sometimes the bewil-
dering, hair-raising experiences that seem to violate commonsense can
also presage enormously positive transformative breakthroughs. After
40 years as a clinical psychologist, Frank Pasciuti learned how to differentiate between the abnormal and the supernormal. In *Chrysalis Crisis*,
he explains why that distinction is vitally important."

—Dean Radin, Ph.D., Chief scientist at the Institute of Noetic Sciences,
and Associate Distinguished Professor at the California Institute of Integral
Studies. Author of *Supernormal, Entangled Minds*, and *The Conscious Universe*

"In *Chrysalis Crisis*, Frank Pasciuti provides techniques for turning life crises into growth opportunities, spicing his guidance liberally with concrete examples from his clients' struggles and from his own. This book will be helpful for both counselors and for people facing critical life junctures. But people not currently in crisis will also appreciate this insightful blend of wisdom and compassion: I know I did. *Chrysalis Crisis* is an invaluable guide to living a more enriched and fulfilling life."

—Bruce Greyson, M.D., Professor Emeritus of psychiatry at the University of Virginia, and one of the founders of the International Association for Near-Death Studies. Co-author of *Irreducible Mind*

"In crisis there is opportunity! Dr. Frank Pasciuti wisely elaborates on this ancient idea. He leads progressively through life's major challenges in the physical, the psychological, and then the spiritual. Through carefully drawn portraits of his patients and his own poignant illustrations, he shows us how to turn the terrifying events of our lives into psycho-spiritual transformation."

—Bernard Beitman, M.D., Visiting Professor at The University of Virginia and former Chair of the Department of Psychiatry at the University of Missouri. Author of *Connecting with Coincidence*

"Dotted with rich case histories, this accessible book explores a big idea: The crises of life are also opportunities for transformation. Dr. Pasciuti gives his reader precious pointers toward learning how to convert their crises into creative advance."

—Michael Grosso, Ph.D., Philosopher and researcher at The University of Virginia's Division of Perceptual Studies. Author of *Soulmaking, The Final Choice, Experiencing the New World Now*, and *Wings of Ecstasy*

CHRYSALIS CRISIS

How Life's Ordeals Can Lead to
Personal & Spiritual Transformation

FRANK PASCIUTI, Ph.D.

RAINBOW RIDGE
BOOKS

Cover and interior design by Frame25 Productions
Cover photos © ArchMan c/o Shutterstock.com and
Avdeenko c/o Shutterstock.com

Published by:
Rainbow Ridge Books, LLC
140 Rainbow Ridge Road
Faber, Virginia 22938
www.rainbowridgebooks.com

If you are unable to order this book from your local
bookseller, you may order directly from the distributor.

Square One Publishers, Inc.
115 Herricks Road
Garden City Park, NY 11040
Phone: (516) 535-2010
Fax: (516) 535-2014
Toll-free: 877-900-BOOK

Library of Congress Control Number: 2019937996

ISBN 978-1-937907-60-0

10 9 8 7 6 5 4 3 2 1

Printed in the United States of America through
The P.A. Hutchison Company, Mayfield, PA

To Lavinia and Italo

Contents

*"If you want to change the world,
start with yourself."*

—Mahatma Gandhi

Preface

Watching a caterpillar transform into a butterfly fascinated the little girl. Each day she would examine the cocoon that was dangling from a tree in her yard. She eagerly awaited the end of its dormant chrysalis stage where it remained inside its silky structure. When the outer shell of the cocoon began to open, the girl's excitement grew. As she witnessed the awakened butterfly reveal its beautiful wings and begin the process of shedding its cocoon, she could hardly contain herself.

While she watched the butterfly struggle to free its wings from the cocoon's hold, she felt sorry for it and thought it might need some assistance. Unfortunately, not knowing the consequence of touching its wings to help free it, she found that after she did, the butterfly fell to the ground and eventually died. She was devastated. She wasn't aware that the butterfly's effort to emancipate itself was *a necessary struggle,* a struggle that had two purposes: One is to free itself from the cocoon, but the other is to strengthen its wings for future flight.

The butterfly's *struggle* reflects the challenges we face when seeking to free ourselves from the impact of a crisis, and how that struggle can contribute to our transformation. We need to adjust to the crisis so that it can also produce the kinds of growth that will strengthen us for our remaining flight through life. That's why when personal growth is acquired in response to a given crisis, I refer to the ordeal as a *Chrysalis Crisis*.

This book is about how your life ordeals can serve as Chrysalis Crises, and how the personal and spiritual development you gain from them can awaken your potential for joy, peace, and happiness.

Introduction

Helping people realize their optimal potential in life has been the primary focus of my 40 years of working as a clinical psychologist. When I'm initially called upon for assistance, the therapy process often starts by addressing the crisis that brought the individual in for help.

Over time, after helping many people adjust to crises, it became evident that most of them struggle with just one or a few key areas of growth while making that necessary adjustment. Some need to become more aware of their feelings; some have to examine and modify their intellectual beliefs; some need to focus on the state of their physical and material wellbeing; and others required growth in areas of social or spiritual functioning, for example.

I also noticed that certain individuals who weren't my clients showed similar kinds of needed development. And when I took a more personal inventory, I saw that I was no less exempt from the need of growth in some of these areas. They're common to everyone. They constitute the obvious, and not so obvious, dimensions of being human, and span the full spectrum of consciousness.

Based on those observations, I sought to quantify where the majority of those areas of growth most frequently presented challenges, and categorized them into *ten key areas of human growth and development*. Though they cover a very broad range of human expression, they're all critical for our day-to-day functioning and overall evolution.

I address each key area in one of three main sections of this book. In the first section, I'll share numerous examples that will show how *physical, intellectual, emotional, moral,* and *social growth* can be prompted by crises. These five areas of growth and development are basic to all people. They enable us to survive, relate, and function in community with others. They're addressed in section one: *The Key Areas of Foundational Development.*

In section two, I examine the next three areas of growth and development. While they're less critical for survival or living in community with others, their growth can aid us on a more individual level. They help us find a personal direction in life, deepen how we function in relationships, and enable us to discover our own meaning and purpose for living. These key areas are *identity, intimacy,* and *existential growth.* That section is entitled, *The Key Areas of Personal Development.*

I'll then move on to address the last two key areas of development. These are the areas of *Intuitive* and *Spiritual growth.* While the names of these two areas are familiar to most, the particular experiences associated with their functioning often are not. For that reason, I'll give them more extensive treatment. That's because when individuals have actual intuitive or spiritual experiences, they frequently can become boggled or frightened. And sometimes, the very foreignness of those experiences can give rise to a crisis.

By their very nature, intuitive experiences tend to be subtle and elusive. They typically lie outside our usual states of conscious awareness and are said to arise from the subliminal levels of our minds. Some manifestations of intuitive experiences can include, but are not be limited to, functions of a psychic nature. These phenomena are widely misunderstood, feared, or rejected. My experience suggests, however, that on certain occasions, they really do occur, so when people report those experiences to me, a good deal of clarity and understanding is needed.

Similarly, while many spiritual experiences are regarded as positive, some of them also can be viewed as foreign or frightening. This confusion partially may be explained by spirituality's long-standing entanglement with religion. I've found that people can have actual spiritual experiences whether they hold religious beliefs or not, yet those with certain religious biases can sometimes misinterpret or distort spiritual experiences by inappropriately sanctifying or demonizing them. In either case, they warrant clarification, too.

Despite misunderstandings, misinterpretations, or confusions, I'll show how actual intuitive and spiritual experiences occur, explain what is known that contributes to their manifestation, and provide credible scientific support for their validity.

I've spent a good part of my professional career as a clinical psychologist attempting to bring clarity to these experiences, disentangling those that are valid from experiences of psychopathology. They're not all delusions and hallucinations. However, they do typically extend beyond the usual boundaries of our personal awareness. I call these: *The Key Areas of Transpersonal Development.* They can be found in section three.

In the final section of the book, entitled *Evolution, Practice, and Synthesis,* I'll share a map of consciousness and show where the ten keys lie on its overall landscape. I'll also provide specific techniques and methods for the higher development of each key and describe how at that higher level they can enhance or detract from the growth of the others. Lastly, I provide an example of how the evolving synergy of all ten areas of growth can contribute to a life of greater contentment, love, and happiness.

Before we begin, however, I want to emphasize one last point. I elected to examine the ten key areas of growth through the vantage point of crises because their drama will heighten your attention and amplify why certain areas of growth are needed. But *you don't have to undergo a crisis to gain personal growth*. While you can pursue it at any time, crises are unique opportunities in which growth is essential to avoid stagnation or regression. Remember, the butterfly needed to struggle in order to break out. Yet whether you seek growth to diminish the pain of a crisis, or aspire to attain it when you're not under duress, understanding the ten key ways it can be acquired will provide you with a blueprint for what you seek.

In summary, my overall intention for this book is to show how people not only adjusted and healed from their ordeals, but in using those ordeals as Chrysalis Crises, discovered their dormant potentials and personally transformed as a result.

CHAPTER 1

How Life Ordeals Can be Used as Chrysalis Crises

For as long as I can remember I've been told there are two things we can count on in this world: that everything changes, and that there always will be a certain amount of suffering in life. I've found that the changes are not always evident, nor the suffering constant, but both are typically present at times of crisis.

We have all faced a crisis at some point in our lives. As you know, they come in all shapes and forms. If a crisis results from an act of nature, like a tornado, earthquake, or hurricane, their impact will be obvious. Hopefully, you'll have ensured your physical safety, battened down the hatches, and picked up the pieces of your life afterwards. But the majority of crises are not so obvious and may not threaten our lives or affect our basic survival. Many take their toll on a more intimate level. Their consequences can be less physically evident and difficult for others to appreciate, unless they've had similar life experiences.

Crises that are more intimate and less physically perceptible can result from the death of a loved one, sudden unemployment, legal struggles, personal isolation, loss of self-direction, the ending of a relationship, or the inability to find meaning in what we do.

Other crises arise from even less evident causes. They result from our own internal perceptions. These subjective experiences can feel foreign or threatening, and because they also may conflict with what culture accepts as real based on shared experiences, they might lead us to question our sanity.

Each of us have different levels of ability in how we adjust to crisis. For instance, if faced with the death of a loved one, we may have varying capacities to emotionally come to terms with that loss. Some may not be able to reconcile the many feelings that get stirred.

But reconciling feelings that result during a crisis is only one area of functioning where we can be challenged to heal. We might also be challenged physically, intellectually, or spiritually, for example.

Our ability to cope with a given crisis will depend on how well those areas were functioning *before* the crisis. If some were lacking earlier, and that deficient area is required to heal, then adjusting to its impact will be that much more of a struggle. But *there's an upside to that struggle.*

For instance, if we suddenly lost someone we loved, we likely would have a host of different feelings. They could be feelings of sadness, fear, anger, or a combination of all. If our ability to identify and express any or all of our feelings was limited before the loss, and we have to learn how to experience them in order to heal, then the suffering caused by the crisis will have prompted us to gain that needed emotional growth.

However, if in the aftermath of a crisis we have the opportunity, resources, and inclination to pursue such growth, then the effort will not only contribute to our overall adjustment, it will also bring forth needed personal development that can benefit us thereafter. That's how a crisis can serve as a Chrysalis Crisis.

I use the analogy of the chrysalis to describe the kinds of crises that can be used for growth and transformation because I believe that the chrysalis stage of a caterpillar's transformation into a butterfly best captures the conditions and requirements of achieving such potentials from crises.

The transformation of the caterpillar into a butterfly has a long history of being used to represent the awakening of our psychological and spiritual potentials. Christians have employed it for centuries. St. Teresa paralleled the silkworm's slow transformation out of the darkness of its cocoon to represent the human journey out of what her protégé, St. John of the Cross, called a "Dark Night of the Soul." She saw that journey out of darkness as a necessary stage on route to further awakening the soul.

The early Greeks also drew a relationship between personal transformation and spiritual evolution. They even used the same word to denote soul and butterfly.

I decided to use the chrysalis metaphor to describe the transformative potential of a crisis for three specific reasons. First, like the caterpillar in the chrysalis stage, we're vulnerable when we're going through a crisis. Once the caterpillar surrounds itself in a cocoon, it's defenseless. It can be invaded and devoured by insects. It can get blown down from its dangling hold, or when ready to open, it can be blocked by an object. Unfortunately, should any of these situations occur, they can lead to tragic outcomes from which it can't recover.

We also can be met with insurmountable consequences from certain kinds of crises, and when that's the case, we, too, may not recover. But if we do, then there's a second reason why I believe the chrysalis metaphor applies.

During the chrysalis stage, the caterpillar undergoes the internal process of metamorphosis, a phase where it liquefies and literally melts down. This stage reflects a process we can go through following a crisis. After we survive and overcome its initial impact, our adjustment also will entail a certain amount of internal changes. But during that period, we too may feel as if we're going through our version of a meltdown.

To pursue the potential for growth and transformation that lies beyond that adjustment requires an additional effort. It requires the willingness to engage in the struggle for growth. Let me provide you with another example.

Recall those early teen years when you or someone near to you went through what Anna Freud called, "the storm and stress of adolescence." Prompted by raging hormones, early adolescence tends to be a challenging time in our development as we learn to identify, understand, and manage the expression of our emotions.

Now imagine if that stage of emotional development never was sufficiently mastered. Imagine if instead of being helped to identify, understand, and modulate the expression of your feelings, you were told you shouldn't have them, that some were bad, or you were ridiculed for their expression. Can you also imagine how over time you might learn to unwittingly keep them out of your own awareness, even when certain circumstances might warrant their experience?

If this were the case, how would you come to terms with the many feelings that can get prompted by a crisis? Like the butterfly attempting to break free from its cocoon, you certainly would have a struggle on your hands. But also like the butterfly, once you gained that emotional growth, it would serve you for the rest of your flight through life.

In this way, a Chrysalis Crisis can be like a stress test from the universe. It can lead to the development of key areas of functioning that will be available for similar crises in the future. However, beyond the assurance of being adequately prepared for a similar future crisis, developing critical areas of needed growth can provide other opportunities as you move through life. They can be used to awaken and expand awareness.

Like the dual meaning the Chinese attribute to their word for crisis, a Chrysalis Crisis can present *danger* and *opportunity*. In a Chrysalis Crisis, the danger comes from the initial threat of the crisis; the opportunity lies in its potential to prompt growth and development.

Should your life be met with a crisis, it too can hold such possibilities. But in order to determine if it has the potential to be a Chrysalis Crisis, you'll need to give it further examination. At a point when you feel that the initial shock and impact have been absorbed, you'll want to start by asking a few self-reflective questions.

First, in adjusting to this crisis, have I discovered areas of my personal development that appear to need additional growth or understanding? If certain areas stand out, then I would ask a second question: How can I gain this increased development? And finally, a third: Can this kind of growth be achieved independently, or would it be more successfully attained if I sought outside help and assistance?

As I've indicated, a crisis may or may not hold the potential to be a Chrysalis Crisis. But when it does, and the opportunity to achieve significant developmental growth can come about as a result, then in my opinion, deriving that benefit can leave you feeling less victimized by its ordeal. While it may be a small consolation, you would at least gain some satisfaction if it awakened you to certain areas of needed growth. Then, if attained, the ordeal won't feel as if it were some random painful event that led to no apparent good.

If you have to contend with the suffering of a crises, why not let it serve as a Chrysalis Crisis? Let its fire temper the steel of your development. Let it prompt you to become stronger than you were before. If you have to accept the inevitability of the change it thrusts upon you, harness its momentum. Let it catalyze your progress along a path of growth and transformation.

Yes, I'm aware that to some of you this may sound a little too much like attempting to make heavenly lemonade out of the hellish lemons of life. You may think it's too optimistic to suggest that the change and suffering accompanying a crisis can actually provide "opportunities" for positive transformation.

I recognize that personal development may not be your first priority when facing a crisis. And I'm not naïve to the many kinds of devastating crises that can occur in people's lives. But when I, as a clinical psychologist, see much of that suffering displayed in the confines of my office, I'm continually amazed at the resilience of the people who share that pain with me: how they not only succeed in diminishing its sting but use it to prompt their growth.

Even if my optimistic encouragement motivates you to consider the possibilities for growth in your crises, you may still ask: Why bother? Where is all this development and transformation leading? Do I have to use this crisis as grist for my growth mill? Why not just get through the ordeal and put it behind me as quickly as possible?

These are legitimate questions and they're certainly worth considering. Their answers are critical to justifying the effort because using a crisis as a Chrysalis Crisis is clearly not an endeavor everyone will elect to undertake—nor should they feel they must. *There's no one right way one ought to adjust to a crisis.* Pursuing personal growth is a choice at any time. And while it may be an occupational bias that leads me to encourage that choice, I truly believe it's one worth making.

I've facilitated and witnessed scores of clients gain significant benefits from the efforts they made adjusting to crises. I've seen them make dramatic changes afterwards. As a result, they not only reinstated a sense of balance and harmony into their lives but actually seemed personally and spiritually deepened by the experience.

Certainly, most would not want to go through their ordeal again, but as inconceivable as it may sound, many will acknowledge that if it wasn't for the crisis, and the choice they made to use it as a Chrysalis Crisis, much of what they needed to learn might never have come to their attention.

I've found that when a particular area of personal growth is needed to resolve a crisis, understanding what constitutes that growth, and what's entailed in achieving it, can effectively be illuminated in the context of a crisis. That's why I've elected to use examples of crises to explore and amplify the areas of growth we'll examine. Different kinds of crises focus and dramatize particular areas of growth. One kind of crisis can reveal how lacking a certain area of development may have caused it to arise, while another will show how the absence of particular area of development undermined the individual's adjustment.

In addition to these purposes, there are other reasons why I employ specific and composite examples of certain types of crises. Some are stories of crises that I professionally treated—the ones that most challenged me to seek understanding about a given area of growth. Some are descriptions of crises I personally experienced.

With those, the understanding and knowledge I gained came as a result of my own struggle. And finally, some of the examples of crises were experienced by individuals who were nearby and related to me. They afforded an ongoing perspective on how they adjusted to their crisis and functioned in life afterwards.

All of these crises contributed to my education. They not only helped me clarify and articulate what I learned, but their examples can serve as a teaching tool. And because it's my intention to show you how to achieve growth from crisis, sharing how others succeeded in doing so will humanize the effort. It makes the struggle more relatable. It instills hope. And it shows that sometimes good things *can* come from crisis situations.

I don't need to venture far to come up with my initial example. The following experience intimately touched my life. It served as my first inspiration for writing this book. Long before I ever imagined a career in clinical psychology, it showed me how personal growth can come from crisis. It evidenced the power of the human spirit, and it helped me gain compassion for those less fortunate to achieve such results.

CHAPTER 2

Lovey's Story

Lavinia was the seventh oldest of 11 children residing in a 14-unit brick apartment building in Newark, New Jersey. Attractive, with pitch black hair and a quick smile, she was a high energy girl whose charm, wit, and outgoingness won her many friends and the favor of her siblings.

Though she had a thirst for knowledge and loved to read, her formal education only went through the 10th grade. It was the 1930s, and she took on full time employment so she could contribute to her family's recovery from the Depression.

Lovey, as everyone called her, dated a number of young men before she eventually won the fancy of Frank. They became increasingly more serious after a few years of dating and decided to make a lifelong commitment to each other. Prior to making that commitment legal, however, it was tested significantly.

Not too long before they were to marry, Lovey started having trouble maintaining her balance. Normally athletic and coordinated, it was foreign for her to not feel in command of her body.

Her sister Sophie noted that on the job, Lovey occasionally would start swaying and had to brace herself so she didn't fall.

Lovey recalled one occasion when she and Frank were leaving a nightclub. As she was maneuvering between the tables and heading towards the door, she stumbled. She felt embarrassed, imagining others thought she probably had too much to drink. That wasn't the case, and the stumbling grew increasingly more frequent.

Soon Lovey's physical condition deteriorated to the point where it was thought she might have contracted Lou Gehrig's disease (ALS). This preliminary diagnosis was devastating. Lovey, Frank, and their families assumed she was facing the possibility of an early death.

In time it became apparent that she did not have ALS, but had developed Multiple Sclerosis (MS). Little was known about the progression of MS at that time, and Lovey feared that it, too, might be fatal.

Her life had taken a dramatic turn for the worse, and Lovey's future was looking bleak. In light of that reality, she told Frank that she would understand if he did not want to marry her. But Frank loved her and held out hope for her recovery, so they went through with their plans.

In addition to Frank's support, Lovey's parents, sisters, and brothers rallied around her. As a family, they had known tragedy before. Two of their other siblings had died, one in his first year of life from a virus, and their oldest sibling, a few years before Lovey was born, by accidently setting herself on fire while playing with matches.

Not too long after Frank and Lovey married, she became completely confined to a wheelchair. Frustrated and frightened, she forged on with what she still thought might be a shortened life.

Lovey was in crisis. She found herself struggling with existential questions about death at a time in life when most young people are in their physical prime. In response, she set out to learn all she could about survival and the afterlife. As it became clear that conventional medicine could offer little hope, she developed an interest in finding any alternative cures for her sickness.

Her quest for answers took her to all available sources. She was open to any avenue for gaining existential or spiritual understanding, not limiting herself to any one particular religious path. She took the same approach in her investigation of alternative cures.

The openness of her search was a little easier to undertake because she grew up in a family that embraced and tolerated different religious perspectives, as well as alternative ideas about healing. That openness, tolerance, and alternative thinking had started with her parents.

Her mother was a committed Catholic. She made daily morning pilgrimages to the nearby church and strongly believed in the power of prayer. Her father, on the other hand was a Protestant and less of a churchgoer. However, he embraced beliefs arising from the spiritualist movement in 19th century Europe.

Her parents' different religious influences and diverse beliefs made for an interesting family mix. Lovey was affected by both. While she embraced her mother's Catholicism, she also found her father's spiritualist ideas intriguing.

One belief of her father's that she found particularly interesting was the notion that the mind can influence the physical world and affect the body. It seemed to her that the miracles of the Catholic saints, and the reported results of spiritualists engaging in activities such as hypnosis, might share a common cause. The possibility that one's mind could heal or hinder the body became most curious to her at the time of her sickness. She already wondered if her thoughts and emotions played a part in causing the MS because just prior to her first symptoms she had been extremely upset by the death of a very close friend.

The ways in which mind might influence matter had long intrigued her. Early in her life she recalled how her father would gather around the kitchen table with certain friends and a few of her brothers, and they'd attempt to move a glass with just their thoughts. Interests such as these, and the general spiritual openness of her parents, all contributed to Lovey's curiosity. It also prompted a search by a few of her siblings. One brother's search had a strong influence on Lovey. His name was Italo.

Like Lovey, Italo's interest in the mind's potential began with the influence of their father, but his curiosity intensified after he had an anomalous experience during the Second World War. When he returned from the war, he was motivated to understand what could explain his strange battlefield event. He shared what he was learning with Lovey, and it inspired her to undertake her own search about what could be learned about the inner workings of the mind.

As a result of her search, Lovey also discovered the benefits of undertaking certain techniques that could aid the self-investigation of her own mind. She began to regularly meditate and keep a journal. And though what she learned and the techniques she employed did not cure her MS, another interesting result came about: they had a therapeutic and calming effect on her. The anxiety she felt about dying significantly decreased, and her overall sense of meaning and purpose in life deepened.

Lovey's crisis, and the lessons she learned in an effort to absorb and integrate its impact, brought about a significant transformation in her life. It affected both the acceptance of her situation and buoyed her overall disposition. Those closest to her said that she largely maintained a positive attitude, displayed a contagious sense of humor, and even when frustrated, quickly returned to her all-is-well smile.

Lovey continued to live well beyond her initial prognosis. And though she contracted a severe form of MS, after a few years, her symptoms stabilized. Once she accommodated to their limitations, she and Frank decided to go ahead and start a family. But not too long after the birth of their first child, Lovey's life took another difficult turn. Again, her inner resiliency was tested. But this time the ordeal was prompted by a crisis brought about by Frank.

Like many men who have difficulty when their wife's attentions turn to the needs of their first child, Frank felt a bit like he got cut out of the herd. In response, he found solace in his long-standing habit of gambling. Unfortunately, the losses he incurred from gambling added to the financial pressures of a growing family. Those pressures grew even more when Lovey became pregnant with their second child. They were also added to by the increasing demands of his job, and in combination, became a perfect storm for what followed.

Frank worked as a bookkeeper for an employer who began to ask more and more of him. From Frank's perspective, his boss took advantage of his vulnerable situation at home and exploited what he knew was a desperate need to maintain employment. He frequently would ask Frank to stay longer during weekdays and put in extra time on weekends. Frank became resentful. He felt as if he was being dealt another bad hand.

His life situation weighed heavy on him. It was a lot of pressure. He felt burdened. But Frank was not one to be aware of his feelings, nor did he manage them well when they surfaced. So he distracted himself from their underlying discomfort by increasingly engaging in his two main forms of coping: compulsive gambling and compulsive overeating.

Eventually, both got out of control. He gained a lot of weight and lost a lot of money. Then, like a lightning bolt flashing out of that perfect storm of dysfunctional conditions, Frank got an idea that would dramatically change the course of his life, unfortunately, for the worse. He conjured up a plan of how he could eliminate his most pressing problem of not having enough money. It led him to make a very poor choice; a choice that took him from the proverbial frying pan into the fire.

Frank decided to "borrow" a significant sum of money from his boss's petty cash fund. He found a clever way he could redirect monies from the business to himself without detection. After accumulating a fairly sizable amount, he told his boss he needed to take an emergency leave of absence. He then flew out to Las Vegas. He figured he could use the cash to make a "big score," and then he'd return the money.

Recognizing that he was engaging in embezzlement, he left behind a confession note. He figured that by doing so, once he returned the money, the courts would go easy on him—especially in light of his situation at home. Predictably, however, in Las Vegas, the house won. Frank lost all the money, and he ended up going to jail for two years.

Still pregnant, Lovey was now faced with single parenting a toddler with another child on the way. Her life became unmanageable. In an incredible gesture of giving, her older sister invited Lovey and her daughter to move in with her family. But with a husband and three children of her own, their two-bedroom apartment burst at the seams.

A few months later, that space became even more limited, because at 4:44 a.m. on Labor Day, Lovey gave birth to me. But her pains did not subside with the coincident occurrence of laboring on that day. Despite her stubborn Taurus nature, her never say die attitude, and her recently cultivated psycho-spiritual resilience, she received yet another blow shortly afterward—and this one was a knockout punch.

In what started to resemble the trials of Job, a few months after my birth she found herself again looking at the possibility of death. This time, from contracting yet another sickness: Erysipelas.

Erysipelas is a highly contagious bacterial skin infection. Mom's already compromised immune system from the MS made her more susceptible to it. She was particularly vulnerable to one of its more virulent forms in her postpartum condition. She had to be hospitalized for a considerable period of time. With dad still 20 months from being released, my aunt and her husband could not care for the three children and two babies, so the decision was made to send me to live with my grandparents.

Mom now found herself enduring a long-term hospitalization, receiving ice baths to bring down her fevers, separation from her children and husband, and for a short while again threatened with the possibility of death.

I recall when she first told me years later about that low point. I was taken aback by the perspective she shared. It seemed to accompany the acceptance she employed at that time and largely exhibited throughout the years I knew her. It established itself in her initial adjustment to the MS and became further strengthened by the life crises that followed.

When I queried her as to how with her fighting spirit she could accept such a life fate, she said she believed it was all a part of a greater plan for her soul's evolution. She had faith in that. And she also said that in light of that belief, she ultimately realized that she had to surrender completely, the kind of surrender that the Alcoholic Anonymous program suggests as the need to "let go and let God."

I asked her if it was hard to forgive my dad for making her life that much more difficult back when he went to jail, and thereafter when his continuing gambling created ongoing financial problems for our family. She said, "He accepted me with my sickness, so I've accepted him with his." Those were powerful words that I'll never forget, and for me they added a deeper appreciation of the vow many of us make in our own marriages: "for better and for worse."

Dad was less inclined to talk about those years, or to be very self- disclosing or self-examining about his life in general. I never heard him reflect about the conditions that brought on his crisis. While he learned his lesson about not stealing, he learned little about his emotional life, nor was he inclined to give much thought to any of the other unconscious drives that led him to lose sight of his moral compass. As a result, he never got control of his compulsive gambling and eating. Both created further suffering and took increasing tolls on his health.

He remained loyal to my mother, however, and cared for her over the next 40 years until her very slow and debilitating disease ran its course. I admired his commitment and sacrifice, and always knew that despite his limited way of expressing it, he loved my sister and me. He did his best to support us, despite the constant financial erosion caused by his gambling addiction.

I don't sit in judgment of my father, but like my mother, I've sought to learn what I can from both their experiences. With regard to dad, I realize that as with the rest of us, he had both saint and sinner within him. Unfortunately, after his crisis, he neither had the opportunity nor inclination to use it for self-understanding. As a result, the cumulative effect of the stress and anxiety led to ulcers, diabetes, chronic heart failure, and end-of-life depression.

One incident in his life indicated to me just how unaware he was of his feelings. It occurred at the end of my mother's life. She had gone into her last of many comas and was in death's imminent decline. Unfortunately, due to his own health problems at the time, he was in another hospital. When I went to see him and told him that mom was dying, a tear started running down his face. With puzzlement, he looked at me and questioned why his eyes were tearing. I was astonished that he had not made the connection and gently suggested that it was probably because he was sad.

A few years later, I came across that notorious confession letter he left behind before heading off to Las Vegas. A good five pages long, it was filled with all the hurt, resentment, and pain that surrounded his life at the time. I felt so much like I wished he would have had someone to talk to. If he had, he possibly could have been able to diffuse the forces that led to that devastating decision.

When I told him I had discovered the letter in mom's personal belongings, he was just as disinclined to talk about those difficult feelings then as he had been years before. It was sad. Though he did show great compassion for my mother, he never really learned how to be aware of his feelings, or how to be intimately open with others.

As you might imagine, my career choice to become a clinical psychologist was significantly influenced by my family circumstances. And as with many of my colleagues in the field of psychotherapy, I believe it's possible to understand what prompts our behaviors and how we can grow from the crises we encounter. I also believe that despite that understanding, we're all responsible for our actions.

But whether we are faced with crises that come to us from what seems to be "out of the blue," or crises that result from our own actions, we can choose to learn from our experiences, or not. We can seek greater understanding of ourselves, or just put it out of mind and, as some say, "let sleeping dogs lie."

Dad was not inclined to seek that understanding, but those sleeping dogs didn't always remain in slumber. They would awaken when he wasn't aware and covertly prowl around his unconscious, gnawing at his wellbeing. Alternatively, mom's search bore many fruits, and what she gained from her self-discovery also became a blessing to my sister and me, because if we, or anyone else showed an interest, she was very willing to pass along what she discovered.

I welcomed her insights and was fortunate to vicariously learn from her ordeals. And yet I also found that dad's plight taught me an important lesson: that you can change some of your ways, (i.e., in his case, the right and wrong about stealing), but not engage in the process of self-understanding, and continue to suffer from the uncorrected causes that gave rise to your self-destructive actions in the first place.

Each of us have that choice to make, whether it's prompted by crisis or just living an examined life. For my mother, that choice translated into developing a new and accepting relationship with her body. She continued to acquire knowledge about many aspects of her growth. She learned more about her emotions. Despite her previous outgoingness, she learned to modify her social interactions in light of her new circumstances. Her identity required adjustment, less attached to her physicality, more anchored to her intellectual, emotional, and spiritual dimensions.

The suffering she endured deepened her compassion and increased her willingness to take greater interpersonal risks by being more open and intimate with others. Her crisis prompted her to seek meaning and purpose in life despite her limitations. And finally, because of her confinement, she was particularly interested to explore ways in which her mind might overcome the physical bounds of time and space, and practiced techniques for experiencing states of consciousness that took her beyond such limits.

I can personally attest to the results of all those efforts because I know that she ultimately found joy in life despite all her difficulties. I frequently would hear her whistling and singing to herself in the kitchen, cracking jokes on the phone with family and friends, or hysterically laughing at a comedy show on TV. She regularly would be visited by others who would come by to offer her support, then end up confiding their problems and seeking her wisdom and advice. In so many ways, she was a significant inspiration in my life.

Yes, I was captivated by my mother and attached to her in ways not uncommon for many of us Italian boys. But it was particularly easy to become charmed and mesmerized in her presence. Her articulateness and passion for what she'd personally discovered and believed could be intoxicating at times. But her inspiration went beyond that of a loving son. Others also spoke of her strengths and the way she impacted their lives, because most importantly, she did more than talk the talk. In ways that far exceeded what she could do physically, she walked the walk.

What she modeled on a daily basis prompted me to want to learn how we all can grow from difficult ordeals in life; how a given crisis might challenge us to learn certain aspects in our own development—aspects needed for our soul's evolution. I wanted to learn how groping for perspective in the aftermath of a crisis can enable us to find a broader sense of meaning and purpose in life; how opening our minds and hearts to a broad spiritual perspective can prevent us from being confined or paralyzed by one rigid religious belief system; and how not remaining myopically constricted by the predominantly accepted boundaries of time, space, and the disproportionate emphasis on materialism, can awaken us to a fuller breadth of our consciousness's potential.

Mom lived a total of 50 years with the MS. The last five were spent confined to bed as her body slowly withered away. But right up to the end, even when she couldn't speak, nurses would comment on how every day, when first encountering her, she'd flash that smile.

During one visit just before she fully lost the ability to speak, I asked her if she still found meaning in such a shrunken world of experience. I questioned if she would rather just throw in the towel than go on living in her condition. I knew that one of the spiritual beliefs she came to embrace was that we lead many lives—that the soul's growth required more experience than one life could provide.

I recall how her dark brown eyes widened and how she intensely looked at me as she slowly mouthed the words in response to my question. She said that as long as she wasn't physically suffering, she was still okay with continuing to live; she still liked keeping informed about my life, my sister's, and the stories of our children; she enjoyed seeing her siblings and other family members who would regularly stop by; and she looked forward to my father's presence and, ironically, worried about his failing health.

Although her days were spent lying on her back, held prisoner by her body, she still found a meaning for living. She never lost faith. The spiritual and psychological lessons mom was forced to learn from her crises aided her throughout her life, right up to the days before it ended.

My mother's ordeal was first precipitated by a physical crisis, but as you can see, it impacted other key areas in her life. It presented an intellectual, emotional, social, identity, existential, and spiritual challenge. All those key areas demanded further development in order for her to effectively cope and adjust to her life situation.

Her example and how she managed to do that prompted me to investigate what it is that we all may need to learn to find peace despite our life crises. In what ways do each of us have to grow when everything around us says give up? Are there certain beliefs that can make us stronger when facing difficult challenges? Can our minds be harnessed to affect the healing of our bodies? Are we really more than physical beings? Do our ordeals prepare us for increased spiritual growth and transformation? And if so, where does it all lead?

I will explore these questions in the following pages and show through examples what others have taught me in their efforts to understand their own crises. I'll also share some lessons I learned when personally pursuing those answers. Some came from working as a clinical psychologist and hypnotherapist in a private practice; some came as a result of certain painful and anomalous experiences of my own; and some came from a very intense five-year pilgrimage where I sought out teachings and learned methods from of a diverse number of healers.

It has been my mission to find out what truth can be discerned from experiences such as my mother's. It's entailed a multi-decade pursuit of ongoing research to integrate and synthesize what I've discovered. I'll share it all with you here and hope that it will inspire you to find personal and spiritual growth from the crises you encounter. And despite the suffering those crises may bring into your life, I'll show you how you can have them serve as the Chrysalis Crises that can lead to your transformation.

SECTION I

The Key Areas of Foundational Development:

Physical, Intellectual, Emotional, Moral, and Social Growth

CHAPTER 3

That Which Doesn't Kill Us: Physical Crisis

"That which doesn't kill us makes us stronger" is a familiar adage, first quoted by the German philosopher Frederick Nietzsche. Recent research has found that while terrible events can produce negative effects, whatever doesn't kill us, or seriously traumatize us, can, in moderation, indeed make us stronger. What's considered "moderate," however, is relative from person to person.

Whether mild, moderate, or severe, there seems to be an endless number of crises taking place in the world. When I hear of them in the media, or have their details shared in therapy, I often wonder: What possible benefit could come from all this suffering? Can it really lead to any good?

I find some comfort in the words of Woodrow Wilson, the 28th president of the United States, who said, "The reward of suffering is experience." While I don't dispute that suffering produces impactful experiences, I would personally need more to come from it to feel "rewarded." For me, it would at least have to result in learning.

Learning from experiences that create suffering, however, can be tricky. If it's the kind of learning that contributes to personal growth and transformation, it can take time to realize. For instance, before you focus on such learning, you'll probably need to give other immediate priorities your attention, like initial recovery and adjustment.

But once those needs have been addressed, if you do wish to derive personal growth from your experience, a certain amount of self-examination will be necessary. That process can add richness to your life. It's the kind of examination Socrates suggested is everyone's responsibility. He said, "The unexamined life is not worth living." In other words, if you examine your life experiences and you attend to the way they personally impact you, worthwhile learning can be derived from the painful ones and the positive ones.

Socrates also believed that this kind of learning will ensure that your life will be a success. And according to the philosopher, a successful life is one which fulfills two primary purposes: personal *and* spiritual development.

I agree with the primacy Socrates gives to these life purposes, and I've found that personal and spiritual growth can be derived from crises. When they are, learning from life's ordeals can make the suffering they produce feel like it was worthwhile.

That certainly was the case for Bob, whose story will illustrate the key area of *physical growth* in a Chrysalis Crisis. Bob was an exceptional athlete in his day, and he worked hard at it. A three-sport star in high school, Bob excelled in football, wrestling, and track. Recognized on numerous state and county teams, he could have pursued any of those sports in college, but he chose to play football. He said he loved the rough and tumble of the game.

When Bob came into my care, however, those athletic days were a good 25 years behind him, and his body had significantly changed during the interim. A sizable man of about six foot two, he looked to weigh somewhere between 250 to 300 pounds. That was well above his earlier playing weight. He had a round face, with an engaging smile, and when he first greeted me, his large hand swallowed mine. His head was fully shaven of what little hair remained, and his broad shoulders and muscular arms showed the signs of someone who had done some serious weightlifting at one time.

Unfortunately, in that well-known effect that occurs with many weight lifters who let themselves go, a lot of that upper body mass headed south. A good deal of it was hanging over his belt. Increasing age, inactivity, and the force of gravity had taken its toll.

But the gravity that contributed to that migration was different from the gravity that brought him in to see me. The reason he sought therapy was to address the psychological and emotional issues that played a part in a health crisis he had a few months before. At that time, Bob almost died from a heart attack.

When it occurred, he was supervising the development of an apartment complex. Bob had studied construction management in college and said he enjoyed playing an integral part erecting large projects. However, this particular project was not running smoothly. A big reason for that was the poor performance of a new subcontractor that his organization had taken on.

Bob had spoken to this sub on a few previous occasions about the shoddiness and slowness of his team's work, but despite his dissatisfaction, Bob gave the sub additional opportunities to make improvements. None were made. When Bob's crisis occurred, the project was well along, and he found himself caught in that well-known spot between a rock and a hard place. He feared that to switch to another subcontractor would put them even further behind, yet the underperformance continued to slow the project down. It was a tough call.

They increasingly fell behind schedule. Unexpected weather also set them back, and Bob felt mounting pressure from his employer. He was told by his boss that their company was facing financial difficulties, and a great deal was at stake with this particular development. If it was unsuccessful, their organization faced potential bankruptcy. That would mean Bob would be out of a job.

The pressure increased. Bob realized that again he would have to confront the subcontractor. He was apprehensive about talking to him because the guy was difficult to deal with. Prior to their scheduled meeting, Bob said he felt emotionally keyed up. Then, true to form, the sub was late, and by the time he showed, Bob was already loaded for bear. He could hardly contain his anger.

As in their previous discussions, the sub refused to take responsibility for his crew's performance. He made excuses and blamed others. Bob quickly became enraged and completely lost his cool. He said he wanted to pummel the guy.

Wisely, he didn't. However, amidst the altercation, he felt a sharp pain in his chest and a numbness in his left arm. Then he began to sweat profusely and became lightheaded. Not sure what was happening to him, he recalled initially falling to his knees and, moments later, collapsing onto the floor. He didn't remember anything after that. He was told that someone quickly called 911, and an ambulance came shortly afterward. As it turned out, he was fortunate a hospital was nearby.

When Bob came to, he found himself hooked up to monitors and lying in a critical care unit. He was frightened. Seeing him awake, a compassionate nurse gently oriented him to what happened. Later he discovered that had it not been for the quick response of the caller and his proximity to the hospital, he probably wouldn't have made it. That sent a chill through his body.

Though he recognized he was nowhere near the physical conditioning of his prime, Bob always felt grateful for his continued good health. It was a blow for him to consider the extent to which it failed. He now realized he had taken that health for granted and had done little to maintain it. That initial bedside conversation was a wake-up call in more ways than one.

Major changes were needed in his life—and more than just physically. His marriage and finances were also failing. After he underwent a few necessary procedures and had time to rehabilitate, he confided his full situation to his cardiologist. It was then that his doctor suggested he seek counseling.

Bob knew his physician's advice was right, but he had never been in therapy, and when it was mentioned, he was uncomfortable with taking the step. The doctor picked up on his hesitance and told him he knew a particular therapist with whom he might easily connect. That's when he encouraged him to see me.

The reason the doctor directed him my way was because we also had a professional relationship. I had my own heart-related event a number of years before, and he'd been very helpful to me.

Prior to this event, I'd been doing a lot of long distance running, my weight was down, and I believed I was in excellent condition, so the irregular heartbeat I'd occasionally experienced never concerned me. I thought it was some benign form of "runner's arrhythmia." I was wrong. It turned out I was having occasional episodes of Atrial Fibrillation (a-fib). Fortunately, however, where a-fib warrants concern and monitoring, it's not the potential "lights out" problem Bob was dealing with. Nonetheless, when your ticker is not running perfectly, it still can be scary.

Because the cardiologist knew I could relate to the vulnerability of having heart trouble, and that I also had an athletic background, he thought I'd be a good therapist match for Bob—two old warriors coming to terms with the realities of aging.

Well, he was right. Bob and I eventually did establish a good therapeutic alliance, but it took time. He needed a number of sessions to get comfortable with the process. It wasn't his way to confide in others, and particularly to reveal his vulnerabilities to another man. Competitors are trained to do the opposite: never show your weaknesses, don't let them see you sweat, never reveal your underbelly.

But Bob was motivated to lower those defenses. Almost dying can have that effect on a person. While he was no longer in danger of another heart attack, nor experiencing any physical discomfort in the aftermath of his surgery, it became evident that he was still in pain. But the pain was of a different nature. It had to do with his failing marriage, his serious financial problems, the potential loss of his home, and a general sense of losing control of his life.

I felt bad for Bob. For a guy who liked to maintain a high level of control in his life, everything was tumbling to the ground around him. He was like Humpty Dumpty who fell off the wall. His world was in pieces and he wondered if he could ever put it all back together again. I was optimistic that he could and had a sense that he would benefit from therapy and make the needed changes.

In my ongoing attempt to learn as much as I could about Bob, I gathered additional information about his family background. He said he loved his mother and father, but believed they had one of those marriages of convenience. His mom would be there for him when he needed her, but he said he wasn't particularly close to his dad. His father was portrayed as someone who was disappointed with how his own life turned out, and put a lot of pressure on Bob to fulfill his unrealized aspirations, in particular having never been a successful athlete.

Like many boys in that position, Bob wanted his father's love and approval, so he sought accomplishment in those areas. Since he was a gifted athlete, he evidenced early potential. Yet he mentioned that despite his performances, his dad would diminish or discount his achievements. He would frequently compare his success to the better performances of other athletes they knew. While Bob found this disheartening, he said it only served to motivate him more to prove his father wrong by excelling even further.

This early dynamic between Bob and his dad helped me understand the intensity of his drive and how it fueled the rage he felt when things were not working as he'd planned. There were no excuses. One needs to improve one's performance, was his mantra!

I helped him see how his emotional blow up with the sub partially might be connected to this earlier dynamic with his dad. I also mentioned that even when we're not consciously aware of the overt and expressed expectations of parents, as children we tend to pick up on them anyway. As a matter of fact, the ones that aren't expressed outwardly can be even more insidious. I shared a quote by Carl Jung, the Swiss psychiatrist, who said, "The greatest burden a child must bear is the unlived life of the parent."

Bob also came to see there were two sides to that dynamic. One side prompted him to fulfill his dad's expectation to become a star athlete, but the other side worked in the opposite direction. It contributed to why he let himself deteriorate physically. That was particularly evident since his father died.

That occurred when Bob was in his early 30s, and it seemed to alleviate the pressure to conform to those expectations. However, even with his dad out of his life, Bob had taken on his father's voice and made it his own. Unfortunately, he did not realize it was still very present in the back of his mind, and as a result, his dad's demands and his rebellion against them were warring inside his head.

For example, he might have passing thoughts, like "I need to get in shape," or "I need to lose some weight." But on the heels of that, he'd have that rebellious side rear up in protest. It might counter with something to the effect of "Get off my back," or "Leave me alone, I'll start tomorrow." The latter voice was easier to follow, especially after a beer or two. Then he would just sink further into the couch and watch more TV.

In recent years, the rebellious side was winning, and the extent of its success could be measured by his expanding waistline. But he refused to see that his body was becoming a time bomb. His blindness to that reality was equaled by his unwillingness to see the deteriorating status of his marriage and finances. And though his use of alcohol had not reached a state of addiction, his level of use contributed to his avoidance and denial of those problems.

At one point in his therapy, Bob and I thought it might be helpful to have his wife join us for a session. When she did, she made it crystal clear that she wasn't happy in the marriage. But as Bob shared what he was learning about himself in therapy, she became more tolerant and compassionate. Almost losing him softened her a bit, but their marriage was still on the rocks.

When I inquired as to how things had gotten so out of kilter, I was struck with how she also seemed to share a degree of obliviousness to their mounting relationship problems and out-of-control finances. They both avoided confronting issues or resolving what needed to be done to solve them. Alternatively, tensions would build, then anger and blaming would follow. They'd blow off the tension, then return to their shared collusion of sweeping things under the rug.

Bob was most inclined to avoid these uncomfortable areas, just as he had come to ignore his burgeoning weight. And he was ashamed. He did not want to see what was gathering all around him, and as a result, everything worsened.

To her credit, his wife had made appeals to begin couples therapy, and even once suggested that they seek a financial advisor. But Bob resisted. He would angrily attack her when she tried to broach these subjects. It was even worse if she dared say anything about his weight.

Although he wasn't that young boy dealing with his father anymore, those little boy feelings were still alive in Bob. They remained charged for years. And now the internal conflict he had between compliance and resistance was getting re-enacted with his wife. But it remained outside his awareness and was wreaking havoc on his life.

Carl Jung suggests that these unresolved unconscious feelings are like emotional anchors that hold such dynamics in place. Even if you have intellectual understanding as to what caused the initial establishment of a given dynamic, if all the accompanying feelings associated to that dynamic are not uncovered, appropriately experienced, and diffused, it's like trying to row a boat out of troubled waters while remaining anchored to the dock.

It was past time for Bob not only to gain these personal insights but pull up those emotional anchors. He no longer could afford to have the dog of his self-destructive behaviors be waged by the tail of his unconscious feelings.

The key area of physical growth in Bob's life needed a major examination. Overcoming his long-standing resistance to physical exercise and dieting continued to pose a challenge. He needed additional support, particularly on the exercise front. I could tell by many of his ongoing comments that he felt a great deal of shame about the appearance of his body. He still had the pride and ego of a once successful athlete.

I suggested that if he could find the resources, he should seek the services of a personal trainer. I had hoped that even with a few sessions, he might be provided a blueprint for improvement. I further suggested that he initiate taking walks with his wife, and told him that the activity could have a dual benefit: someone to share the exercise with, and a time for them to talk.

At one point, he referred to not being the athlete he used to be, and that no amount of conditioning and weight loss would bring back his youthful appearance. I acknowledged that reality, and mentioned that while we all want to look and perform our best, we need to accept that when we get up in our years, we're never going to recapture that 25-year-old body we once had. Rather, it's less about vanity or turning back the clock of aging. It's more about increasing vitality; improving your sense of wellbeing; using your body to throw off the tensions of too much mental and emotional exertion; and experiencing the confidence that comes from maintaining your health.

"Be the best conditioned 47-year-old Bob you can be," I said. "Do it in the body you presently have. If it's true that our bodies serve as the vehicle for our minds and spirits, keep yours limber, healthy, and conditioned as long as possible. Then, when that day comes where you need to lay it down, have the satisfaction that you got the most mileage out of it. Use it all up. Leave nothing on the field." I suspected that in his days as an athlete, he'd heard that last statement before.

I also said, "After you get past the years where the motivation for optimal physical conditioning is no longer about improving athletic performance, exercise can be embraced as a form of physical hygiene and health maintenance. While it may not be the competitive fun it used to be, it's still necessary. It's like taking care of your teeth. You don't have to floss all your teeth. Just floss the ones you want to keep." He got the message. He didn't want to come out of the game.

This particular juncture in Bob's life was very challenging. Like the butterfly that struggles to release itself from its cocoon, he worked hard to emancipate from old negative feelings and habits. He had to throw off outdated patterns that were holding him back from taking flight in his life.

Being in therapy took a lot of effort for Bob. He wasn't a very personally insightful guy, nor was he previously inclined to do much self-examination. But he was coachable. He let me do some mindfulness training with him, and as I requested, he began keeping a journal about his day-to-day moods. These activities all helped him increase his level of self-awareness.

Bob had been frightened and depressed when he first came to see me, and while he never did put his old humpty dumpty self back together again, he found a better solution: he transformed into a newer version of himself. He got to look death in the face, return to living life more consciously, and became more mindful of that which made him tick—and not just his heart.

He became more attentive to all the neglected aspects of his physical world. Besides his body, he stopped binge buying things he couldn't afford. He learned to live within his means and paid more attention to his finances. And because he and his wife began to communicate better, they not only worked more effectively as a team, but their sex life dramatically improved.

Bob's health crisis almost took his life. It literally had him on his back. But he pulled one of his old wrestling moves on it. He maneuvered a reverse and got on top of the situation. He turned his heart attack crisis into a Chrysalis Crisis, and made needed changes in many aspects of his physical world.

Maintaining a healthy body and sustaining a balanced material existence is critical if you wish to give focus and attention to developing the nine key areas of growth that follow. The good news is that the knowledge you need to master your physical world, as well as the information that's necessary for growth in the other key areas, is available. Some of it can be found externally, but some of it will need to be discovered internally. All of it, however, will contribute to the area of development examined in the next chapter: the key area of intellectual growth.

CHAPTER 4

Meltdown Before Transformation: Intellectual Crisis

Chrysalis Crisis. Just saying those words produces a cutting expression. They don't flow easily, like "cellar door." They have a jarring effect. Their enunciation is sharp and hard on the ears. The double emphasis of the "cr" sound brings to my mind the *cr*ashing and *cr*acking of *cr*ystal.

But that piercing effect is well suited for capturing the harshness of the ordeals they describe because Chrysalis Crises can often feel as if our lives are *cr*ashing, when what we value is *cr*umbling around us, or when the very structure of our existence is going through a form of *cr*eative destruction. And after the crash, there's the burn, when the world we once knew and the stability it provided feel as though they've gone up in flames.

However, a fire can be purgative. It can burn away the dross from gold. It can sterilize and purify. For instance, where a forest fire can threaten both lives and structures in its path, it also can remove the underbrush and debris that inhibit new growth in the forest, open it to additional sunlight, and nourish its soil.

Once we get past the shock of a crisis, adjust and accommodate to any losses we've incurred, it also can reveal openings for new growth and awareness in our lives. If one sheds light on areas where personal development is needed, then gaining that growth can nourish our future evolution, and like the phoenix that rises out of its ashes, we can transform into new versions of our selves.

Sue did that. She was at the start of a life altering change when we first met, but growth and transformation were the furthest thing from her mind. She was still adjusting to the shock of hearing that her husband, Bart, was having an affair. It took her completely by surprise.

She noticed Bart had been withdrawing over the past year but thought it was primarily due to his business falling off during the recession. As the sole breadwinner, she suspected he was feeling financial pressure. But Bart wasn't one to share his feelings so she never knew for sure.

When Sue first suggested to Bart that they get into couples counseling, she didn't imagine an affair would become the issue. She thought they just needed to communicate better, have a therapist arbitrate some of their more contentious decisions, and get some help managing their emotional reactions toward each other.

Recognizing the impact of Bart's revelation on Sue, their couple's therapist suggested she seek additional individual support. He made the same recommendation to Bart, but he was resistant to the idea. Bart felt one shrink session a week was enough for him. Sue welcomed the help.

At our first session, Sue was still visibly shaken when she disclosed why she sought my support. Her eyes filled with tears and she had a panicked, questioning look on her face when she considered the possibilities of her future. Animated and articulate, she needed little help getting in touch with her feelings. Her emotions flowed easily.

Sue was an exceptionally beautiful woman with stylishly cut auburn hair, high cheekbones, hazel eyes, flawless skin, and a perfect set of very white teeth. It was easy to see why she once briefly worked as an actress. She also had the shape of a model and carried herself with the posture of one. Though she was in her mid-forties, she looked at least ten years younger.

But her youthful appearance and beauty could not conceal the vulnerability she was feeling. With three adolescent children still navigating their way through school, the idea of being a single parent was overwhelming. Up to that point, her role as a parent had not gone well.

Sue favored a tough love approach and ruled her household with a heavy hand. She was similarly firm when making decisions with Bart. That led to many confrontations where she would draw lines in the sand or give ultimatums. When Sue told me about her conflicts with the children and Bart, I got the impression that she caused a lot of the emotional storms. But the storm she was now in was more like a category five hurricane.

Amidst the pain of being betrayed, Sue could not conceive how she would ever be able to forgive Bart. She felt deeply wounded and needed time to sort through her feelings. However, at a point when I thought she might be receptive, I tried to help her see how it is possible to not only heal from such a hurtful experience but grow personally and even improve her marriage. At first, she wasn't buying it.

Before those latter outcomes could occur, however, there was a lot of work to do. Because in addition to working through her feelings, she had to confront another area in her development. Sue was about to undergo a Chrysalis Crises with the predominant emphasis on the key area of *intellectual growth*.

She was a very rigid thinker who embraced a number of entrenched beliefs about how people or life *should* or *ought* to work. That kind of thinking not only posed a barrier to healing her marriage but also explained why she frequently got into emotional conflicts with Bart and the children. In light of that propensity, I determined that Sue would benefit from a more cognitive approach to her therapy, one that would give greater emphasis to what she thought, as opposed to what she felt.

Sue held one belief in particular that required attention. It had significant implications for whether her marriage would survive its present ordeal. She long maintained that if her husband ever cheated on her, it would justify divorce. But that wasn't the only belief that created problems in her life. She had other rooted ways of thinking that alienated herself with him and others. There were stereotyped beliefs about men, fixed ideas about how relationships should function, and exacting notions about how adolescents ought to behave. In general, she held many strong opinions with little tolerance for disagreement.

During the earlier sessions, I took a more supportive role with Sue, and as a result, she came to see me as an ally. So later, when she'd profess some of those beliefs to justify a position she'd taken, she assumed I agreed with her. I frequently didn't. But as it became all the more evident that many of her rigid beliefs contributed to conflicts in her life, it was clear that I would have to openly find a way to challenge them while maintaining a therapeutic alliance.

I didn't pivot in that direction until I trusted that our connection could tolerate some discordance. When I began to tread those grounds, I did so with a lot of prefacing and a good deal of tact. I initially assured her that I wasn't trying to dismantle her whole belief system. I said if she ultimately wanted to stick to her position after she heard me out, that would always be her prerogative. I also emphasized that I wasn't suggesting she be so open-minded that her brains fall out, but that she make room for other opinions, and not reactively shoot high and to the right. With that understanding, she granted me permission to challenge her when I thought it was necessary.

On one occasion she was emotionally reacting to a particular incident where the reality of what was taking place was not likely to change. It had to do with some established procedure at her children's school that was mandated by the state. It was one of those situations well suited for the serenity prayer: "God, grant me the serenity to accept the things I cannot change…"

But Sue was not about to find that serenity. Instead she continued to bang her head against the wall of non-acceptance. However, once I gave her the needed time to vent her feelings, I was able to point out how it was she who often suffered the most from the rigidity of her thinking. She seemed open to my message, so I decided to do a little teaching. I introduced her to a clinical approach called Rational Emotive and Behavior Therapy (REBT).[1]

REBT rises out of the field of cognitive behavioral therapy. It's been around for years. The earliest versions of the technique were developed by Dr. Albert Ellis back in the 1950s. In a nutshell, REBT offers a way to analyze a given situation so your behavioral responses can be better understood and potentially changed. It emphasizes that the "incident" (the antecedent), and your "reactions" to it (the consequences), are often affected or shaped by the beliefs you hold about the incident.

Often times such beliefs can lie outside your conscious awareness. They may get unwittingly adopted into your belief system as a result of earlier life indoctrination from parents or culture. Alternatively, they may be taken on and harbored consciously. However, if those beliefs happen to be inaccurate, stereotyped, or rigidly held, they can constrict or undermine your ability to handle situations that require flexibility or new thinking. Let me give you an example.

I once worked with a couple where the wife consistently had trouble being on time. When she would run late, her husband would get agitated, annoyed, and become aggressively impatient. He believed that her lateness was a sign of disrespect, that she was being inconsiderate, or that she was being passive aggressive because he was such a stickler for punctuality.

During our couple's session, I explored his assumptions. She sincerely denied them all. He wasn't convinced. She willingly admitted that time management had always been a problem for her, but said it existed long before she knew him.

With further assessment, we discovered that she struggled with an Attention Deficit Disorder (ADD). One of its symptoms is difficulty with time management. Knowing that another reason existed for why she was always late enabled her husband to change his beliefs about what he thought explained her lack of punctuality, and it helped him begin modifying his impatient behavior.

When I use this approach with suitable clients, I give them further instruction on how they can have success employing it themselves. I suggest that the technique can be remembered and undertaken by using what is referred to as the A, B, C, and D of the process. I'll share it with you now.

First, if you're faced with a situation that causes disruption between you and your partner, identify the incident or **A**ntecedent that started the problem. For example, maybe your husband failed to notice you had gotten your hair cut and styled. Then, determine the **C**onsequences that came about as a result of that antecedent. Those would be your reactions and behaviors that followed. You may have felt hurt, ignored, or decided to be quiet and withdraw from him. Next, put on your therapist hat and flesh out what **B**eliefs effected those consequences. Possibly, you believe you're getting older and he isn't attracted to you anymore, or you've put on a few pounds, and that's why he's not paying attention to how you look. Finally, be prepared to examine and **D**ispute those beliefs. If you check them out with him, and they don't apply, they may require modification. Maybe he was just tired, preoccupied, or generally not very observant that evening.

If you maintain beliefs that do require change, and you continue to abide by them, you can end up frequently painting yourself into a corner. They limit your freedom of movement. It's like those early skeptics who continued to insist the earth was flat. They probably didn't sail far into the horizon.

Certainly, many beliefs are valid and need to be maintained, but with increased awareness and an openness to change, those that are outdated, faulty, or rigidly adhered to may warrant being discarded or modified. That can make your life and personal relationships run smoother.

Sue needed to intellectually grow in this way so she could at least tolerate beliefs that differed from hers. For example, shifting her posture in this manner would enable her children to make some of their decisions in ways that might not align with her. That would give them a greater sense of their own agency and lead to less locking of the horns.

But in order for Sue to get through her present marital crisis, it was going to take more than her willingness to be more accepting of Bart's different beliefs. No one was suggesting she believe it's okay to have an affair. Yet according to their couple's therapist, for Bart, the affair was also a symptom of deeper problems, and in order to fix their marriage, he would need to make some major changes. Unfortunately, when that was made clear, Bart decided it was more than he wanted to take on. He again said he wasn't going to get into individual therapy, and he ended his couple's therapy, too.

Bart's unwillingness to make the needed changes negatively affected Sue's ability to work through the affair, and it cast a bleak shadow on any hope for a reconciliation. But she stuck with her therapy and continued her process of growth. For instance, she learned how to avoid confrontations in other relationships and how best to manage them when they arose. She showed an increasing willingness to examine other beliefs she held that might warrant modification. And she began a process of self-education by reading relevant books about making marriage work, parenting, and personal development.

Though all those efforts contributed to Sue's intellectual growth, Bart was unwilling to make any further changes, and while it saddened her to do so, she ultimately decided to seek a divorce. But that decision was made in a way that was less predicated on her previous belief about what one *should* do when an affair occurs in a marriage. It was a choice she felt was right in light of the concerns she had about the kind of relationship they would continue to have in the future.

Now, in addition to the loss of her marriage and its significant impact on her children, Sue was also faced with the reality that after the divorce, there would be few financial resources to fall back on. She and Bart had not accrued any significant savings, they had limited equity in their home, and what they did have would need to fund two residences.

Though Bart could pay some monthly alimony, due to his bad investments that got brought to light in the divorce proceedings, his income was more limited than Sue realized. What little money he directed to Sue was insufficient for her and the children, so she was now faced with having to enter the workforce.

It had been years since Sue found employment. Throughout her marriage, she and Bart agreed to have her primarily be a stay-at-home mom, taking care of the children and domestic needs. Other than limited involvement with various aspects of acting earlier in her life, Sue had little other work experience. And while she had a good deal of native intelligence, she never pursued her education past high school.

But Sue was not without resources. She had plenty of what psychologist Martin Seligman at the University of Pennsylvania calls "signature strengths."[2] These are areas of interest and aptitude that, once identified, can help a person select a line of work or certain activities that they're best suited for. According to Seligman, when an individual is engaged in undertakings that employ their signature strengths, they will be using abilities that align with an authentic part of who they are. And when they become involved in those activities, they can find "Authentic Happiness" in life.

Sue had such strengths. For instance, she was an articulate and excellent communicator, and had a certain flair about her. She'd light up a room when she entered. Sue had what people call "a presence." Her emotional nature also came across in the sincere warmth she expressed when she engaged people, and her outgoing, charming, and charismatic nature made her effective with groups.

In addition to the intellectual growth she was gaining in therapy, Sue needed to acquire other knowledge, like how to turn those strengths into employable skills, and once she found work, she had to learn how to keep a budget. She had a lot to learn about a lot of things, and Sue summoned the courage to meet that challenge. By doing so, she continued to turn her marital crisis into a Chrysalis Crisis, undergoing a major transformation as a result.

I continued to help her address areas in her life that required change, and as I did, I discovered that other beliefs needed modification. Many of them were self-limiting beliefs. One was that she believed she wasn't very smart. Despite what seemed evident to the contrary, Sue felt that if it wasn't for her looks, she had little else to offer.

Though in reality she was smart, there were limited opportunities to make decent money with just a high school education. However, one day she had an idea. Sue realized that some of her strengths could be used to earn money. She recalled how at one point in her husband's developing business, she was able to help him and a few of his employees sharpen their presentation skills when they would attend and speak at conferences.

Using the knowledge she gained from acting classes and some part time work she did as an acting teacher, Sue remembered how she was able to help them, how much they benefited from the help, and how good she felt providing it. She started imagining that other professionals might also welcome a similar kind of support.

Sue then took the entrepreneurial initiative to put together a package of specific techniques she could teach people who might want to develop their presentation skills. As she pulled together her menu of services, she told a friend about her idea, and that friend advised her to consult the nearby university's school of business where free guidance was offered to market ideas.

At first, Sue was a little apprehensive that someone "in the know" might say her idea was dumb, but once she overcame that insecurity, she contacted a business consultant and was pleasantly surprised to find he not only liked her idea, but provided some great suggestions for getting her business up and running.

With that validation and direction, Sue began sending out flyers and following them up with phone calls. Soon, a few people employed her, and after she had success with them, they became references, and more work followed.

Another individual in the community heard about Sue's training techniques and thought that Sue's teaching methods could enhance the job interviewing skills of people in her program. She discussed her needs with Sue and was as much impressed with Sue as she was with her training techniques. She offered Sue half-time employment.

The additional job turned out to be a great fit for Sue. It provided more predictable income, and she loved the work. Sue also felt particularly resonant with the plight of the people in the program. After all, she said, "I'm just one step ahead of them." She could hardly believe someone was willing to pay her to do something that felt so timely, natural, and meaningful in her life. The job not only offered regular income, but its part-time status enabled her to continue pursuing her other work and have the time flexibility for her family. It was a win/win for all.

Meeting her need for employment and earning her own income made Sue's confidence soar. Her depression lifted significantly and so did her energy level. She became a very busy lady, hitting on all cylinders. Her sense of self-sufficiency, potency, and the feeling of being more in control of her life was an experience she'd never really known before. She said it was like she personally came to discover what it means when people say that knowledge is power. Sue was finding her intellectual muscle and felt strengthened as a result.

Her children noticed the changes, too. They became her biggest fans. Their mom was growing and transforming right before their eyes. She was blossoming into the woman she always had the potential to be. Her increasing internal strength added radiance to her beauty.

Toward the end of therapy, Sue reminded me of an earlier session when she said she was "all over the place." At that time, Sue wasn't sure who she was anymore. I told her that when people are undergoing significant personal change, they often feel that way. I shared that a Polish psychologist and psychiatrist by the name of Kazimierz Dabrowski calls that experience "positive disintegration."[3]

According to Dabrowski, there are times when your personal development will require that you break down certain existing structures of your personality. New growth will sometimes necessitate its partial loosening or dismantling. During that process, you *can* feel as though you are *all over the place*. But with effort, you can modify or replace those structures, re-assemble them, and transform yourself into a higher version of your potential.

That's when you're like the caterpillar that completely melts down in order to transform into a butterfly. It can be a distressing process and it may take time. When you find yourself in the middle of such a transition and you're suffering, it may be hard to trust it can lead to any good. There may be the tendency to flee the struggle rather than stick with it long enough to acquire the growth.

But if that struggle is undertaken in the right way, it can bring light to key areas that are lacking in your development. They could be areas of deficiency that contributed to bringing the crisis about, undermined your ability to cope with it while it went on, compromised your capacity to adjust in its aftermath, or limited your inherent potential thereafter.

Once you gain knowledge of the transformative process and undertake it with growth and development as your goal, you can derive the specific knowledge you need to turn your crisis into a Chrysalis Crisis.

The key area of intellectual growth will always be critical when seeking this kind of development because the body of knowledge that pertains to the other nine keys differ from each other. There will be a continued need for the acquisition of additional information to bring about their development.

It's also important to realize that while the growth of each key area requires gaining more information about their particular kind of development, it takes more than an intellectual process to gain their further mastery. A number of the key areas require an additional component: actual experience. That is particularly the case in the *key area of emotional growth.*

CHAPTER 5

A Tsunami
of Feelings:
Emotional Crisis

Donald was a slightly built man with curly brown hair and penetrating blue eyes. He wore dark rimmed glasses, a buttoned-down shirt, and grey pants. Though he was 38 years old, he still had a youthful look about him. He spoke with a reserved intellectual style and gave considerable thought to my questions before responding. Married ten years with two small children, he lived near the university where he was employed as a physics professor.

Research and writing were Donald's predominant focus in life. He enjoyed the mental challenge of solving complex equations and could become so absorbed conducting experiments, he'd often remain in his lab for long hours. Donald relished the world of scientific discovery. He enjoyed attending conferences and looked forward to learning from others.

Though his work was given priority, he said he appreciated being married. Donald described his wife as an exceptional woman who was happy to be a stay-at-home mom, and his children as well-behaved and curious. He felt grateful his wife was content to be at home because it enabled him to concentrate on his profession, and it provided stability for their family.

One spring, however, all that changed. Donald's wife began having pains in her abdomen. She first thought they might be related to her monthly cramping, but when they persisted she made an appointment to see her family practitioner. He couldn't explain the cause, so he referred her to a specialist. After diagnosing the problem, the specialist told her she had a very aggressive form of cancer and only months to live.

Donald was shocked by the news. Like an unexpected earthquake that suddenly shook his life, when his wife died six months later, it was as if the ground opened below him, and his whole world collapsed into a deep, dark chasm.

When Donald came to see me in therapy, he was anxious and depressed. He and the children were in crisis, and he was overwhelmed with what he was facing. Not only did he have his own adjustment to make, but he had to help the children with theirs.

Recognizing that they had to be his utmost priority, he wanted to initially focus on what his children needed in order to accommodate this dramatic change. He now had to start taking on many of the responsibilities his wife had previously assumed. And while he needed to maintain employment, he knew it would require a significant change in how he approached his work.

These weren't easy adjustments, but he began making them. But the greatest personal difficulty Donald had with this crisis was dealing with the many emotions that he and the children were experiencing.

Donald didn't do feelings well. Addressing the family's emotional needs had been his wife's domain. She and Donald were very different in how they approached them. He tended to be the rational one, always seeking solutions and finding reasons for people to not have feelings. She freely expressed hers, easily empathized with others, and showed great compassion for those encountering life's difficulties. Now he had to assume those roles.

It's been my clinical experience that when children are facing upsetting events in their lives, and emphasis is placed on rationally dealing with the emotions that arise, feelings can be seen as experiences that need to be brushed aside. If their expression is discouraged or chastised, then the child learns to suppress them. Consequentially, they become inclined to tune out their feelings when they have them, and lack experience learning how to appropriately express, manage, and understand emotions.

Unfortunately, this had been the case with Donald during his formative years. In his family, a greater priority was placed on elevating his intellectual IQ, and it resulted in him having a very low emotional IQ. His present crisis, however, became a Chrysalis Crisis as he developed his *key area of emotional growth.*

In a well-received book entitled *Emotional Intelligence,* Daniel Goleman defines Emotional IQ, or what he calls EQ, as one's ability to recognize and understand emotions in yourself and others.[1] Those who have a sufficiently developed EQ use emotional awareness to manage their behaviors and empathically respond to the feelings of others. Fortunately, these abilities can be taught, and Donald needed learned them.

Up to this point in his life, Donald had managed to function in a predominantly cerebral manner. In the framework of Jungian Psychological Types, he was an extreme "thinker." Now, however, he had to develop his auxiliary function of "feeling." But for Donald, tuning into his feelings and showing empathy for the feelings of others was like using his left hand when he was right handed by nature.

During his married years, he relied on his wife to raise his emotional awareness. She'd try to point out what feelings he or others might have about certain work situations, feelings that would be present in their relationship, and feelings the children were struggling with at any given time. But these were foreign waters for Donald to navigate alone, and now he was dealing with a tsunami of mixed feelings.

Donald was deeply grieving his wife's loss, fearful for the welfare of his children, ashamed he was unable to emotionally connect with them, and angry that his world had been turned upside down. But he was motivated to successfully get through his crisis. He wanted to support and nurture his children and was willing to grow and change where necessary.

In addition to lacking an awareness of his feelings, Donald also had the face of a poker player. When he would talk about an experience where I suspected he might have a certain feeling, there would be few overt signs. I'd have to imagine what most people would feel in the situation he described, then wonder aloud if he might have had that particular feeling.

For example, when he was telling me about the occasion when he broke the news to his children that their mom had died, I asked how he felt when they started crying. He looked at me stoned faced. He couldn't recall having a feeling at the time. However, when I wondered aloud if he may have also felt sad when he witnessed their pain, his eyes welled up. Just like his wife, I initially had to help him make those connections.

But over time, Donald increasingly recognized that feelings usually accompanied many of his experiences, and he found his own way to identify his emotions. After he'd share a particularly poignant or troublesome incident, he would logically deduce that it probably prompted a feeling. And even if he wasn't initially in touch with it, upon further reflection, a feeling would begin to register.

Despite the roundabout way he got there, Donald began awakening to his emotional life. He found he could use his strong suit of thinking to assist him in identifying feelings. It was an interesting process to witness. When he succeeded, it would be as if he recalled a dream he'd forgotten. He'd bring into his awareness an emotion he'd once experienced, but one that eluded his conscious detection.

As Donald became more aware of his feelings, his deductive approach was needed less and less. He increasingly began to label and experience what he felt more directly and immediately, developing what I call the ability to "feel on your feet."

Feeling on your feet is akin to thinking on your feet. When you think on your feet, you're able to produce relevant thoughts at the time they're needed, many times right in the flow of conversation. Feeling on your feet works similarly. You're aware of what you're feeling in the moment something or someone is prompting an emotion.

For instance, if someone were to say something to you in a conversation, and you felt hurt as a result, being aware of what you feel in that moment would enable you to better manage that situation. If you wanted to address what was said at that time, how you felt about the exchange, it could be done while the feeling is still fresh.

Alternatively, being mindful of a feeling that's triggered in the moment can help you be aware of what might otherwise unwittingly prompt you to react in ways you'll regret later. It gives you a little more space between the hassle and how you register it—time to make the best conscious choice in how you wish to respond. This is similar to thinking before you act, only here you're also taking your feelings into consideration before you let them lead you in a certain direction. It's like consulting an emotional compass.

In addition to using your feelings for guidance in an emotional exchange, when you learn to consciously register, manage, and appropriately express them, you can diffuse their energy when needed—clear them as you go. This clearing process can be all the more necessary if the feelings you accumulate are the difficult ones you tend to avoid. If you let them build up, they increasingly occupy space in your heart. That can cause you to get depressed. So why give them free rent there? Why not address and diffuse them as they arise, leave more room for joy, happiness, and love?

These were lessons Donald was learning, and over time registering and expressing most of his feelings became less of a problem. However, there was one particular feeling with which he still struggled. While he showed greater comfort experiencing his sadness, openly expressed shame about regrettable choices he made in the past, and readily expressed his fears, he still had a problem getting in touch with his anger.

Donald would resist acknowledging he felt anger even when everything he described about a situation would suggest he was experiencing the affect. When I'd note that he may have been angry, he would diminish it by saying he was only a little frustrated. He was just uncomfortable owning up to being angry.

One reason for his resistance was that he held beliefs that being angry was wrong. Unfortunately, that belief contributed to his suppressing the feeling when he had it. When I explored his thinking about how he understood anger, he said he was raised to believe that any expression of anger was inappropriate and destructive, and that if you're an angry person, it shows you have a defect of some sort.

Donald's inability to identify and learn to appropriately express anger was being inhibited by his intellectual understanding about the feeling. It's a good example of how one key area of growth can affect another. I had to challenge his beliefs as I had with Sue. Only in his case, it was his thinking about the expression of a feeling that needed to be modified so he could allow himself to realize it and learn to work with that feeling.

Donald so much valued his intellect and his ability to think problems through, that experiencing anger particularly offended his sense of reason. To him, it was an irrational affect. When I challenged him about some of his reasons, he provided additional arguments. He said that he'd seen people get out of control and look foolish when they were angry; he'd heard people say things that were hurtful; he watched anger lead to fights; and he believed that anger could be deadly if it was allowed to escalate to rage.

I listened to his beliefs and acknowledged that those outcomes are indeed possibilities. I also empathized with his strong feelings about expressing anger, most of which seemed to be based in shame or fear. But I stressed that when anger is recognized and managed appropriately, it can be expressed in ways that avoid such negative consequences.

He looked unconvinced but receptive, so I entered his rational world and gave him a few reasons. For instance, I said, if anger is tempered and expressed in the right manner, it can have a mobilizing affect. It can be channeled into non-aggressive assertion. If done tactfully and diplomatically, it can prompt change.

I also said that if people unwittingly harbor a great deal of anger and haven't consciously registered, experienced, or expressed it when needed, they'll be less likely to examine its causes and eradicate its influence. Additionally, I shared with him that I've often found anger to be the first layer of feelings someone may have about a situation, and that it's not uncommon for a feeling like grief or fear to lie below. It can be hard to access and release those feelings if a person is unwilling to move through the anger's initial layer.

Donald's beliefs about anger were long entrenched, so it was a tough sell to get him to see that any benefit could come from exploring and experiencing its effect. He needed further convincing, so I continued to make my case.

I told him that anger can be even more insidious and destructive when it's not recognized or appropriately diffused. Though he'd never talked of suicide, I mentioned how unexpressed anger can often lie behind the act of taking one's life. When that's the case, the unconscious anger can devolve into a quiet, helpless, hopeless, and despairing rage. Then that rage gets turned onto oneself.

Also, because I knew Donald had a strong Christian upbringing, I ventured into that area to see if I could shift his intellectual position. I reminded him that even Jesus was noted to have gotten angry with the merchants who set up their tables in the temple. And finally, since he often alluded to the minds of great thinkers, I shared one of Aristotle's quotes: "Be angry with the right person, to the right degree, at the right time, for the right purpose, in the right manner."

I completed my appeal by saying, "It's not that you shouldn't express your anger, Donald, it's about doing it in the right way. Anger is just a form of emotional energy. Think of it as you would nuclear energy. If it's harnessed, contained, and effectively channeled, it can light up cities. If it's used destructively, it can blow them into oblivion."

I made the choice to enter Donald's rational world, to present what I hoped would be a cogent argument for him to reconsider his beliefs about anger. Like the deductive approach he needed at the start of our work when he attempted to identify his other feelings, I hoped that by engaging his intellect first he might change his attitude in its regard.

But despite my success at intellectually convincing him that anger was an okay affect to feel, it still took considerable time before he could register it or give it expression. He had buried his anger for so long that unearthing it required a good deal of experiential work. That's because having the intellectual understanding that a given feeling is okay to express, and being able to actually experience that feeling, can still be a difficult gap to bridge.

Even if you know that expressing a feeling the right way is acceptable, and you know the cause of why you have the feeling, you can't "think" a feeling. That knowledge is only partially helpful in learning to experience a given feeling, and it often lies at the heart of why certain life issues remain unresolved. When it comes to laying long standing issues in life to rest, both the thinking and feeling related to those issues need work. Neither can exclusively get the job done.

But we civilized and rational people place a high emphasis on our intellect. Feelings can often seem messy and less easily packaged and put away, particularly the feelings that we believe are less flattering. Again, however, I find myself in agreement with Carl Jung where he believed that feeling serves as the anchor to complexes.

Granted, it can be uncomfortable experiencing emotions you'd rather avoid. That's especially the case if they've accumulated over time. Their potential expression can feel like a threat from the inside out. But just intellectualizing about them doesn't get the job done, and actually, too much intellectualizing about feelings can become a defense against their experience.

I personally learned about this propensity as a result of a crisis I once had. Ironically, it came in the midst of gaining an intellectual understanding about psychology and psychotherapy. The crisis occurred during the four-year period I was pursuing my PhD. I was 28 years old at the time, living in East Lansing, Michigan, and about midway through my program.

That four-year stretch was the first extended period in my life where I lived far away from my childhood home and family. When I first moved to Michigan, I was excited about pursuing my degree and discovering another part of the country. Initially, the program's demands, my teaching position, and meeting new people kept me busy. But the new acquaintances could not make up for the absence of the many close relationships I left behind. After the novelty wore off, I became lonely. The dark winter seemed to drag on. And then I met a woman with whom I quickly became attached.

That relationship quelled those lonely feelings, but as I would find out later, it didn't solve the underlying problems that gave them rise. I had yet to fully understand their cause, but that effort got put on a backburner because I became consumed with the good feelings that accompany the start of a new relationship. Then I took part in a premature decision. In the words of the song made famous by Johnny Cash, "we got married in a fever, hotter than a pepper sprout," and we weren't living far from Jackson, when suddenly that fire ran out.

Unfortunately for both of us, it was a flash fire. We impulsively moved in together, got engaged, got married, and almost as quickly as it all started, it ended. The whole experience lasted about 20 months, and everything I needed to come to terms with before I took that detour came back with the additional complications of a divorce.

I would have to say that the ordeal was my first personal experience with a Chrysalis Crisis. It led to uncovering and clearing a lot of unconscious emotional baggage I wasn't even aware I was lugging around. I was glad to be in a program learning about psychotherapy because I had plenty of therapists to choose from, and I clearly needed to get on the other side of the couch at that time.

It was a humbling but very important experience to go through because not only did I make some important discoveries about myself, I learned something else that I've never forgotten. No matter how astute therapists are in detecting what may be going on in their client's unconscious, that which lies in their own unconscious can remain hidden until given self-examination. Even Sigmund Freud had an unconscious. We're all vulnerable to that human condition.

That growth didn't come easy for me. It took time and a lot of work. But its effort led to a rapid period in my development. And as I said previously, for me it underscored that just "knowing" the cause of your problem is not enough. You can connect the dots and even be trained at tying them together for others, but it's very different to experientially release the emotions attached to those causes —to actually pull up those anchors.

You can't pick and choose what emotions you will or won't elect to feel. Life will bring you experiences where any number or combination of feelings can get activated. You need to get familiar with all your feelings, know when you're registering them, understand why you're having them, use them to give you guidance when needed, and most difficult of all, learn to actually express them in a manner that's appropriate when warranted.

They don't just go away, and it takes energy to keep them out of awareness. But part of your healing process may require revisiting some of those emotional experiences under a managed and safe situation, finishing what was left incomplete. To not do so and attempt to move on would be as effective as trying to put a crown on a damaged tooth when a root canal is needed to be done first.

Sorry for such a painful analogy, but in certain situations unresolved feelings require being revisited, felt, and finally diffused. Yet like a root canal, it doesn't mean you have to be laid raw to the pain. There are ways to ease the suffering when you do that kind of work and procedures that avoid being re-traumatized by the process.

It's unfortunate when life brings you lemons, but when it does, in addition to learning what you can from the ordeal, you need to experience and metabolize the feelings associated to it. Forgive another unattractive analogy, but if you don't, you could go through life emotionally constipated. And you might be also be surprised just how long unresolved and undiffused feelings can remain buried in your unconscious. Never was this made clearer to me than when I worked with a 75-year-old man by the name of Nick.

Nick came to see me because he was experiencing unexplainable intense anxiety accompanied by chest pain. His doctor and a cardiologist examined his heart and said he was healthy as a horse for his age. Both suspected something else might explain what was contributing to the symptoms.

Nick was a short, dark-haired fellow of Greek descent, who once worked as a mason. He'd been retired for 10 years and, until recently, had lived most of his life in a city up north. But Nick and his wife had decided they wanted to move closer to their daughter and her family. He was happy to have made the move and now enjoyed spending time with his grandkids.

After taking his history and getting a picture of how his life was presently going, I found nothing that would initially explain why he was feeling anxiety. He didn't have any threatening sickness, nor did he appear to be struggling with any apprehensiveness about death. His wife was also blessed with good health, and their finances in retirement seemed more than sufficient to sustain their present lifestyle.

I explored when he had what sounded like his first mild anxiety attack. He said it occurred while he was with his grandson at the park. They'd become very close and had been spending a good deal of time together. Nick looked forward to their one-on-one time when they would go on walks and various outings.

I recalled when I had asked Nick about his family of origin that he said his dad died when he was young. He mentioned that he and his two older sisters were raised by their mom. She never remarried. Nick described his mom as this strong, stoic type of a woman who was somewhat reserved. He said she wasn't the soft and cuddly type of mom who was openly affectionate, but he knew she loved him. He had few memories of his dad.

When I asked how his father's death was handled, Nick spoke admirably of how his mom just pulled her life together, found work, and forged on. He also said something else that caught my attention. He said that his mother told him that he had to be strong, too, because now he was the little man of the house.

Nick's dad died when he was 6 years old, the same age as his grandson. I inquired if he recalled how he felt when his dad died, but he said he couldn't remember. At that point, I suspected that there may have been some unresolved feelings about that loss, so I asked if he would be willing to allow me to employ a light hypnotic trance to assist his recollection. He agreed.

While in trance, I took Nick back to the tender moment when he was first told that his dad died. He was able to specifically place himself in the kitchen of his childhood home, even describing details of what that room looked like. I then gently asked him to slowly take a breath and check within himself how he felt upon hearing the news. In a moment, his eyes started watering, and with little additional prompting on my part, he began to weep.

Soon the weeping built into deep guttural crying. He cried so hard that he had to gasp for air on occasion. It was like he was that little boy who was once told he lost his daddy. I sat there next to him as he continued weeping, my own eyes brought to tears. I knew he just needed to let those emotions flow and finally be done with them.

Nick had been sitting on those feelings for nearly 70 years! He said he could hardly remember a time when he cried, not for his dad, or for anything else for that matter. It wasn't okay for men to cry in his day, he said. One could only imagine the cost he paid for shutting off those tender feelings for so long.

My sense was that those inhibitions about crying lessened with age. And also, through the open-hearted love he felt for his grandson, and the retrospective identification he developed with him at that same age he lost his dad, Nick's long repressed feelings got reawakened and started percolating back to the surface of his mind.

I've seen this occur before. Forgotten memories and feelings can get reawakened when parents open their hearts to children, and their children reach an age where the parent had some unresolved issues. They come alive again. Yet when it leads to the parent's growth or healing, I think of that line in the Wordsworth poem, "The child is the father of man."

Nick missed his father, but he only needed a few more sessions with me after that breakthrough. It quickly became evident that the anxiety and chest pain were no longer an issue. For the most part, his life was in a good place. He was not only a good example of how you can need an intellectual understanding and an emotional release to fully resolve a problem, but also how those two key areas in life can bring about symptoms in the key area of physicality.

Where Nick's resolution required retrieving his ability to cry, Donald's Chrysalis Crisis led to a more overall awakening of his key area of emotional growth. However, Donald's changes went beyond just opening his emotional life. He was also forced to change his reclusive ways. No longer could he just isolate himself by reading or spending extended periods alone in his lab. His children required that he engage more with them and others, like the parents of friends and his children's teachers. As he did, he became more open. And with those he could trust, that openness included sharing feelings.

Donald's road to healing took him in directions he never conceived of before his wife's death. The growth he achieved came in areas that remained out of sight until the crisis brought them into his awareness.

A crisis can be like a stormy sea that stirs the ocean's depths. It brings previously buried objects to the surface, leaving some scattered on the beach. But if not examined when exposed, they can get drawn back under or covered over. With us, however, out of sight is not out of mind. And that can be concerning, if what lies in those blind spots contributes to creating additional problems in our lives.

CHAPTER 6

Driving Blind:
Moral Crisis

While some people believe in the saying "ignorance is bliss," it's not one I personally endorse. I've incurred too many negative consequences in my life due to a lack of information. Bliss certainly wasn't the outcome. I imagine if you've ever been given a speeding ticket because you weren't aware of how fast you were going, the maxim "ignorance is no excuse for the law" was the one most driven home.

Similarly, traveling through life without sufficient self-awareness can also lead to negative consequences. For instance, not being mindful of where your chosen path may be leading can leave you unprepared for its hazards. Not knowing what lies in your intellectual or emotional blind spots can cause you to drift into dangerous places. And making critical life choices that are motivated by unconscious drives can result in suffering for yourself and others.

Brad's story serves as a perfect example. He had the misfortune of having all these possibilities become a reality. He was increasingly drifting into activities that were bound to create difficulties in his life. They led to problems he failed to envision. And the choices he made one evening resulted in an agonizing ordeal with a painful awakening, one that was both literal and figurative.

When Brad commenced therapy, he still was noticeably shaken by that ordeal. A well-built young man who stood about six foot two, he had light brown hair, blue eyes, and was very handsome. When he settled into the brown chair across from me, he sat upright and looked lost for where to start. As he began to speak, it appeared he was having trouble maintaining eye contact. He frequently gazed down.

I got the impression that it was difficult for him to say what prompted his call, and I had a sense that he might be feeling some shame in its regard. Once he got into the details, it became evident why.

Brad recently had undergone a very traumatic experience. Reviewing it again was painful. It was as if a nuclear bomb had just gone off in his life and the initial flash was still too blinding. And like the mushroom cloud that follows, the burgeoning effects of his trauma held serious consequences for his future.

A few weeks earlier Brad and his closest friend were sitting around his apartment on a Friday evening when they impulsively decided to take a late-night drive to Virginia Beach. The trip typically takes about three hours. Halfway there, Brad lost control of his car and it resulted in a serious accident.

He still wasn't clear how it all came about but suspected he had fallen asleep at the wheel. According to the police, the car veered off the road before hitting a concrete barrier on the passenger side. There were no skid marks prior to the point of impact.

Brad's first recollection upon awakening was being pinned down in his overturned car, struggling to breathe. When he came to, he was dazed and confused. He recalled seeing a blur of flashing lights and hearing the voices of the rescue team. He also noticed his friend's body lying nearby. He was later horrified to hear that his friend had died.

His friend's death weighed heavily on him. Having had too much to drink, Brad knew he shouldn't have been driving a car that night.

Other than a concussion and some bruising, Brad was extremely fortunate not to have incurred serious injury himself. But he was not spared the mental and emotional wounds. They ran deep. He was experiencing a heavy sense of guilt, and profound grief. He also was filled with anxiety, anticipating consequences that had yet to unfold. Though it was too early to determine if he was suffering from a post-traumatic stress disorder (PTSD), he was certainly experiencing an acute stress disorder.

The consequences he was anticipating certainly warranted concern because Brad was facing a DUI manslaughter charge, the likelihood of jail time, and potentially significant financial and career damages. At the age of 25 and just starting out in life, he knew these damages would have major implications for his future.

Tragedies were foreign to Brad. Other than his parents divorcing when he was in grade school, he'd led a pretty uneventful life. Hailing from a small town in Central Virginia, he was the youngest of three boys. They all resided with their mom who was depicted as a hard worker and somewhat reserved.

Brad had little recollection of his father. He said his dad was hardly ever around following the divorce and, after a year or two, abandoned the family completely. Brad heard through the grapevine that his father eventually moved out of state and ultimately became a derelict alcoholic.

Throughout his school years Brad had a history of athletic success. After he graduated college, he quickly found employment and moved into his own apartment, and it appeared as if his life was on a positive trajectory.

Once I gathered his family history and background, I decided to first address Brad's level of stress. Overwhelmed by all that happened, he was depressed and highly anxious. The acute stress disorder Brad was experiencing extended beyond a month and ultimately warranted the full diagnosis of PTSD.

Brad was having intrusive recollections of the moment he discovered his friend's body lying next to him. At times this image broke into his awareness during disturbing dreams, causing him to awaken in panic attacks. The anxiety led him to avoid any stimuli that would arouse recollections of the incident. For instance, he became highly anxious just being in a car. He was having persistent symptoms of arousal, occasionally experiencing increased heart rate, cold sweats, and rapid breathing.

Adopting a therapy approach where I conveyed support without judgment, I helped Brad carefully examine how he thought about the event, label feelings associated to it, and develop strategies for adopting behaviors that would enable him to resume full functioning of his needed activities.

I also employed hypnosis to help Brad desensitize the memory of the traumatic moments following the accident. Through the use of trance, and the establishment of a safe place to go in his mind should he become overwhelmed by the memories, I was able to gently and progressively re-expose him to those memories so he could diffuse their charge and not become re-traumatized by the process. In time, he was able to file those memories away as representations of past events and allay the associated emotions so they would not intrude into his present.

As the PTSD symptoms subsided and therapy proceeded, it also became apparent that Brad had another major concern to address: his relationship with alcohol. Despite what he told me when I initially inquired about the extent of his drinking, he finally acknowledged that it had gotten out of hand. Like his father and his grandfather before him, Brad was an alcoholic.

Brad resisted being thought of as an alcoholic. Despite his level of consumption and daily pattern of drinking, he still denied the label applied. In his mind, being an alcoholic was being a derelict drunk like his dad. He believed his proven record of success and his ability to maintain his employment would attest to the contrary. He also rationalized that his level of drinking was no different than the kind of partying he did in college.

I granted him that many college students do a lot of drinking, but if taken out of the context of that lifestyle, it probably would qualify for a diagnosis of substance abuse. However, I said, the majority of students who indulge to that extent during those college years usually break out of that pattern after they graduate and take on added responsibilities. Those who don't—or can't—are usually headed for serious problems.

Despite my perspective, Brad continued to struggle with the idea that he'd become an alcoholic like his dad. Accepting that would be to admit he had no self-control, and he would feel shame that he'd succumbed to the same problem. So in order to help him accept that reality without the self-judgment and contempt, I informed him that there's a significant body of research that supports a genetic link to becoming an alcoholic. I suggested that if he viewed his alcoholism as a disease, one that needed to be treated, we could move into the kind of work required for its amelioration. Reframing it that way softened his resistance.

I also recommended that in light of his possibly being an alcoholic, and due to the severity of the pending charges that had yet to be tried in court, there were a few good reasons to start attending an AA group. He saw the sense in that, and once he began attending AA, he not only found it helpful, but not too long afterward admitted that he was indeed an alcoholic.

In time, however, it became apparent that his alcohol addiction was just the first layer of problems he faced. Brad needed psychological and emotional growth in several areas. Much of it had been brought to light by his recent ordeal. It's the kind of growth that often follows PTSD. It's called posttraumatic growth, or PTG.

This kind of growth has been given a considerable amount of attention in the past 20 years. It arises out of a more recent turn toward what is referred to as Positive Psychology, an emphasis that focuses on positive growth rather than pathology.

PTG results in five major areas of growth: increased inner strength, an openness to new possibilities in life, closer and deeper relationships, an enhanced appreciation for life, and a stronger sense of spirituality. A few of these areas overlap with the ten key areas of growth examined in this book, and that's why I include PTG under the umbrella of Chrysalis Crises.

With regard to Brad's growth, I helped him see the potential of how he could use this traumatic event as a Chrysalis Crisis. He liked the idea and welcomed the challenge but, as it turned out, that effort needed to be put on a back burner.

Though Brad had excellent legal representation and conveyed sincere remorse for what transpired, only so much could be done to lessen the consequences. Taking everything into consideration,

Brad was shown some mercy. Although he was given jail time and leveled a substantial fine, the judge told Brad that if he conducted himself properly in jail, at a certain point he would be allowed to return to the community and complete the balance of his time on weekends. Those allowances, however, were contingent on two expectations: that he continue attending AA both during and after jail, and that he resume his therapy upon release.

After his period of full-time incarceration, Brad returned to my office. When he first showed up, he appeared changed. He was no longer feeling as much fear and grief, and the PTSD symptoms were virtually gone. The whole ordeal—the death of his friend, his time in jail, and the other consequences he faced—sobered Brad in ways beyond giving up alcohol. He really wanted to change his life now. He was ready to use his crisis as a way to grow and mature—ready to use it as a Chrysalis Crisis.

In pursuit of that goal, the time in jail proved to be beneficial in two other ways. First, he didn't have access to alcohol; that assured a needed period of abstinence. And second, attending the AA group helped him stabilize around his sobriety.

That was helpful for the work we undertook, because in order to address the kinds of problems that lay below his addiction, I had to stir the very feelings and anxieties he used the alcohol to anesthetize. While such depth work is often required to address the underpinnings of addictions, unearthing those feelings and memories before abstinence is stabilized can prompt an individual to relapse.

Brad showed much less vulnerability to that potential. He seemed stronger, well anchored in his abstinence, and he was prepared to do the kind of work that was needed. And while he was independently motivated to take it on, I took some comfort in the fact that since therapy was mandated by the court, if the process got difficult, he would still have to stick with it.

Once we resumed our sessions, we quickly regained the trust and comfort level we had achieved earlier. Brad seemed hungry for my male mentoring, and in addition to other impressions I perceived, he also appeared humbled by his recent life events. He softened and came across as more mature. Having been away from the anesthetizing effects of the alcohol for some time, he also seemed much more emotionally accessible.

While incarcerated, Brad said he gave a great deal of thought to how and why his successful life had taken such a bad turn. What boggled him, and what was most difficult for him to accept, was how he could elect to do something he clearly understood was wrong. He imagined how others might make such a dumb mistake, but he said he knew better than to drink and drive. And furthermore, he still considered himself to be an ethical and moral person.

I told him that such ethical and moral inconsistencies are not uncommon in people. I shared research from a book that's fittingly entitled *Blind Spots*.[1] It reveals how biases in our thought processes effect how we view the ethical actions we take. Those biases can lead to three inconsistent positions on how we respond to ethical dilemmas: How we think we'll act before we're faced with a given ethical dilemma, how we actually choose to act in the moment we confront it, and how we retroactively view ourselves after having made an unethical choice that's contrary to what we imagined we'd do.

Interestingly, the authors note that despite knowing better beforehand, and acting in a manner that we know was wrong, we may nevertheless still see ourselves as an ethical person afterwards. It underscores how inconsistent we can be as humans, and how despite those inconsistencies we can simultaneously hold conflicting perceptions of ourselves.

It's been my clinical experience that when those contradictions occur, it often indicates that unrecognized aspects of an individual's unconscious are operating at cross purposes with how that person consciously wants to conduct himself.

The authors of *Blind Spots* also provide additional research on "behavioral ethics," a field of study they say that "seeks to understand how people actually behave when confronted with an ethical dilemma."[2] They found that making the right ethical or moral choice in any given situation is often influenced by a couple of common-sense variables. One is just taking sufficient time before making that choice, and another is giving the choice adequate consideration. In Brad's case, on the evening of the accident, his inebriation and impulsivity compromised both of those variables.

But even if you're given sufficient time to consider an ethical decision, and you have the knowledge of what *is* right and wrong, whether you will choose to act in an ethical manner is also influenced by your stage of cognitive growth. Lawrence Kohlberg was an early pioneer in this field of research.

Kohlberg's theory on the stages of moral development run parallel to the cognitive lines of development that Jean Piaget outlined in his research. Kohlberg defines six identifiable stages, and he groups them into three different levels. They progressively unfold as the person intellectually matures, and they can overlap as they evolve.

At the first level, what he calls the *pre-conventional level*, obedience, punishment, and self-interest are of primary concern. Questions like, how can I avoid punishment, or what's in it for me, are considered when making an ethical decision. At the second level, called the *conventional*, interpersonal conformity, social concern, and the acceptance of the social order drive ethical decisions. This is referred to as the "good boy/good girl attitude," where one wants to be seen as a law-abiding citizen, respecting authority and following the law of the land. In the third *post-conventional* level, we recognize that there is a "social contract" we all have with each other, and that there are universal principles that exist which should ultimately govern the ethical decisions we make. Determining what is ethical and moral is arrived at through abstract thinking, adherence to values, and governed more by one's individual conscience.

Let me give you an example of how an ethical decision might be made at each level. Imagine that you're thinking about taking a bribe from someone who wants inside information on a potential stock purchase. At Kohlberg's pre-conventional level, that ethical decision will be driven by considerations like, will I get caught? Or, what's in it for me if I take this risk? At the second conventional level, that decision will be driven by the acceptance of society's conventions of right and wrong. You might not take the bribe because of the potential social embarrassment of being seen as a corrupt official, or because it's against the rules and you're good soldier who respects authority.

Lastly, in the post-conventional stage, even if those laws were hardly ever enforced and it is well known that everyone is doing it so no one would care, you might still not take the money. Because at that higher level, your decision would be driven by how it sits with your personal conscience. You might not do it because you believe in abstract principles like fairness.

Interestingly, at this third level, you might alternatively not choose to abide by an existing law because you personally believe it does not meet your standard of a higher universal principle. For instance, you may elect to defy a law based in prejudice because it fails to uphold a higher abstract principle like "all people are created equal."

Some of the critics of Kohlberg's theory suggest it doesn't consider other influential variables that underlie ethical decision making. I tend to agree because I believe that emotions play a significant role in effecting ethical choices. One obvious feeling would be fear of getting caught, but I think it goes beyond that. Other feelings can also influence doing something that you "know" is wrong.

For example, irrespective of whatever intellectual level Brad was operating on, or whether he would have had adequate time to give his decision additional consideration, I suspect that the choice he made to drive under the influence, as well as other choices he was making to engage in illegal activities, were driven by a host of unconscious emotions.

Those unconscious emotions were anchored in his mind long before the accident, and he effectively kept them out of his awareness by his continued drinking. On that night, Brad was not only too drunk to drive, *he was driven to drink*. And it was becoming clear that it was all part of a self-destructive pattern that had been long standing in his life—a treacherous unconscious pattern—that stood in direct conflict with what he consciously undertook to make his life a success. In a way, Brad was leading a double life, a life that up until that evening remained largely separated.

Investigating, unearthing, and integrating the feelings that contributed to that separation became the challenge of our work. Brad needed to identify those emotions because, as the authors of *Blind Spots* state, "the difficulty of changing ethical behavior comes from the lack of awareness."[3]

The investigation of emotional influences on ethical and moral decision making initially was given prominence by Martin Hoffman.[4] His theory of moral development is predicated on the primacy of "affect," the ability of an individual to imagine or empathize with how their ethical choices will make others feel.

For example, even if a person is not intellectually clear about what is right or wrong in a given situation, if he can imagine how his ethical choice will make other people feel before he acts, it can provide an alternative moral compass to consult. More recently, Jonathan Haidt, another renowned researcher in the field, also emphasized the importance of feelings in ethical decisions. He noted that emotional reactions *precede* moral judgments.[5]

Both of what these researchers point out applied to Brad. He wasn't an outright sociopath. He could show empathy for others and had a conscience. He also seemed to have a host of feelings that effected his moral judgments. However, many of those feelings had been long buried, and I discovered that alcohol wasn't the only substance he used to keep them out of his awareness. He had a dual addiction, which included the use of numerous illegal drugs, some of which he would occasionally deal for money.

This darker side of Brad also revealed itself in other depraved behaviors, for example in the way he treated women. When he discussed his relationships with them, he depicted himself as a "player," the kind of guy who would manipulate or lie to a woman to get what he wanted. He saw women as sexual objects, giving little thought to how his behaviors made them feel.

A good deal of Brad's entitlement and attitude toward women appeared to be driven by a motherlode of unconscious feelings. He held a lot of resentment toward his mom. Once we got into a deeper exploration of that relationship, he ranted about how he perceived she treated him and his brothers. He said she spent little one on one time with them outside of overseeing their schoolwork. She expected them to do a lot of chores and generally follow her iron clad rules.

Though it was uncomfortable for Brad to explore those feelings, they were more accessible now that he wasn't abusing substances. Once he expressed and reconciled them, he was able to shift his attitude towards his mother. He could see how her withdrawal and reticence was probably due to a longstanding depression that followed his father's abandonment of the family. And he could appreciate that single parenting three boys while being the sole provider left little of her for much else.

But it wasn't all about his mom. There was a "fatherlode" of emotional confusion, too. Those buried feelings, along with their associated toxic beliefs contributed to the difficulties he was experiencing in his life. He lacked the self-awareness of how it all took a toll on him.

It was a real awakening for Brad. He came to see how those unconscious beliefs and emotions contributed to the darker side of his nice guy front. They comprised that part of him that Carl Jung refers to as the "shadow side" of the personality, the side that lies behind the persona or mask we present to others.

Brad was not unique in being oblivious to this darker side of his makeup. It's difficult for most people to recognize. Even when identified, it's hard to face. It can cause embarrassment and shame to admit, and takes a good deal of humility and courage to share it with others, even a therapist.

But whether it's guilt or shame that keeps us oblivious to these shadow aspects, it's important to recognize that it's only human to have some. They're like barnacles that inevitably get picked up on the underside of a boat. For us, they remain below the waterline of our awareness, yet like a boat, if they accumulate, they can slow us down as we attempt to sail through life.

Together, Brad and I were able to help him shed many of the darker feelings and thoughts he'd been carrying around. He came to see how their detrimental effects led to the ethical choices he made. All of these insights and changes contributed to his development in the key area of moral growth.

That was no small accomplishment for Brad. He put in an extensive effort to achieve that outcome. But as a result of that success, he could now trust his own moral guidance system—no more driving blind.

When clients successfully undertake this kind of depth-work and eliminate their buried self-destructive patterns, I'm often reminded of what Jesus once said in this regard. It comes from the Gospel of Saint Thomas: "If you bring forth what is within you, what you bring forth will save you. If you do not bring forth what is within you, what you do not bring forth will destroy you."

This certainly was the case with Brad. He chose to use his crisis as a Chrysalis Crisis and opted to avoid any further life destruction. But now that he wasn't inclined to do any more tearing down, he wanted to do some new construction. Namely, build a healthy relationship with a woman.

Toward the end of our work together, he expressed a desire to find a woman he could share his life with. He felt ready and better equipped to succeed at making a relationship work. Brad came to see women in a more respectful light, no longer just as objects to meet his sexual needs. And when he had occasions to first meet one, he no longer came across as some suave ladies' man. Instead, he tried to be more sincere, transparent, and authentic.

Though Brad had his father's blood running through him, he realized he could bring more to a relationship than his dad brought to his mom. While he had to keep an eye on his use of alcohol, he wasn't genetically destined to blindly drive himself down a road to destroying relationships. And he could consciously make decisions to improve his life in other ways. One was his decision to not resume friendships with people who still abused alcohol and drugs. He sought new social connections. He revived his athletic interests, joined sports teams, and strengthened friendships made in AA.

All of these changes came as the result of a cumulative effect from the work he undertook to turn his life around. It not only required the gains he made in the key area of moral growth, but Brad had to acquire further development in a number of the other key areas we've examined, too.

He addressed his key area of physical growth by taking his body back from the grasp of alcohol and drug addiction, and he learned to not let his sexual desires lead him to exploit women. In the key area of intellectual growth, he sought the information and self-knowledge he needed from me, AA, and books. He eradicated self-limiting beliefs and changed his thoughts about his future.

Brad also worked very hard in the key area of emotional growth. He not only quieted the feelings surrounding the accident, but uncovered and resolved many of those unconscious feelings he carried toward his mom and dad.

His overall transformation required growth in a number of key areas, some more than others. He is a good example of a point I made earlier: all ten key areas of growth are interdependent, and to varying degrees influence each other. But one key area Brad did not need help with is social growth. Brad was outgoing by nature, could engender a positive response from others, and was good at getting included in new groups. But not everyone has developed that ability.

CHAPTER 7

Out of the Woods:
Social Crisis

Rona was excited to start college. She worked long and hard to gain entry to the University of Virginia in Charlottesville. Her folks were happy she chose the state's flagship institution because while it's one of the nation's top public universities, the in-state tuition was much easier on their pocketbooks.

Though she was accepted into some highly ranked Ivy League schools, Rona felt most comfortable staying in Virginia. She didn't want to venture too far away from home. But even at that, UVA was a good three-and-a-half-hour drive from where she lived in the southwest corner of the state.

At first, Rona soaked up the newness of the college experience. The campus was every bit as beautiful as she recalled from an earlier visit: the Jeffersonian architecture, the beauty of the central lawn, the splendor of the nearby mountains, and the historic small city that surrounds the university. It was all eye candy. However, compared to her small town, moving to Charlottesville was like heading to the big city.

Initially, freshman orientation provided plenty of structure and activity to help Rona settle in. Housed in one of the older dorms in the center of campus, she had a short walk to most of her classes. Her roommate was nice enough, but like Rona she was more of an introvert.

Rona found her courses thought-provoking. She liked learning and took a great deal of pride being the only student from her high school capable of gaining admission into UVA. But the learning environment at UVA was competitive, and the professors were demanding. There were no easy grades. Even the courses that sounded less rigorous required plenty of reading.

Success in school had come pretty easy for Rona in the past, but now she was being academically challenged in ways she'd not previously experienced. Like a star athlete in high school who joins a high-caliber college team, she was competing with other gifted individuals. And as with a sports team, there were a limited number of starting spots in the position she hoped to occupy. Everyone was working for A's. That was particularly the case in the pre-med classes. Due to their difficulty, they were typically graded on a curve, and only so many A's were available.

Adjusting to an academic environment where more than 90 percent of accepted students were in the top 10 percent of their high school classes was a little daunting for Rona. And because her anticipated career drew such an elite group, she worked harder than ever and still got more B's than A's. She wasn't used to that. It was sobering and disturbing, and it began to take a toll on her confidence.

A large part of Rona's identity and self-esteem was based upon being a top student. Excelling in academics was virtually her sole focus during her formative years. She sacrificed a great deal to attain that success, and most of that sacrifice came at the expense of engaging in other school and social activities.

For Rona, however, it was an easy sacrifice to make, because she wasn't much for joining groups or partying. Neither was she athletic, so she didn't partake in any sports teams. As a matter of fact, the only group she did affiliate with in high school was the chess club. That suited her mental keenness but required very little of her interpersonally.

In those days, Rona was your classic loner. If she needed any personal interaction, she would seek out her mom. Like Rona, her mother was more of an introvert, but she was a good listener. Compared to her dad, however, Rona's mom was a social butterfly. Her father was described as what we might diagnose in the clinical trade as a schizoid personality, someone who avoids social activities and consistently shies away from interactions with others.

While it wasn't clear at first whether Rona fit that same description, there were definitely some similarities. On the upside, however, she inherited her dad's exceptional intelligence. They both were noted for their crisp logical and analytic thinking abilities.

Socially, Rona's mother and father had little need for affiliation. And for that matter, according to Rona, they hardly spent time interacting with each other. They rarely got together with other couples, and their extended families lived out of state. Contact with relatives was infrequent.

Rona's mother was a writer and her father worked as an accountant. Even their jobs required considerable alone time. Rona had no other siblings, so in their home, all three frequently would go off into their own worlds: mom would write, dad would pore over spreadsheets, and Rona would occupy herself with schoolwork or reading.

The family lived at a decent standard of living. They drove new cars and owned a nice home back in the woods. But despite their wherewithal, they did not own a television. Both parents believed that it was a waste of time to watch TV, and when the mom home-schooled Rona during her primary years, she preferred to not have its distracting temptations around.

While this environment was optimal for intellectual learning, it did little to help Rona grow socially. She didn't learn basic inter-personal skills or how to navigate social situations. It wasn't that she suffered from social anxiety; she was just significantly lacking in social development. This deficit, however, became more of a handi-cap once she was out in the world and living away.

By the later part of her first semester, Rona began to feel increas-ingly more isolated. Without access to her mom when needed, she also began to feel lonely. Conversations over the phone and using Skype helped, but it wasn't the same as having someone she knew nearby.

She and her roommate never quite bonded. The girl grew up in Northern Virginia and socially gravitated toward a few of her long-standing high school friends who also came down to UVA. Little effort was made to include Rona into her activities, and Rona didn't know how to initiate getting herself included. And because the roommate spent a lot of her time away from their room, Rona took that as a sign that the roommate didn't like her. That led Rona to start feeling bad about herself.

As the social isolation and pressures of the academic demands began to mount, Rona came to wonder if she had made the right decision going to UVA. She became increasingly unhappy, and it started to undermine her performance in school. Just when Rona was feeling most disheartened, she received what amounted to a high D and a low C on two mid-term exams.

Such grades were foreign to Rona. Seeing them in black and white was almost surreal. She panicked. Embarrassed to tell her mom and ashamed of what her dad would think, she had no one to whom she could turn. Now, she was not only lonely, but she also was feeling like a failure. It all resulted in her becoming depressed.

Fortunately, Rona had an astute Resident Advisor working on her dorm floor. The young woman noticed that Rona tended to go it alone. Occasionally, she would try to throw out a hook to engage Rona in conversation, but Rona wouldn't bite. Despite the lack of response, however, the RA persevered. She had good instincts and noticed that Rona's body language and demeanor suggested she was down. The RA's continued efforts finally paid off, and when Rona eventually opened up to her, the suspicions were confirmed: Rona was troubled.

The RA recognized that Rona needed professional help with her depression, and she suggested that Rona go to the university counseling center to seek their services. There Rona was provided a limited number of therapy sessions, and then was referred out to the community for additional help. That's how Rona came into my care.

My first impression of her in my waiting room was that she looked younger than a first-year student. When I approached her and introduced myself, she stood up, shook my hand, and gave me a nervous smile. Petite and frail in appearance, Rona looked no more than five feet tall. She had long brown hair with bangs covering her forehead, wore dark rimmed glasses, and had brown eyes.

After she settled into my office, I outlined the conditions of our professional relationship and began conducting an assessment. It was quickly evident that Rona was depressed. She revealed many of its diagnostic signs. She'd not been sleeping or eating well, was often sad, randomly became weepy, experienced low self-esteem, was unable to concentrate, derived little pleasure in life, and generally felt helpless and hopeless about changing her situation.

When I queried her further as to just how bad things had gotten, she admitted that the thought of killing herself had crossed her mind. I asked how far that thinking had progressed and was glad to hear that it was mostly a passing thought, not an act she'd seriously considered.

I didn't need to be a Sigmund Freud to see that Rona was in crisis. And while it soon became evident that she lacked in social development, her emotional growth was also limited. But because she was suffering, she was highly motivated to change. I suspected her motivation and intellectual abilities would enable her to make good use of therapy and in essence told her that this life ordeal could serve as a Chrysalis Crisis. She felt encouraged by my optimism and embraced the challenge.

The first of those challenges required taking risks with me. Professional or not, opening up to me was not easy for her. There were lots of stops and starts, and I frequently found myself saying, "Can you tell me more about that?" or "Can you elaborate?" Even though she knew revealing herself was necessary for the process to work, it just wasn't in her nature to talk that much. However, over time, trust developed and she slowly opened up.

When I gathered more information about her family, she described her relationships with her mother and father. She depicted a good deal of distance between herself and her dad, and I could see how that contributed to the difficulties she had relating to men. I realized that it was probably difficult for her to open up to a male therapist, so I tried to be sensitive and patient with her.

My work was clear. If I could help Rona establish a strong therapeutic alliance with me, then our professional relationship could serve as a vehicle for the kind of growth she needed. But I knew it would take more than I could provide in one-on-one therapy. While I trusted she eventually could gain increasing comfort with me in the safety of my office, I believed she would need opportunities to transfer that knowledge into social situations outside.

She was coachable and showed a quick understanding of strategies when we discussed managing certain interpersonal situations, but she had a lot of social blind spots. She needed more real-life practice to open her eyes.

Rona was severely lacking in the area that Daniel Goleman refers to as *social intelligence*.[1] He suggests that one's *social IQ* is predicated on two main functions: *social awareness* and *social facility*.

According to Goleman, "*social awareness* refers to a spectrum that runs from instantaneously sensing another's inner state, to understanding her feelings and thoughts," and generally "getting" complicated social situations.[2]

He lists four main areas that contribute to a heightened sense of social awareness: *primal empathy*, or sensing non-verbal emotional signals; *attunement*, or listening with full receptivity; *empathic accuracy*, or understanding another person's thoughts, feelings, and intentions; and *social cognition*, or knowing how the social world works.

Rona was quick to grasp this knowledge, but her ability to empathize and her accuracy for understanding the feelings of others was lacking. Through more practice in social interactions, that learning could contribute to the second key function articulated by Goleman: *social facility*.

Social facility builds on social awareness. It allows for smooth and effective interactions, which also includes four areas of adeptness: *synchrony*, what Goleman describes as one's ability to interact smoothly at the non-verbal level; *self-presentation*, or presenting oneself effectively;

influence, or shaping the outcome of social interactions; and *concern,* or caring about other's needs and acting accordingly.

These were all skills and abilities that Rona needed to learn, and she was motivated to develop them. Over time in our work it became apparent that she had a real hunger for more personal connection with others and, like her mom, appeared to have the capacity to be more emotionally open. Rona just didn't know how to go about getting what she wanted from people.

Rona was like a plant that needed watering. She'd been socially wilting. Even her gifted intellect began to wither due to the absence of other needed nutrients that were lacking in her life. And because I knew she needed more than I could individually provide in our therapy, I asked that in addition, she consider joining a therapy group.

I knew that a psychotherapy group would provide her with more hands-on social experience in a safe and facilitated setting. There she could start gaining interpersonal skills like synchrony, or learn to understand nonverbal interactions with others, and become more emotionally attuned in her interactions.

If Rona didn't gain these abilities, she would be at a disadvantage in life. She would run the risk of suffering from what Goleman calls "dyssemia." He defines dyssemia as "a deficit in reading, and acting on, the nonverbal signs that guide smooth interactions."

For example, a socially dyssemic person who's conversing with another individual who needs to end the interaction will miss the subtle and not so subtle signs that the person wishes to terminate the conversation. The person needing to exit might initially shift his eyes away as if he were looking to locate someone, or glance at his watch.

Having a basic level of *social synchrony* enables a person to pick up on these not so subtle cues. Then with further facility, she could employ some *social caring* by reading the other person's need and contribute helpful *interactive influence* by making statements to assist the disengagement. Alternatively, not picking up on the cues, nor offering any help, just tends to lead to more awkward or abrupt departures.

A professionally led psychotherapy group geared toward inter-personal and social development would provide Rona the opportunity to hone all these abilities. Additionally, it would offer another safe and confidential forum for her to explore and understand the kinds of intimate feelings that she and others of her age experience.

Despite the potential learning a psychotherapy group could provide, however, Rona was predictably hesitant to join one. Initially, just the thought of doing so scared her. But in time, she mus-tered the courage to seek one out and, as I hoped, began to learn what she needed. As a result of her growth from group therapy and her continued work with me, Rona began to flower.

Witnessing her flower was very gratifying. I find it heartening to see someone her age who's motivated and malleable succeed in mak-ing needed change. College age students are good examples of young adults who evidence that capacity. Though they comprise a small part of my practice, I enjoy having a number of them on my caseload.

I first discovered their energy, intellect, and ripeness for growth when undertaking my doctoral internship at the Michigan State University counseling center. There I was taught a variety of thera-peutic approaches and instructed on how to utilize numerous psy-chological instruments in my work with students. One particular instrument I used also was employed to help individuals with the kinds of interpersonal problems Rona presented. That instrument is called the Myers Briggs Type Indicator (MBTI).[4]

The MBTI is not a test where you find out if you pass or fail your personality, nor is it a heavy-duty clinical instrument constructed to determine psychopathology. It's more of a personality inventory that measures individual preferences on a few key functions that all people employ.

The instrument is based on Carl Jung's theory of psychological types.[5] It primarily measures four key areas of how we personally function. The first area measures a person's *basic orientation toward the world*. Jung identified two distinctly diverse ways we direct that orientation. He coined the words *introversion* and *extraversion* to differentiate them.

According to Jung, the *introvert* is oriented inwardly, stimulated by his internal world of ideas and concepts. When presented with new people, ideas, or situations, for example, the more introverted person will be inclined to give them further thought, mull things over, and feel no particular need to verbally express his thoughts.

Alternatively, the *extravert* tends to be more stimulated by what goes on around him. His focus is oriented outward. If the extravert were presented with new people, ideas, or situations, he would be more inclined to socially extend himself to others, verbally express his thoughts and ideas, or throw himself into the new situations.

These two types of orientation are familiar to most people, and like right-handedness and left-handedness, introversion and extraversion typically reveals itself early in life. However, an individual's preferred orientation is just one of four areas measured by the MBTI.

Two of the other three areas were also identified by Jung, and he considered them to be the *core functions* of psychological type. Those functions are *perception* and *judgment,* and within each of them, lie their two different preferences.

The *perception* function is defined as the process of *how we perceive the world, how we become aware of information, or generally, how we behold that which is around us.* Jung found that there are broadly two ways people employ their perception function. Some of us prefer to use what he called *sensing,* while others favor employing *intuition.*

Those who favor *sensing* as their preferred style of perception rely more on their five objective senses in how they register what they perceive. Because of that they're inclined to focus on what they actually see, touch, smell, taste, or hear. Sensing types have a more practical, realistic style of responding to the world. They're typically the "show me" kind of folk.

Intuition, on the other hand, employs perception in a more indirect manner. An individual who favors intuition also would be capable of registering what they see, hear, smell, taste, or touch, but would spend less time focusing on what's specifically available to the senses and be more aware of the impressions, associations, or the possibilities of what they're perceiving. Jung suggests that this kind of awareness comes by way of the individual's unconscious. Intuitive types are your visionaries. They *see* what has not yet manifested to the objective senses.

Research on psychological type has found that, overall, the majority of Americans prefer and predominantly favor the sensing function over the intuitive function. That imbalance stands at about 80 percent preferring sensing and 20 percent intuition. This is important to keep in mind because the kinds of experiences that are intuitively registered will have implications for what I'll discuss later in the book when I examine the key area of intuitive development.

In addition to perception, the other core function of *judgment* is defined as the process by which we come to conclusions about what we perceive. Another way to think about the judgment function is to consider how you go about making decisions. There are two different preferences of how we go about employing the judgment function. Those two different preferences are *feeling* and *thinking*.

Individuals who prefer to employ *feeling* in the judgment process will favor their own subjective likes and dislikes when making decisions. Alternatively, those who prefer to employ *thinking* will be more inclined to make their decisions by using an impartial, analytic, or a pros-and-cons approach. Feeling types also are noted to be more attuned to their feelings and the feelings of others, while thinking types are more attuned to cognitive considerations, rationality, or the logical flow of thoughts.

Finally, in the creation of the MBTI, Clarence Myers and Isabell Briggs determined that there was a need to distinguish one more difference that contributes to an individual's psychological type. They noted that not only do individuals display different preferences *within* the core functions of perception and judgment, but preferences exist *between* the two core functions. In other words, a given individual may have a stronger preference for employing the function of perceiving over judging, or visa-versa.

For example, a preference for perception over judgment would incline the individual to extend the process of taking in information, be less likely to move toward making a decision, or hold off coming to a conclusion. A strong preference for perception may prolong the process of deliberating and considering and, at times, even lead to procrastination.

Alternatively, the person who prefers the judgment function over the perceiving function is more inclined to make decisions and be less inclined to spend time in the deliberation process. They likely would abbreviate the consideration phase, push to make a decision, or quickly come to conclusions. A strong preference for the judgment function can lead to premature decisions, or coming to conclusions before sufficient information is gathered.

All these different MBTI preferences are assessed by subjects filling out a questionnaire. The responses are then quantified and appointed to one of 16 different psychological types. For instance, a person whose results reflect a preference for **I**ntroversion over extraversion on the orientation function, **S**ensing over intuition on the perception function, **F**eeling over thinking on the judgment function, or the preference for the core **P**erceiving function over the core judgment function, would be designated as the psychological type: ISFP.

That ISFP personality type would then reflect an individual's combined preferences and reveal certain characteristics or inclinations of how he might conduct himself in light of the dimensions measured. But it's important to realize that one has access to *all* these functions and preferences. It's just that when certain preferences are predominantly employed or favored, it can lead some to become highly developed and others to be left lacking.

This was the case with Rona. When employing the MBTI in my work with her, I was not surprised to find that she had strong preferences for introversion and thinking. Of the four functions, those two revealed the areas where she most needed to grow. She needed to further actualize her extroverted potentials and develop greater facility understanding her feelings and the feelings of others.

Like a number of students I worked with at the counseling center, Rona's trouble socially acclimating correlated with a strong preference for introversion. That is *not* to say that all introverts will have social problems when going away to school because extraverts can have their kinds of difficulties, too. But I've found that highly introverted students took a little longer to establish new friendships. They seemed to need more time and shared experiences to develop the quality of connection that for them might warrant the title of "friend."

The good news about all the different dimensions of psychological type is that, according to Jung, we not only innately have access to all of these different functions and preferences, but with effort we can develop each one. Like handedness, practice at developing our auxiliary preferences can help us become "ambidextrous" in psychological type.

Sometimes, the need to cultivate those less developed preferences get prompted by a crisis. Though there were different reasons for doing so, Donald, like Rona, had to develop more of his feeling function to balance his strong thinking bias. He also needed to exercise more of his extroverted abilities when he no longer had his wife to mediate his and the kids' interactions with the world. Sue is a good example of someone who needed to be less of a premature judger, and open her mind to alternative ways of perceiving herself and others.

Changing life situations, with or without crisis, also can prompt us to shift or develop the other preferences in type. Let me share a personal experience I had in this regard. It took place when I was working at that counseling center.

At the time, I was providing MBTI testing and interpretations for numerous campus and community-wide applications. As part of my employment, I also was receiving supervision from the center's director to assure my work was being conducted properly.

During one session, my mentor asked how I was progressing on my doctoral dissertation. I shared that I was mostly feeling anxiety about the undertaking, waffling between a few different topics being considered, and generally working in fits and spurts. After a few years of working together, he knew me well. He'd seen my strengths and weaknesses, so he approached my angst within the context of our shared knowledge of the MBTI.

Knowing that I was an extreme **Extravert**, an extreme intuitive (**N**), and having clear preferences for **Feeling** and **Perceiving**, he gave me the following advice. He said, "As an ENFP, you're going to need to develop your ISTJ functions, especially if you want to successfully undertake and complete your dissertation."

He went on to explain that I would need to forego much of the "extraverted" time I spent socializing with others and spend more "introverted" time reading and writing. And after I "intuitively" envisioned the possibilities of a given dissertation topic, I would need to employ my "sensing" functions so that when reviewing the related research on my topic, I'd be sure to zero in on the relevant details and facts that needed to be gathered.

Then, he said, despite my personal "feelings" about what results I hoped to find, I would have to employ my "thinking" function to assure I treat the data that's actually discovered with impartial and logical analysis. And lastly, because he knew how I might fall prey to the less helpful tendencies of a preferred "perceiver," he emphasized the need to draw upon my "judgment" function. He said that function is instrumental for instituting the structure, time management, and organization required for carrying out such a task. Despite my perceiver inclinations, he added, "You can't just 'go-with-the- flow' if you want to undertake and complete a dissertation."

It was sage advice, and it was on the mark because completing my dissertation indeed required employing all my *auxiliary* functions. At times, however, I felt like a right-handed basketball player who had to start using his left hand to get the ball up to the basket.

Employing my auxiliary functions to complete the dissertation was a challenge, but I was able to make the needed changes. So was Rona. She developed some of her auxiliary extroverted skills and increased her ability to gain greater awareness of feelings.

Prompted by her depression, threatening grades, and even passing thoughts of suicide, Rona pursued what she needed to learn. She used the adversity of that first year's adjustment in college as a Chrysalis Crisis. While she didn't necessarily transform into a flaming extrovert, or someone who began wearing her feelings on her sleeves, she did learn to make better connections with others.

Rona also took another couple of courageous steps that were an outgrowth of the gains she made. She sought out and was granted membership in a sorority, and began a friendship with a young fellow she met at a fraternity get-together. Rona began reaping the benefits of increasing her social IQ.

Developing the key area of social growth is important if we wish to fully actualize as humans. Goleman suggests that our sense of positive well-being and our sense of fulfillment in life comes from good quality relationships. He says, "Resonant relationships are like emotional vitamins, they sustain us through tough times and nourish us daily."[6]

Finding the right balance between social connection and time alone, however, is an ever-changing need. Yet it's optimal if we can feel comfortable when doing either, because each has the potential to lead to deeper self-discovery and both can lead to continued growth. While that development can be realized in a number of ways, one area where it can be particularly helpful is in the area of *Identity growth*. It's one of three areas we'll now move on to explore in Section Two: *The key areas of personal development.*

SECTION II

The Key Areas of Personal Development:

Identity, Intimacy, and Existential Growth

CHAPTER 8

Who Am I Now?
Identity Crisis

Jim was a first cousin and five years my senior. He was only 16 years old when his devastating crisis occurred. I'll never forget that early fall evening when my father came home and announced the news.

Dad alternated working the night shift at the luncheonette he owned with Jim's father. When he came home at that late hour, he'd usually find my mother, sister, or me watching TV. Typically, before he'd open our front apartment door, we'd hear the jingle of keys as he fumbled with the lock. Then he'd push the door open, step into the room, and greet whoever was present. But this time, he just closed the door behind him and stood there. That drew our attention. The look on his face raised our concern. After a moment, he said, "There's been a serious accident. Jimmy Boy's been critically hurt."

Jim was the oldest of three children in my Uncle Jim and Aunt Angie's family. In those days, we sometimes referred to him as "Jimmy Boy" to differentiate him from his dad. But just shy of turning 17, Jimmy looked nothing like a boy. At six feet tall and about 200 pounds of solid muscle, he was a handsome young man with dark hair and a smile that could light up a room. He also had an outgoing and fun-loving personality that added more wattage to his glow.

At the time, Jim was starting his senior year at Immaculate Conception, a small co-ed Catholic High School in Montclair, New Jersey. As a successful athlete in football, basketball, and baseball, Jim already had gained the notice of a number of colleges for all three sports, but it was football where he excelled the most. In his junior year, he was appointed to all-state and all-conference teams, and based on that performance he'd already been extended full athletic scholarships to schools like Boston College, The University of Miami, and Holy Cross.

Many had great expectations for how he and the team would fare his senior year. The first official game of the high school season was still a week away, and on this particular evening Jimmy's team was scrimmaging the behemoth all-boys regional high school in Newark, Essex Catholic. It had nearly 3,000 students enrolled at one time and played in the larger parochial division. Coincidentally, a first cousin from my mother's side of the family was playing on the other team. Both were senior captains.

On the night of the accident, Jim was playing in his two primary positions: fullback on offense, and linebacker on defense. The play where he was injured took place on a punt return. Jim's team was kicking the ball away. After blocking to protect the punter, Jim made his way up-field to seek out the ball carrier.

The fellow returning the ball was speedily weaving his way through a number of prospective tacklers when he came into Jim's proximity. Jim rolled off a block, turned in the up-field direction, and suddenly came to find that the oncoming runner was right in front of him. At that point, the ball carrier had a full head of steam. Instinctively, Jim did what he'd usually do in his linebacker role. He steeled himself like a bull then thrust forward to tackle the runner. Both positioned themselves for impact. Their heads met first.

The intense smashing of their helmets was punctuated by the popping sound of metal on metal. The collision took them both to the ground. Unfortunately for Jim, speed trumped strength, and the crashing of their heads caused Jim's to snap back. He incurred a spinal cord injury that left him a quadriplegic for life.

Hearing my dad describe this event seemed surreal. It was hard to take in. Jim was my hero. I aspired to be like him. We worked side-by-side at our fathers' luncheonette. I would watch him as he would kid around and make small talk with the customers. Many were the blue-collar friends of our fathers' who wanted to keep apprised of Jim's athletic accomplishments.

I closely followed his successes, too, and had a number of memorable Thanksgiving days watching him play football. I was proud to be his younger cousin, but what ultimately impressed me about Jim was what he did with his life after that accident.

At first, we all worried that the severity of the injury would be fatal, but thankfully it wasn't. Afterward, Jim worked as hard at his rehabilitation as he did to become a successful athlete.

I'll always remember the benefit dinner that was held on his behalf. Fellow Montclair resident Yogi Berra, and another New Jersey resident, Yankee teammate Phil Rizzuto, donated their time and renowned personages to make the dinner a great success. It raised needed money for Jim's rehabilitation and enough to cover Jim's tuition at Seton Hall University. There, Jim received an undergraduate degree, followed by a Master's degree in rehabilitative counseling.

How Jim handled his crisis, and how he moved on afterwards, provided me with an early model of two very important lessons. The first was witnessing the difference between a *deficit* and a *handicap*. The deficit for Jim was primarily his inability to walk, but the handicap was the extent to which he allowed that disability to compromise his life.

Jim strove to minimize the extent to which he would allow his inability to walk stop him from fully functioning, and one function he refused to surrender was the capacity that most 17-year-old boys look forward to securing: the ability to drive a car. With the support of his family and some of the funds he gained from the dinner, Jim bought a car that was fitted with hand controls.

I recall the day in his driveway when he gave me a demonstration of how they worked. First, he showed me how he could negotiate transferring himself from his wheelchair into the car. Even with the compromised functioning of his upper body, he was able to press down his hands on the wheelchairs armrests like a gymnast raising himself up between parallel bars. Then, after a moment of locking his elbows and stabilizing his balance, he used his still muscular arms to shift himself across the divide onto the front seat of the car.

Once settled in, he pulled his wheelchair over toward him, collapsed it, and lifted it into the back seat behind him. It was clear to me that I was to watch and not assist. Afterwards, he gave me a brief explanation of how the hand controls worked, and then looked up at me with that smile—a smile that spoke volumes. Jim was not going to let himself be identified as a passive victim to life's events. That was my second lesson.

Not being defined by his deficit, and not identifying with being a victim to life's tragic events, were just two ways Jim had to work with his identity. At a time in life when searching for one's identity is a front and center developmental issue, Jim had some major adjustments to make. Even under normal circumstances, the adolescent years are, according to the developmental psychologist and psychoanalyst Erik Ericson, a time of a "normal identity crisis."[1] For Jim, that developmental process became much more difficult.

In the blink of an eye, Jim's identity as an elite athlete heading to college on a football scholarship came to an abrupt halt. So did his identity as a man who could walk. He also was at that age when young adults seek to emancipate from family, head out into life, and start discovering their own separate selves. He was in those emancipating years when teens move from dis-identifying with family to increasingly identifying with friends—the years when a teen may feel clearer about who they don't want to be like when they get to be their parents' age but are not quite clear about who they wish to become.

In those later adolescent years, teens also can go through a phase of what is known as "hostile dependency." It's that transitional period between adolescence and emerging adulthood when they still need the support of parents but don't want to need them. For instance, they still require their parents' financial assistance, but they don't want to be told what to do with their lives; a period when older teens seek freedom but can't pay its price. The tensions and interpersonal tremors that can prevail during that stage are like a death rattle that precedes a transitional state of release.

Jim's accident threw a wrench into this whole process and made the transition into fully independent adulthood much more difficult to navigate. All the more now, he needed his family, and they certainly were there for him, but he also wanted to be his own man. He didn't want to be dependent and unable to care for himself. It wasn't in his nature. He wanted to be independent, self-sufficient, and potent. Ultimately, that's exactly what came to pass.

Despite the advice of the rehab physician who told Jim to "not raise the bar too high in his life," Jim set his sights skyward. Though it was recognized that the physician's advice was probably said with the caring intent to protect Jim from future disappointments, it only served to fire Jim up. It triggered his, "I'll show him" nature. That was a mark of his character.

One area where Jim did set that bar high was in his pursuit of a relationship. He sought out, courted, and married a wonderful woman. She was cut from the same character of cloth as Jim. Aware of Jim from his earlier high school days, she had occasions to interact with him a few times after his injury. For her, the early connections started off with little thought given to where they might lead. She already envisioned a path in life which would have taken her away from a committed relationship. But like a linebacker with his eye on the ball, Jim pursued her company, and she ended up leaving the convent to create a life with him. They were married for over 40 years, raised two beautiful daughters, and were blessed with eight grandchildren.

In addition to fulfilling his vision of being married and having children, Jim also developed an amazing career. This was another area where he set the bar high, and it was one where he most creatively turned life's lemons into lemonade.

After he completed his degree in rehabilitative counseling, Jim found work at a specialized children's hospital. There he initially functioned as a counselor. Eventually, he climbed his way up the administrative ladder to become the hospital's vice president. During that period, Jim also began conducting disability assessments for adults.

On occasion, Jim would be summoned to present the findings of his assessments at court ordered depositions. At one point, a judge noted Jim's professionalism and confident manner. He suggested that Jim make himself available to provide expert testimony for court room cases.

This appealed to Jim because earlier in his life he had once imagined being a lawyer. But that dream seemed to have gotten lost and derailed by life's events. However, once Jim began serving as an expert witness, he loved being in a courtroom, and the shift in his career took off.

As envisioned by the judge, Jim was a natural. Over time, word spread, and attorneys throughout the country began hearing of Jim's effectiveness in a courtroom. Those who were trying cases against individuals making fraudulent disability claims sought him out. Jim often delivered a crushing blow to the defense. Not only did he confidently provide a professional assessment of the defendant's *actual* capacities, but when he rolled up to the witness stand in his wheelchair to provide his testimony, *he served as a model of someone who was functioning at a high level despite his disability.* Just his appearance made the testimony he provided that much more impressionable to the jurors.

Jim's success as an expert witness enabled him to have major impact in his new role. It became evident to everyone that Jim's intellect, communication skills, and confident demeanor were all aspects of psychologist Seligman's notion of "signature strengths." While they could never substitute for his ability to walk or express his athleticism again, he discovered a profession where he truly shined, one where he found continued purpose and meaning.

In addition to evolving his career, Jim developed and sustained many loving relationships until his death at age 66. Though he lost his ability to walk, it didn't stop him from continuing to make great strides in life, and they all contributed to the kind of happiness and joy he was able to find. He found what both Freud and Seligman suggest can be discovered if we're willing to grow and actualize our potentials: the ability to love and work.

Jim had to make major adjustments to redefine and continue to refine his identity. That success enabled him to turn his crisis into a Chrysalis Crisis. It wasn't easy. It required a good deal of struggling at times, and though I wasn't privy to the inside plight of that struggle, I've been told that it demanded growth in all the foundational areas we've examined, and in many of the other areas as well.

Jim dug deep within himself to find an identity where he could again feel whole, an identity where he transformed an initially bleak situation into one of purposeful work, love, and prosperity.

Like Jim, the search for one's identity can often translate into the choice of a fitting career, but one's identity also can be challenging to define in other ways. Take clarifying one's sexual identity, for example. For some, clarifying their sexual identity may come with the realization that their sexual orientation is not what they initially thought. This can be a difficult discovery to make, particularly if it leads to realizations that run against the grain of what others would prefer.

I've worked with a number of men and women who struggled to reconcile the discovery that their sexual orientation was more congruently identified with being gay, lesbian, or bisexual. Years ago, when society was much less accepting of these alternative lifestyles, realizing and disclosing that discovery could lead to a crisis in relationships with family, friends, and others. It took much greater courage to come out in those times.

Yet while we are freer now in our culture to be who we are, discovering that your sexual orientation is not what others would prefer can still be difficult to disclose. Making that discovery can result from a painful process of peeling back the layers of a self that doesn't feel true.

Even with the kind of effort and struggle the process of self-discovery can entail, identity formation is not a one-and-done process. Discovering one's identity is a process that goes on throughout the life cycle, and it affects numerous areas of our existence. As Erikson once said, "Identity is like a good conscience: it is never maintained once and for all, but continually lost and regained."[2] And I would add, is continually reworked and revised.

We saw this with Sue. After years of working as an actress, she gave up her career to become a stay-at-home mom. She then happily took on the identity of a mother, nurturer of children, and supportive wife. After the divorce, she had to again reconsider the question: Who am I, now that I'm no longer a wife? While she still held onto her identity as a mother, and no longer wished to reassume her identity as an actress, she had to explore new potential avenues for herself. Part of that process entailed taking an inventory of her strengths, and then considering where those strengths could best be suited for the transformation of who she then wanted and needed to become.

Sue's dilemma is not uncommon at that time of life, even when it is not triggered by a divorce crisis. Similar questions can arise when prompted by a mid-life crisis, empty nest, or at retirement.

When I consider how the progression of uncovering deeper layers of the self proceeds throughout the life cycle, I'm reminded of what a professor once told me during a clinical practicum. He said, "Life is a continual process of separation and individuation." By that he meant, we are constantly evolving, shedding skins of who we used to be, and moving more and more toward greater *individuation.*

The notion of individuation is a principle put forth by a number of noted philosophers and psychologists, most notably, great minds like Jung, Nietzsche, and Schopenhauer. Jung viewed individuation as "the process by which individual beings are formed and differentiated."[3] As a matter of fact, he believed that *identity's highest expression is individuation.* In essence, it's how we come to consciously identify the part of our self that is individually distinct from others.

That process of separation and individuation starts out early in life. It begins when we separate from our mother's womb and take on our own separate physical existence as an independently breathing entity. It carries on in infancy as we further come to realize we are separate from our mothers. Later, after we gain mobility and greater cognitive ability, we separate further. We explore the physical world with increasing independence from our mother's embrace.

That continuing separation and individuation leads to discoveries that we are physically different than the opposite sex. Our self-discovery takes on identifications with our family, our race, our culture, our religious (or no religious) affiliation, our national identity, and beyond.

This process also unfolds cognitively as we consider the beliefs we come to hold about ourselves. Some of those beliefs may be consciously or unconsciously adopted during the impressionable years of childhood and adolescence. They can result from the mirroring or feedback we receive from significant people around us, like parents, extended family, or teachers.

Certain beliefs that we hold about ourselves may be accurate and derived from the valid feedback of people who shared their impressions of us during our development. Yet some feedback may not accurately reflect who we are. In both cases, however, that input gets incorporated into our evolving identities, so it's ultimately our responsibility to separate the wheat from the chaff. If we don't, we may establish an inaccurate foundation upon which our identity is built, and that can lead to making career choices or other choices in life that are less suitable.

When the significant voices early in life are strong, they can overly influence your emerging identity. While some of that input can be helpful, if it's too loud or influential, it can create too much external noise, and that can distract from your ability to listen within yourself for direction.

Each of us have our own internal guidance system. It can serve us when seeking knowledge about our identity or direction in life for other purposes. Its internal impressions and guidance can be subtle and come into awareness in a more intuitive manner. For instance, when it comes to discerning a given vocational course, that direction may come in the form of hunches, clues, or flashes of insight.

Economist Herminia Ibarra wrote a well-received book about the struggle of initially identifying or redirecting one's career. It's called, *Working Identity*.[4] There are a number of helpful books on that topic, but what I liked about hers is that she describes the challenge of identifying a line of suitable work as a *career crisis*.

According to Ibarra, when a career crisis occurs, we're required to change ourselves. "The key to making that change," she states, "lies in first knowing—with as much clarity and certainty as possible—what we really want to do, and then using that knowledge to implement a sound strategy." She goes on to state, that this kind of "Knowing ... comes from self-reflection, in solitary introspection."[5]

For example, as a result of a solitary self-search, I came to realize that my interest in working with people, and my earlier interests in subjects like consumer behavior, marketing research, and motivational management, had more to do with a curiosity about people's psyches. But that discovery resulted from a process of self-investigation and an extended period of time while I actively groped for a direction. During that process, I had to tolerate not knowing an answer while I remained committed to the process of finding out.

What I've learned about this process is that career choice frequently grows out of self-understanding, because as you gain greater knowledge about yourself, you get a clearer idea about what kind of work might fit most suitably with your interests, aptitudes, and personality.

But determining your vocational direction is just one way you can benefit from a further clarification of your identity. That search can also lead you to discover how to broaden the range of your other inherent potentials. Some of those potentials will even extend what you imagine are the limits of your particular gender.

Jungian psychologist June Singer addresses the scope of potentials in men and women in her work on *androgyny*.[6] Androgyny describes the combination of masculine and feminine characteristics within every individual. According to Singer, as we become more conscious of *who we are*, "we gain awareness of the dualities that have molded our psyches." She says those dualities are "activity-passivity, competition-cooperation, independence-dependence, logic-intuition, and many more." However, Singer notes, there is one duality "that appears to be the generator of all psychic dualities, that of male-female."

In essence, Singer suggests that *men and women each have both masculine and feminine characteristics*. Jung refers to these dual attributes as our *animus* (the male qualities) and our *anima* (the female qualities). While we are typically more inclined to express the qualities predominantly associated with our gender, a person with greater androgyny can access and employ the predominant qualities of the opposite gender when it's more appropriate for a given situation.

For example, while a man will be more naturally inclined to express his dominant male characteristics like aggression, assertion, competition, and independence, according to the theory of androgyny, he can also learn to employ his feminine attributes when needed. So if being competitive is inappropriate for a given situation, expressing the more feminine attribute of cooperativeness may prove most optimal.

Similarly, if being assertive, dominant, or aggressive is not the best way to handle a certain problem, then the more feminine approach of being receptive, collaborative, and willing to compromise may produce a better result. Should a man lose his way on the "road" of life, rather than blindly forging on independently, he can avoid making a lot of wrong turns if he is willing to accept support by asking for "directions."

I've found at times that rather than employing my predominant masculine tendency to be assertive and take action, if I heeded the words of that famous Beatle's song "Let it be" and just cooled my heels, things turned out just fine in the long run. Not surprisingly, those "words of wisdom" come from the Mother Mary, the great feminine.

Women can also benefit by cultivating and employing their auxiliary masculine attributes and characteristics. While the freedom to develop and express them has a long history of being denied and discouraged, I've seen significant changes in the course of my lifetime. In this country, for instance, women have claimed their right and ability to be assertive. They have more opportunities to be competitive. And if they wish, they can now live more independently than past generations.

Another way to increase your range of effectiveness would be to cultivate those functions of Psychological Type that tend to get ceded to the opposite sex. For instance, if you're a man and neglect to develop your intuition because you've heard it's "women's intuition," then I remind you that intuitive abilities are equally available to you.

Alternatively, if you're a woman, you also may want to reconsider accepting any sex biased limitations. For example, men don't have a gender advantage to being clear "thinkers" when emotionally laden decisions need to be made. You are just as capable of being logical, rational, and impartial at such times.

Whether you're a man or a woman, expanding your identity to include the full spectrum of your potentials will enable you to achieve a greater balance and a wider range of success in life. According to Singer, "the message of androgyny is that the human psyche is comprised of many dualities that must be kept in balance in order for the individual to be whole, to be truly human."[7]

Shifting life situations also will require flexibility in how you identify yourself. For instance, a promotion at work may necessitate a change in your identity from line staff to a supervisor. If you marry, your identity will change from being single to being a husband or a wife. Should you have children, your identity will morph again into that of a parent.

Most of these shifts in identity come easily. They can be slipped in and out of like changing garments in a wardrobe of potential selves. However, some adjustments in identity may be more difficult, like the change in identity that can come about in retirement.

Redefining one's identity at retirement can be particularly hard if the greater part of that identity had been previously tied to work or career. That was the case with Jack when he first came to see me. For him, *retirement was the crisis*.

Jack was a charming and vital man in his late seventies. Well over six feet, he was handsome, lean, and scrappy looking. He had a thick crop of grey hair, and a demeanor that reminded me of the actor Harrison Ford.

At the start of therapy, Jack already had been away from work for a few years, but his retirement had been accompanied by a number of significant changes. When he worked, he was a well-known and well-paid TV broadcaster. Due to his notoriety, he received a good deal of adulation from others. His wealth also enabled him to live a lifestyle that most of us can only dream about. The perks of his job allowed him to travel widely, fly first class, and stay at the best hotels.

Unfortunately, after that career ended, the perks ceased too, and a good deal of his wealth evaporated in the recession. His financial wherewithal decreased significantly, and with it his ability to live in the lap of luxury. His world dramatically changed, and that change required a great deal of adjustment.

The adjustment ushered in a host of questions. Questions like, who was I now that I no longer worked in such a prestigious career? Who was I now that I was no longer a man of exceptional financial means? And who was I now that my previous healthy and athletic body showed increasing signs of deterioration?

These questions all loomed large for Jack, and he had all the signs of a late life depression. Fortunately, he had the wisdom to know that what he was struggling with had a lot of moving parts. Recognizing that, he sought help and used his retirement crisis as a Chrysalis Crisis.

First off, Jack had some grieving to do. Though he felt guilty and somewhat sheepish about admitting it, he was attached to the lifestyle and image he once enjoyed. The wealth and excitement were sorely missed, and so was the loss of his identity of being special. While it was a status that others bequeathed upon him, it was one that he relished wearing.

In addition to the notoriety and lifestyle, he also missed the health he once took for granted. It was hard not being able to do the physical things that used to come so easy, like walking up a flight of stairs without having pain in his knees.

During our work together, Jack got in touch with other losses, too. He had feelings about certain experiences he'd never actualized. One was not becoming a father. And while he had some experiences on his "bucket list" that he still hoped to realize, a number were now beyond him financially and physically. However, he ultimately was able to make peace with them, and at one point, laughingly said they would now have to go on his "fuckit list."

Other questions also began to occupy Jack's mind. There were existential questions like: What was the meaning of this life I've lived? How will I deal with being alone if my wife dies before me? And most frighteningly, where will I be in the future, when like many of my friends, I lay this body down?

These were questions he'd previously given little time to pondering, but now they were at the forefront of his thinking. While he was open to exploring them with me, one person he neglected to discuss them with was his wife.

When I questioned him as to why he had not broached these concerns with her, he said he wanted to get clear about them first. I accepted his right to do that, but challenged his thinking and suggested that maybe discussing them with her could also help him get clear. Then he leveled with me. He said it just wasn't his way to share such concerns with his wife.

Though I got the sense that Jack really loved his wife, it appeared that the way they ran their marriage contributed to maintaining a certain amount of physical and emotional distance. It was a pattern that started early. When they first met, they were both older and had already become successful professionals. They each valued their autonomy, and the demands of their careers required extended time apart.

Now they were continually in each other's company. That required an adjustment. I mentioned to Jack that the upside to being more constantly together could provide opportunities to broach some of those existential topics. Jack saw the sense in what I was saying and agreed to give it a try. Once he did, he found that his wife welcomed the opportunity to explore those questions, too.

Jack eventually sorted out many of his thoughts and feelings, and got the therapeutic lift he needed from our work. He became more optimistic and was no longer depressed. Having made peace with his new status in life, he realized he still had many blessings. Once he embraced his new identity, he began volunteering to help others. He worked at remaining open with his wife, and their ongoing conversations deepened their intimacy.

Being intimate with another person requires sharing the very thoughts and feelings we hold close. Yet sometimes sharing them can feel scary. But as Erikson states in his writings on The Eight Stages of Man, when one "emerges" from a successful search for identity, "one is eager and willing to fuse his identity with others." Then, "He is ready for intimacy."[8]

As you become clearer, more realistic, and more self-accepting of your identity, you'll feel more comfortable revealing yourself to others. But when you're unsure of who you are, or harbor inaccurate and negative beliefs about yourself, you'll be inclined to hold back from letting other people get to know you.

So if you seek a relationship, or are presently in one that you'd like to deepen, expanding your range of self-disclosure and emotional openness will help it develop. Alternatively, if you limit how much you're willing to share, then like a tree that can't extend its roots to meet its needs for nurturance and stability, your relationship, like the tree, will fail to thrive. This was the course that relationships tended to take for our next case study, Amy, and that's what gave rise to her Chrysalis Crisis.

CHAPTER 9

Up Close and Personal: Intimacy Crisis

It was early September when Amy first arrived at my office. In a college town, it's the time of year that harkens new beginnings. It accompanies a palpable uptick of energy and activity. The traffic gets heavier as students move in, and lines get longer at grocery stores.

The early fall also marked the beginning of a new year for Amy. She had a recent birthday, and although she lived in town, she wasn't experiencing any uptick in energy. Her life was feeling quite the opposite.

Amy was depressed and discouraged. Having another birthday was just a painful reminder that she was now further into her thirties and had yet to find a lasting relationship. While she had gained a reasonable amount of career success, she still wanted to get married and have children. The way she saw it, time was running out. Her biological clock was winding down.

When I queried Amy about the extent of her depression, I got the sense that revealing personal information was difficult for her. She was cautious. For instance, after briefly answered my questions, she'd hesitate, her eyes would widen, and she appeared to measure my reaction before proceeding.

At one point during her most extended response, Amy paused abruptly. She then took a long breath, sat back in her chair, and adjusted her skirt over her knees. It seemed as though she suddenly realized she'd gone on talking for a while and feared she may have revealed too much.

I sat with the silence and let her initiate resuming. When she did, she raised a concern that I've heard from a number of people at the start of therapy. Amy questioned if, with all the serious problems in the world, hers justified attention.

I asked if she wondered whether I might find her problems trivial and unworthy of my time. She acknowledged that rationally she knew that probably wasn't the case but still seemed to question if her concerns were sufficiently grave.

Clinically, there were a number of avenues I could have taken at that juncture, but my sense was that she was continuing to have difficulty settling into therapy, so I decided to address her question. I agreed that while there is a great deal of suffering in the world, it was my impression that her problems warranted attention too, especially since they were contributing to her depression.

Amy's blue eyes welled up and she continued to tell me what concerned her. She shared that all her relationships with men had ended in disappointment. They initially held promise, she said, but after she invested a great deal of energy to make them work, they would fail.

I said I could see how that must be very frustrating and discouraging. Her head dropped a bit and she looked toward the floor. Silence prevailed again. Then Amy began to weep gently. Despite appearing uncomfortable expressing her feelings, she seemed unable to stem their flow.

I remained still and decided to give her whatever time she needed to experience them. Not too long afterward, her shoulders lurched back as she reached for a breath, and she broke out into a cry. Amy buried her face in her hands. Then she slid up in her chair and rested her elbows on her knees. The shift in position caused her long blond hair to fall forward. It surrounded her arms and head, enclosing her like a cocoon. I felt for her pain.

Not much time elapsed before she again looked up to make contact. When she did, her eyes were moist and red. Though there were tissues nearby, she didn't reach for one. Instead, she ran the side of her thumb along the lower edges of her eyes to clean away any makeup that might have run.

Amy appeared to relax a bit after that cry, but I could tell it was difficult for her to be so exposed and vulnerable. But like the sun's appearance after a passing storm, Amy revealed a brief self-conscious smile. Then she acknowledged that she'd been keeping a lot of that inside.

With so much raw emotion close to the surface, I wondered if it was just having a birthday that prompted her to come in at that time. When I questioned Amy about it, she said there was something else. Over the Labor Day weekend, she and a guy she'd been dating since the spring abruptly broke up. She thought he might be the one, so its ending was unexpected and particularly disappointing.

Amy knew that men found her smart and attractive, and she realized she would have plenty more opportunities, but getting into relationships wasn't the problem. What perplexed her was why she couldn't get any of them to go the distance.

She did have a brief marriage in her twenties, but like all of her other relationships since, the marriage got off to a hot and heavy start, then just fizzled out. Amy said she stuck with the marriage because she felt the formal commitment justified additional effort. But she bemoaned the wasted time, now seeing those lost years as even more precious.

I asked her if she had any insight as to why her many relationships ultimately ended. She said she eventually finds fault with the men and the luster wears off. Once she becomes dissatisfied, she ends up pulling the plug. In the most recent relationship, however, that wasn't the case. She was the one deemed lacking, and in an intense altercation she received an earful about her shortcomings, then *he* ended the relationship.

Amy had little more to say about that breakup. She appeared reluctant to go into it any further. My sense was it still hurt too much to discuss, so I pivoted and asked additional questions about her background. I inquired about her experiences in school, friendships, interactions with siblings, relationships with parents, and perceptions she had of their marriage.

She willingly answered my questions but rarely elaborated unless I prompted her. I often found myself asking if she would tell me more. Though she'd never been in psychotherapy before, she knew I'd have to delve into her background. Yet answering personal questions seemed to continually take her out of her comfort zone.

It was becoming evident early on that treating Amy's depression and addressing her other relational problems was going to require focusing on her capacity to be interpersonally intimate and self-disclosing.

In our next few sessions, Amy continued to avoid broaching personally sensitive issues. She would slip into talking about other people's problems, difficulties that her employer's business was facing, or try to get me to take the stage and assume the role of a teacher—anything to stay away from her having to talk more personally about herself. There were stops, starts, and numerous digressions, but I remained patient. I was resolved to keep her on track, so when she'd flee to safer ground, I'd gently call it to her attention and redirect her back to herself.

Amy was at the forefront of her struggle with intimacy, and she was experiencing it in the room with me. Therapist or not, it was difficult for her to open up, and that presented her with a quandary: She wanted to use therapy to learn how to become more intimate so she could effectively sustain relationships, but deriving that benefit from therapy required she continually push out to the edges of her discomfort by revealing herself to me. As a result, Amy continued to sputter during that early stretch of therapy, but she had the will and courage to stick with it.

She had gumption, and I liked that about her, yet I knew it was still going to take some time before she could consistently let her guard down. That's because her patterns of drifting to safer topics and keeping her cards close to her chest had a long history.

From what I could discern, those patterns largely came about as the result of two main causes in her family. The first was a product that was conditioned by the predominant communication style that took place in her home. The second seemed to be more of a defensive behavior that Amy established so she could avoid being emotionally wounded.

The first cause became clear when she described how people in her family interacted. While she depicted most everyone as outgoing, Amy said self-revealing conversations were rare. For instance, when her two younger brothers, parents, and she would sit around the dinner table, the topics they talked about were always superficial and safe. They'd discuss current events, sports, weather, or activities at work and school.

She couldn't recall her parents sharing many personal stories of their youth, or talking about their past difficulties and failures. She said she never really knew how their individual lives were going. When I asked about her parents' relationship, she depicted a fairly normal marriage, and emphasized that they hardly ever openly expressed frustrations or disappointments with each other. Her sense was that any disputes that may have existed between them, got settled behind closed doors.

If there was an outward emotional event, it usually had to do with something that started with Amy's dad. She said that most of the time he spent his evening hours reading or watching TV. But if he had a few beers, he could become very critical and judgmental—particularly of her. The boys didn't draw that kind of attention from him, and her mother would go off by herself if she knew he'd been drinking. However, Amy recalled a number of times when he made it painfully clear where she failed to measure up.

In her early years, he mostly criticized her grades. It was classic. If she bought home a report card of all A's and one B, he would focus on the B. Nothing was ever good enough for him, she said. As she moved into adolescence, he criticized her clothes, music, and friends, often leaving her hurt by his comments.

Unfortunately, when those interactions would occur with her dad, Amy's mother offered no protection nor consolation afterwards. It sounded as though her mom had limited ability to emotionally nurture the kids. Apparently, she had grown up in a stern family and was raised to just "suck it up" when life proved difficult. She was not inclined to be empathic, nor lend a compassionate ear when Amy was in need.

Despite knowing this about her mom, Amy continued to reach out to her after her dad's attacks. But she recalled her mother always saying the same thing: she just needed to recognize that her dad had high standards, that he really loved her, and that he just wanted what was best for her. For Amy, hearing that didn't help. It was more like seeking nurturance at her mother's breast, only to come away with sour milk.

When I asked how she felt about her mom's response, she only would say that she was disappointed with her mother for never having the courage to take on her father when she needed defending. No one took him on, Amy said, except one time in her early adolescence when she dared to try. And that didn't go so well.

Amy had been smitten with a young fellow who would become her first love. Unfortunately, her father was critical of the boy's culture and religious background. But Amy was developing feelings for the guy, so at one point, when her dad made one of his offhanded critical comments, she just reacted and lost her cool.

Her father's response was intense. She was met with a barrage of indictments and a laundry list of her failings. It was painful to recall. She choked up as she shared it. After that occasion, Amy said, she never took him on again. Instead, she just hid more and more of herself to avoid his disapproval.

It wasn't hard to see why her recent breakup created a crisis. It re-enacted that earlier experience with her dad and resurrected much of the pain she felt over the years.

As our therapy proceeded, it became all the more apparent why Amy learned to protect herself. While she stayed safe inside her shell, no one could reach her. And yet Amy's fear of connecting more deeply, sharing feelings, or being vulnerable contributed to why her relationships did not thrive. But while that was a central problem, it wasn't the only one. Other offshoots also arose as a result, and they all needed to be identified, examined, and changed.

Because Amy was willing to do the work required to make the needed changes, I could see how this crisis could serve as a Chrysalis Crisis. Amy *could* develop the capacity to be more intimate, and that was starting to occur with me in therapy. She'd already experienced making headway, even if she wasn't exactly clear about what it intellectually meant to be intimate. But a clearer understanding of what it entails to be intimate can be helpful. It can define what you're striving for, so I suggested some reading.

The first book I directed Amy to was a national bestseller written by Harriet Lerner: *The Dance of Intimacy*.[1] In it, Lerner states that "Intimacy means that we can be who we are in a relationship, and allow the other person to do the same. Being who we are requires that we can talk openly about things that are important to us, that we take a clear position on where we stand on important issues, and that we clarify the limits of what is acceptable and tolerable to us in a relationship."[2]

This kind of latitude in relationships was missing in Amy's home. She never learned nor felt confident that it would be safe to truly reveal herself and be accepted. That fear became an inhibiting block and contributed to why she withdrew into herself.

I also recommended another book I thought she might find helpful: *Why Am I Afraid to Tell You Who I Am?*[3] It's written in an easy to digest style by John Powell, who answers the question in his title by saying, "I'm afraid to tell you who I am, because if I tell you who I am, you may not like who I am, and that's all I've got."[4]

I hoped Amy would appreciate the simple but profound implication of this dilemma because it stood at the heart of her caution in opening up to others.

As Amy increased her intellectual understanding of what it meant to be intimate, and continued to stretch her level of openness with me, I took occasion to give her some input on what being more intimate with others might entail outside our sessions.

I shared with her that being intimate and self-disclosing with others does not mean wearing your feelings and concerns on your sleeves. On the contrary, when meeting people for the first time, being too open too soon can actually be off-putting. If the setting calls for light conversation, then talking hair-and-nails or sports-and-weather is fine. But when you're with people you trust, and the conversation takes a more self-revealing turn, then if you're so inclined *you want to be able* to engage in that level of personal sharing.

As Learner says, it's a dance. You don't always have to accept an invitation to go out on the floor. But if you want to, then it helps to learn the steps so you don't end up tripping over your feet, or stepping on those of others.

Amy didn't have problems engaging people in light conversation. Actually, she was outgoing by nature. Amy was an extrovert and had a high social IQ. That enabled her to work in public relations where she had contact with scores of people. But she just wasn't comfortable making a deeper connection, and sometimes when we'd talk about it, she confused being talkative versus being intimate.

I've found that a number of extroverts fail to realize the difference between being talkative versus engaging on a more intimate level. There's a qualitative difference. Verbally expressing a lot of personal information that's safe, distant, or pretested can be easy for an extrovert. But sharing vulnerable or new personal information, along with the whole spectrum of difficult feelings and thoughts, is another ball of wax. I can recall when I first learned about the difference.

My discovery came as the result of some training I undertook at the start of a master's degree in counseling and group dynamics. In order to learn how to facilitate and develop groups, my classmates and I were required to participate in a number of intensive group encounters. They usually took place over a weekend. We were told that, as with our other mandatory courses, a grade would be given, and it would be based on being an active and sharing participant.

I really enjoyed my first group experience. I was amazed at how strategic exercises and skillfully employed techniques could produce a deep level of intimacy in a group of eight people who had been virtual strangers. In just three days, most everyone was sharing personal experiences and feelings that few, if any other people in our lives, had heard.

But when I received my grade, I was surprised I hadn't done better. I thought I'd been my usual outgoing self and an active participant throughout the weekend. Perplexed, I brought this up to my professor. I was told that while I did contribute and frequently came to the support of others, I didn't put as much of my personal self into the group.

It was his impression that I never really revealed anything that took any significant risk, nor made myself as vulnerable as some of the others. For instance, he said, while I did share some personal information, it was safe, limited, and had probably been shared with many before. And I appeared cautious to reveal anything about myself that might be perceived as a shortcoming.

Though he was very tactful and gentle when giving me that feedback, it was still a little hard to hear. I wanted to do well and truly wasn't clear about the difference between intimate sharing and general sharing. In time, however, I came to know that difference, and in future group intensives, I took greater risks, and grew a lot from taking them.

This professor was very authentic and open with people. I liked that about him. He also was a big fan of Canadian psychologist Sidney Jourard. He suggested I pick up Jourard's book, *The Transparent Self*.[5] Once I did, I found its information consistent with what I was learning.

I particularly appreciated Jourard's explanation about the ways men have difficulty being open and vulnerable. He said our inclination to be competitive and dominant can present an obstacle. It can feel counter-intuitive to show weakness, reveal inadequacies, or expose our underbelly. With that perspective, I could see this was an area that would require more work on my part.

Getting my professor's feedback was a needed awakening. Taking part in his groups provided me with a valuable learning experience, and as physician and author Larry Dossey says in his book *One Mind*, "If a picture is worth a thousand words, an individual's experience can be worth a thousand pictures."[6] Thankfully, I got the picture.

Amy was learning from her experiences, too, particularly her experience in therapy. She was discovering that if she wanted to continue getting to the bottom of why she wasn't sustaining relationships, she would have to take additional risks with me.

In time, she did, and as her cautiousness about being open and vulnerable diminished, additional feelings arose. She expressed more sadness about the loneliness and isolation she felt growing up, and the lack of companionship presently missing in her life. She shared fears that she might be deficient, unworthy of a man's love, or destined to be single and alone. Then, she moved into feelings of anger. They seemed hardest for her to identify and express.

The anger initially emerged when she talked about her ex-husband and other men she dated. Then Amy recognized the disappointment that she felt towards her mom for not being more emotionally available, or defending her from her dad. But when Amy got in touch with the hurt and anger she felt towards him, well that's when we hit the fatherlode.

During that stretch of therapy, the full force of her hurt, fear, and angry feelings toward him dominated our sessions. While those feelings were on the surface, I became the occasional recipient of some not-so-friendly-fire. Collateral damage, you might say. No longer was Amy just happy to have me accept her and listen to her. At times I was viewed as the proxy for all the men who had hurt and failed her in relationships.

This was a critical juncture in Amy's therapy, one that I anticipated might occur. As we navigated our way through this phase of her treatment, I worked hard to be clear about my statements because her heightened sensitivity raised the possibility she might misconstrue what I said.

But it was good that Amy reached this point in therapy with me because now, when those hurt and angry feelings got expressed in the room, I could help her learn to manage and understand them. In the past, she didn't have the tools or perspective to cope with them, and these were the feelings that tended to trip her up in relationships.

Paradoxically, the fact that she felt freer to express this shadow side of herself with me was also indicative that on some level she felt safe in our relationship—confident in the strength of our alliance. She didn't have to maintain a front with me, worry that I might think less of her for venting her darker feelings. Amy trusted that if she needed to express her anger with me, or even at me, I would not abandon her, nor retaliate like her dad.

It's often counterintuitive to think that expressing anger in a relationship can lead to any good. That's because when it arises, it can be experienced as threatening and distancing. But if you withdraw from a person as a result of holding unexpressed anger toward them, the stability of your relationship will suffer.

If the problems that underlie your anger aren't resolved, then those feelings will be left to simmer and seethe. Even if you unwittingly relegate them to your unconscious, they're still down there. Out of awareness does not necessarily mean out of mind.

Furthermore, it takes energy to repress emotions. Fatigue and depression are often the symptoms of that effort. Yet repression isn't always failsafe. Sometimes that emotional energy can't be contained, and in the case of anger, it can erupt in rage. At other times it may escape in less intense but consequential ways. It might trickle out in sarcasm, disgust, or contempt. When that becomes a pattern of how you interact with your significant other, then your relationship can really get into trouble.

John Gottman, the renowned researcher on relationships, produced some interesting findings about why relationships fail. In his book *What Predicts Divorce,*[7] Gottman and his colleagues discovered that contempt and disgust are two of the four most negative marital behaviors that corrosively contribute to the destabilization of a marriage.

It's been my experience working with couples that when they're faced with any of the many problems that can arise, if they don't know how to effectively engage in the process of conflict resolution, the accumulation of unresolved feelings and problems can cause them to shut down. When that happens, emotional and physical intimacy suffers.

I recall a time when the need to confront issues in a marriage was made humorously clear. My wife and I were on a cruise at the time, and we were being entertained at one of the many shows held on the ship. This particular show was a comedy act. In an attempt to encourage audience involvement, the comedian asked everyone who of us were on our honeymoon. A number of hands went up. Then he proceeded up the line to ask who of the couples in the audience were married for 5, 10, 25, and then 50 years. Declining amounts of hands were raised, and when he got to 50, just one little old couple sitting in the back acknowledged they made it to that milestone.

The comedian then asked if they would come up to the stage. They were a little hesitant, but the audience encouraged them on, so they did. Walking up the aisle and across the stage, the petite wife supported her husband who appeared to be a little less mobile. Everyone gave them a big applause when they finally made it up onto center stage.

The entertainer asked where they were from and how many actual years over their fiftieth anniversary they were married. Then, in a respectful, jovial, but sincerely inquisitive manner, he said, "Tell us, how did you keep your marriage going for 50 years?" With little time given to her answer, the woman said in the most confident voice, "we fought it out when we had to." Everyone roared at her candidness. I looked at my wife and smiled, taking note of the wisdom of those words.

It can be difficult to effectively confront problems that arise in relationships, and just fighting to let off steam is not the same thing. Entering into a process of conflict resolution can entail expressing and managing a host of different feelings. Yet, *being intimate includes sharing all feelings*, even the scarier ones like anger. However, expressing anger towards those you love can be done without excessive damage, and if done effectively, it can even strengthen the relationship.

When I worked with couples who were cautious or opposed to expressing anger in their relationships, I would often use the following analogy: When any two of us imperfect human beings come together to form a relationship, we're like the rough material of an evolving sculpture. Giving that material the shape and form we each envision for our relationship requires the mutual and skillful use of a hammer and chisel. Your hammer is your *assertion, energized by controlled anger*. Your chisel is your *feedback, tempered by tact*.

Like a hammer and chisel, there is nothing inherently bad about assertion and feedback. They're just tools. And just as you would no more place the chisel in the middle of the sculpture and smash it as hard as you can with your hammer, you don't want to pummel your partner with rage, saying the most hurtful things you can think of in the exchange.

When it's necessary to confront certain issues in relationships, it requires the skillful use of assertion and feedback. Channeling your anger into *non-aggressive assertion* will be sufficient to bring needed attention to the area of concern. And tactful *feedback focused on behaviors* will specifically address what can or needs to be changed.

What I am talking about here is the *process* of how you go about confronting issues in your relationship. In another one of his books, *The Seven Principles for Making Marriage Work*,[8] Gottman identifies some key ways people succeed or fail at this process.

First of all, it's worth noting that Gottman believes that "Anger between a husband and a wife does not in itself predict a marriage meltdown." He emphasizes it's more "the way they argue" that becomes the problem.[9]

Gottman suggests that when you begin to address a problematic area, it's important to not start up harshly. Next, he suggests not turning your complaints into criticisms. For example, if you want your spouse or partner to help keep the house clean, you could specifically identify behaviors you want to see change. Ask that they not leave dishes around, for instance. Saying something like "you're such a slob" amounts to a character assassination and only compromises the process.

He also describes other negative tendencies people fall into when attempting to confront problems in their relationships. Gottman calls them his *Four Horseman*. They are: expressing *contempt*, becoming *belligerent*, being *defensive*, and *stonewalling*. Stonewallers shut the person out, the way Amy learned to relate to her dad.

Regulating and modulating the expression of anger, and the process of effectively communicating when confronting issues in a relationship, can be difficult. Amy had a lot to learn in that area. For her, the first challenge was just broaching such intimate feelings and thoughts. Then it was knowing what to do with them when she did.

These were skills that were never taught nor modeled by her parents. The only experience Amy had with confrontation in her home was at the hands of her dad. That experience just left her feeling victimized and wounded, and led to her stonewalling ways. Unfortunately, in addition to having a shut-down relationship with her dad, Amy incurred other consequences from having him as a father, and one of the ways he had impact on her was still in her blind spot.

Amy adopted his critical voice. She also could be very critical of others, particularly of men with whom she was in a relationship. In much the same way she often felt with her dad, no man was ever good enough for her. But the one who suffered the most from that critical tendency was Amy, because she constantly ran criticisms down on herself. That also contributed to why she was reluctant letting people get to know her. They would discover all those qualities about her that failed to measure up.

Another way Amy was affected by her father was that she had a similar temper. Both as a result of modeling and the luck of the genetic draw, she had a propensity to lose her cool when under emotional pressure. Though she learned to suppress her anger, Amy said she'd occasionally snap at her mother, but she learned the hard way what could come of being angry with her dad, so she restrained herself there. However, no such restraint was assumed in her relationships with men. In those relationships, her criticalness and reactiveness took a toll.

These were important realizations for Amy. Had she not been willing to reveal more and more of herself to me, some of these areas of needed growth would have not been brought to light. As a result, she learned a great deal about herself and how she functioned in emotionally significant relationships. However, this kind of learning is not just the province of psychotherapy. Much of this type of growth can be learned in other healthy functioning relationships, too.

If you wish to derive such learning, relationships can also serve as people growing arrangements, but a key requirement is a willingness to be more transparent and open.

Back in those group encounter days when I was first learning about the kind of growth that could come from interpersonal relationships, I was introduced to an interesting communication model. It depicted how personal growth could be derived when individuals revealed themselves to each other and were open to receiving feedback. The model is called the Johari Window.[10]

The Johari Window was developed by Joseph Luft and Harry Ingram in the 1950s, but don't let its datedness mislead you. It's still as applicable now as it was then, and it provides a nice explanation of how we humans can grow through intimate exchange.

Basically, the Johari Window is just that—it's a window through which you view how you can grow from a process of revealing yourself to others. In order for you to get a sense of how this model works, you need to first imagine a square window divided into four window panes. In that quadrant of panes, the upper left pane is called the Open Area. This area represents what you know about yourself and what I know about you.

For example, Amy knew that she was intelligent and that others experienced her that way. She shared with me that she had done well in school, and the fact that she was bright was also evident to me. This knowledge about Amy was "visible" to both of us, and that's why it belonged in the open area of the Johari Window.

The next of the four panes in the Johari Window lies below the open area just described. The bottom left quadrant of the window is called the "Hidden Area." This area contains information I know about myself, but you don't know about me. It might be information that I'm not ready to share or may never share. In Amy's situation, this was information she revealed only after a few sessions elapsed, like the extent of difficulty she had in her relationship with her father. Typically, this kind of personal information is riskier to reveal.

In the upper right quadrant of the Johari Window is the pane called the "Blind Area." That area consists of information about ourselves that others can see but of which we're not aware. In Amy's case, this was information about herself that she didn't fully realize until I pointed it out to her. For instance, I told her that it appeared that she had taken on her father's critical voice. She came across as very self-critical and, as a result, further inhibited herself from opening up to others in fear they would discover her self-regarded shortcomings.

The last pane in the Johari Window lies in the bottom right quadrant. It's referred to as the "Self-Discovery" area. In this area lie the insights and revelations you never knew about yourself and I never knew about you. They come into view as a result of the process of our deepening and more intimate disclosures. In a sense, *we discover them about you together* for the first time.

One example of this kind of discovery came about during Amy's therapy. She realized that she wanted to pursue a different career. She'd become discontent with her work and wanted to do something where she could help people. In further discussions and exploration, Amy realized that she might like to get a degree in law and then move into child advocacy. It made a lot of sense in light of her background, but neither of us saw that one coming.

When viewing the Johari Window as a whole, you come to see that as you become more self-revealing with those you trust, and you welcome their constructive feedback, you increasingly expand the upper left pane, the Open Area. That area increases as you share more of what you've held back from others. As people get to know you better, and you're open to their feedback, more of what they see can be bought to your awareness.

Finally, as you deepen your intimacy with others, engaging in what philosopher Martin Buber calls the authenticity of an "I-Thou" relationship, such interactions can lead to continued discoveries of your potentials, those that neither you nor others may have known you possessed.

Alternatively, as Eric Erikson says, "The counterpart to intimacy is *distantiation*: the readiness to repudiate, to isolate, and if necessary, to destroy those forces and people whose essence seems dangerous to one's own."[11]

But if you are willing to engage in what Jourard calls "the dyadic effect," where your self-disclosure begets my self-disclosure, then as we share and learn more about each other, any barriers that exist between us are more likely to break down.

In the words of Jesuit priest and author John Powell, "If I am willing to step out of the darkness of my prison, to expose the deepest part of me to another person, the result is almost always automatic and immediate: The other person feels empowered to reveal himself to me. Having heard of my secret and deep feelings, he is given the courage to communicate his own."[12]

When this occurs, the depth of connection can bridge the gap of the loneliness, isolation, and alienation we can often feel in this world. That level of intimate exchange also can be conducive to exploring other closely held areas of personal concern—areas that are critical to our being but frequently ignored. These areas can include questions on the meaning and purpose in our life, or even the nature of our continued existence.

These later questions fall under the heading of existential concerns: questions about existence and survival. Attending to them can contribute to our *existential growth*. But like the other areas of growth we've explored, this key area of personal development may not get our attention until a crisis thrusts it upon us.

CHAPTER 10

Human Being,
or Human Doing:
Existential Crisis

Imagine one morning unexpectedly awaking up in a magnificent old forest. Having comfortably slept on the moss-covered ground by the roots of a tree, you open your eyes and see yourself surrounded by towering redwoods and lush vegetation. Leafy green ferns spread out before you. Like nature's shag carpet, their unfolding fronds fill the forest's floor.

The sun shines through the treetop canopy lighting the place where you lie. Its rays warm your skin and gleam off the dew-covered leaves. Chirping birds rhythmically respond to each other's calls. A cool passing breeze caresses your face as your senses continue to waken.

While taking a breath of the sweet morning air, you sit up and wonder: *Where am I?* Searching your memory to make sense of it all, you reflect on the evening before: *Am I somehow responsible for being here?* As you rise to your feet and see nothing but forest, you ask yourself: *Am I all alone?* And when you realize that indeed that is the case, a sobering thought gives you a chill: *Will I be okay?*

If in reality you awoke in such a situation, it would make sense that questions like these would arise. Their answers would be critical to orienting yourself, adjusting to your conditions, and recognizing the potential gravity of your situation. However, there are other times in life when you may consider similar questions—times when you're not coming awake in some foreign place, but times when you can also feel like you're "lost in the woods."

These questions can arise when life's crises overwhelm you and you're not sure how you're going to navigate your way out. They can come to mind at less critical times, when you need to re-evaluate where your life is heading. And sometimes such questions can be entertained when you're just reflecting on life in general.

For instance, have you ever considered the reason for *being* in your life, or do you just keep plugging away at what you're *doing*, giving such questions little thought? Do you wonder if you have authorship of your life's events, or do you believe that most of your experiences occur randomly? When you hear it said that we enter and exit this world alone, does the idea of such aloneness raise anxiety? Have you ever fully let in the fact that someday *you* will die, or is that too frightening to face?

These are the existential questions of life—the questions of being. They can include other questions like: What is the purpose of my life? What will occur after I die? Does my life have any meaning? They address the very foundations of our existence. While they can be broad, they're critical to how we view our time on this Earth, or for that matter, afterward.

At various points in your development, you'll likely confront some of these essential issues. They can be challenging. However, when those questions are addressed, considered, and answered to the extent that they can, their implications will influence the way you spend your time in life.

New life situations can bring these questions to the forefront. Certain rites of passage in life's normal development can prompt their consideration. As seen in some of the previous cases we've examined, a given crisis may demand their attention.

Jack's retirement crisis, for instance, prompted him to seek new meaning and purpose in his life. Rona's crisis challenged her to confront her isolation and aloneness. Brad's ordeal forced him take a hard look at the responsibility he held for his life's predicaments. And while Bob's crisis implicated the many ways he neglected his physical world, his greatest wake-up call was in regard to his mortality.

You may not be inclined to give existential questions any thought until a crisis brings them to your attention. Should that be the case, and you use it as a Chrysalis Crisis, then effectively addressing those concerns will contribute to another key area of your development: *Existential growth.*

Existential growth is gained when you derive the needed knowledge, perspective, guidance, and acceptance that's appropriate for the stage of life you're in when such concerns arise. Addressing the existential questions of life, and discovering what answers can be found, will benefit your overall sense of wellbeing.

Here are four examples of how that can happen. If questions about death come to mind, finding an assuring understanding or a comforting perspective about its transition can allay some of the anxiety that underlies its apprehension. Addressing questions regarding the meaning and purpose of your life can guide you toward more satisfying work or activities that better align with your values. Examining and recognizing where and to what extent you're responsible for your life will help you find those areas where you can bring about desired change, and be at peace with those areas you can't. And lastly, learning how isolation and aloneness can sometimes be a part of life will help you accept those periods and possibly even allow you to use them as opportunities for retreat and development.

Like the other key areas we've examined in this section, your existential growth can be a very personal undertaking. Whether you seek to examine these concerns, need to accept some of their realities, or are disinclined to consider such matters, you'll likely be influenced by your own level of curiosity, personal experiences, or living conditions.

For instance, if your day-to-day living conditions are preoccupied with basic survival, your time likely will be focused on keeping yourself safe, fed, and sheltered. You'll probably give a lot less thought to death or the afterlife, and a good deal of thought to the ways of avoiding it.

On the other hand, if you're not preoccupied with physical survival and are favorably positioned to entertain existential questions about death, when or if you go about it will be less affected by your living conditions.

That was the case for Brian. When he considered his existential questions about death, he didn't perceive his life situation as all that favorable.

Brian initially sought my help for more immediate clinical concerns. He was depressed and having difficulty adjusting to some recent losses. The nature of his clinical concerns ushered in existential questions he had about death, and since he wanted to address both areas in his treatment, I approached his therapy in a manner suggested by the writings of Irvin Yalom.

Yalom was a professor of psychiatry at the Stanford University School of Medicine. In his book *Existential Psychotherapy*,[1] he provides therapeutic understanding of how to identify and work with existential concerns in therapy. Existential Psychotherapy is defined by Yalom as "a dynamic approach to therapy which focuses on concerns that are rooted in the individual's existence."[2] His therapeutic approach addresses four existential concerns: *Death, Freedom, Isolation, and Meaninglessness.*

Yalom recommends that individuals pursuing an understanding of these existential concerns should give them deep personal reflection in solitude and silence, away from the distractions of life.

Brian would have welcomed such conditions when exploring his existential concerns about death, but he was still having trouble stabilizing his life in the aftermath of the ordeal that first prompted his seeking help.

When he first came into my office he appeared shell-shocked. At 55, he looked as if he was ten years older. His salt and pepper shaggy locks were wind strewn and untrimmed. Hair grew out the back of his neck and ears. His eyebrows were bushy and wild, and his face was unshaven.

He had not been giving his appearance much attention. Even the clothes on his back had that worn-many-times look. They were heavily wrinkled, like they never felt the touch of an iron. If they had, they looked like they were probably slept in a few times. Though it was mid-summer, the paleness of his complexion suggested he spent most of his time indoors.

Brian might have stood about six foot three when erect, but when he greeted me, he surrendered a few inches to his slightly bent stature. As he walked back to my office, he moved slowly and had a labored gate. I suspected he might be having trouble with his back, but I also got the impression that he was feeling the weight of the world on his shoulders. After he sat down on the couch, he asked if he could use one of the side pillows for lumbar support. He said he had recently thrown out a disc. My hunch about his hunch was confirmed.

As Brian shared his story, it was apparent he was a very sad man. He had just undergone a long and gruesome ordeal of being the primary caretaker for his dying wife. After a long-drawn-out sickness, she passed away; it had happened just a few weeks before he came in. Unfortunately, she wasn't the only significant loss he had in the recent past. His mom also died a few years earlier.

Brian really loved his wife, and it was painful to witness the suffering she went through before she died. It seemed to suck the spirit out of him. He also loved his mother, so losing her was another blow. He felt a lot of grief for both, and because his wife's illness overlapped his mother's death, my sense was that he had not fully grieved either loss. He was very depressed, and it was understandable why.

He also felt alone in his grief. Even though his father was still alive and Brian had a brother living abroad, neither offered much comfort when he called them. His dad was still struggling with the loss of his wife, and Brian's brother just didn't know how to connect around such painful issues.

Brian also had two college-age children who just returned to their lives on campus after their mother's death. He didn't want to burden them any further with his problems or negatively affect their college experiences any more than they had already been.

Having never lost anyone close to him before his mother and wife, Brian had not been directly touched by death. He'd also had a pretty uneventful life up to that point.

Working in the real estate business, Brian made a good living. It enabled his wife to stay at home until the kids went off to college, but shortly thereafter, she developed cancer. Brian said that along with adjusting to the realities of where her cancer was leading, she grieved that she would never move on to actualize some of her dreams, many of which he shared.

Helping his wife come to terms with her impending death and accept these losses was a challenge for Brian. He wasn't good at grieving. It was usually his wife or mother who would provide him with the compassion and support to absorb life's disappointments. They were his pillars. In the wake of their loss, he felt as if his world had come tumbling down upon him.

We spent a good deal of time addressing the many feelings and thoughts that he had about losing them. With the help of an antidepressant and attending regularly scheduled sessions, he was able to lift out of the depression and re-engage his life. But he needed more. Brian was shaken by their loss in other ways. That's when he brought his existential questions about death to the floor.

Yalom states that concerns about death serve as "a core existential conflict between the awareness of its inevitability, and the wish to continue to be."[3] Death both prompted Brian's crisis and became a focus in his adjustment afterwards. As he attempted to make peace with it, he would speculate at times whether his mother and wife still existed in some non-physical dimension. He questioned what would happen to him when he died. He reexamined the beliefs about death and the afterlife that he had been exposed to in his early religious upbringing.

Though he had not given much consideration to these kinds of questions before, they occupied the forefront of his thinking now. Yet Brian also was at that time of life when they would most likely arise. Jung suggested that it is the recognition of our own ultimate demise that ushers in a midlife crisis, and at 55, Brian was still in the age range of what would be considered midlife.

Jungian analyst James Hollis refers to the midlife developmental period as the "Middle Passage."[4] It's when existential concerns about meaning and purpose in life, isolation, and aloneness can most prominently surface. For Brian, however, questions surrounding death took center stage.

You don't need to be at midlife to give serious consideration to death, though. It can occur at any time in the life cycle. Nor are children exempt from this concern, says Yalom. Dealing with terrifying fears of obliteration can be a major developmental task.

I can recall when such questions first came to my mind as a young boy. I was seven, and two people I knew died within a short period of time. One was a schoolmate, the other was my grandfather.

The schoolboy's name was Alfred. On numerous occasions during first grade, we'd cross paths and walk the rest of our way to school together. By the end of that year we became increasingly acquainted and enjoyed each other's company. Though we only lived a short distance away from each other, we lost touch during the summer months; so when second grade started I looked forward to resuming our friendship. But on the first day of school Alfred was nowhere to be found. I discovered he had died that summer from leukemia.

When I heard the news about Alfred, I was perplexed and upset. And when later that year the second event occurred, my young mind struggled to make sense of it all.

That second event took place as I was walking back from school one day. While I was coming down the last long block, I noticed the lights of an emergency vehicle ahead. It appeared to be in the vicinity of my apartment building. When I got closer, I realized it was an ambulance double parked out front. As I drew nearer, I saw two men in uniforms carrying someone in a stretcher down the steps of our stoop onto the sidewalk. I can still vividly remember the concern I felt.

Coming upon the scene, I saw my mother looking out from the opened window where she'd often sit in her wheelchair. My first concern was dispelled, but I was still curious. Who was on that stretcher? Then I noticed my grandmother standing among a few other neighbors by the opened back doors of the ambulance. I discovered it was my grandfather being carted away.

He never returned. I was sad when I heard he had died. I had a close relationship with my grandfather in those years. He lived right across the hall from us, along with his wife and my two unmarried uncles. They supported our family and were a constant presence. That support was particularly helpful during the first year of my life when I was separated from my mom and lived with them.

Grandpa's death and the death of Alfred confused and frightened me. How could life suddenly come to an end, I wondered, particularly for someone as young as I was? Where were they now? Did they just disappear? I recall how my mother attempted to sooth my feelings and concerns. She tried to simplify some of the answers she arrived at when she faced similar questions years earlier during her ordeals.

Giving consideration to death and the afterlife is qualitatively different when you believe you are the one standing at the threshold of that great beyond. Such was the case for my mother. Yalom distinguishes this difference by referring to it as "my death"—an experience we can't really appreciate until it is ours. "A confrontation with one's own death," Yalom wrote, "has the power to provide a massive shift in the way one leads his life."[5]

Short of having that impending experience ourselves, losing people who are close to us, or letting in the reality of our own mortality as we age, will bring questions about death more into focus. Even if we can't know for sure what will happen to us when we die, it can prove helpful if we give attention to this issue when needed.

But even when prompted by close losses or the effects of aging, many people will ignore this concern. Some believe it's too morbid to contemplate, too frightening to face, too futile to imagine what might occur at death, or too presumptuous to consider an afterlife. Nevertheless, Yalom suggests those who don't ponder these questions are not exempt from the impact of their existential reality, and those who ignore them may pay a price by experiencing an unconscious undercurrent of anxiety. In order to keep that anxiety at bay, many will establish defenses that serve their denial, and the consequences of those defenses can create their own problems.

He suggests there are two main defenses people employ to engage in this denial about death. One defense comes in the form of believing in your *personal specialness*, and the other is in harboring the belief in an *ultimate rescuer*. "These defenses," he says, "originate early in life and greatly influence the individual's character structure."[6]

Yalom depicts the individual who believes in an ultimate rescuer as someone who "will look for strength outside himself or herself; will take a dependent, supplicant pose toward others; will repress aggression; may show masochistic trends; and may become deeply depressed at the loss of the dominant other."[7]

The individual whose defense is oriented more toward personal specialness "may be narcissistic; is often a compulsive achiever; is likely to direct aggression outward; may be self-reliant to the point of rejecting necessary, appropriate help from others; may be harshly unaccepting of his or her own personal frailties and limits; and is likely to show expansive, sometimes grandiose trends."[8]

Brian wasn't one to employ the defense of personal specialness, but he did exhibit signs of employing the defense of the ultimate rescuer. Both his mother and wife were rather dominant in his life, and losing them both pulled the carpet out from under his feet. Each loss had its own unique, yet cumulative impact on how he came to terms with his own beliefs about death.

According to Yalom, the loss of a parent, for instance, will put us in touch with our own vulnerability. "If our parents could not save themselves, who will save us?" he says. And in regard to the death of a spouse, he goes on to note, "the loss of a significant other (sometimes the dominant other) increases one's awareness that, try as hard as we may to go through the world two by two, there is nonetheless a basic aloneness that we must bear. No one can die one's own death with one or for one."[9]

These were difficult existential realities that Brian needed to confront. In our continued work together, he sufficiently came to peace with them, and there was a payoff for doing so. He was able to achieve an outcome that Yalom suggests is possible. "The integration of the *idea* of death saves us," he says, as "it acts as a catalyst to plunge us into more authentic life modes, and it enhances our pleasure in the living of life."[10]

Brian rediscovered his joy in living. Though it took him some time to get back on his feet, he made major adjustments to his life in the process. He shifted his career to more meaningful work; found another relationship where he functioned less dependently and with deeper intimacy; he improved his relationships with his children; and he eventually moved to another region of the country to start a new chapter of his life.

Lily Pincus, a social worker at the British Institute for Human Relations and good friend of the philosopher Martin Buber, once said, "Thinking and talking about death need not be morbid; they may be quite the opposite. Ignorance and fear of death overshadow life. Knowing and accepting death erases this shadow."[11] I believe that at some time in our life we will be responsible for addressing this inevitable concern, and taking responsibility for our lives is itself an existential issue.

Responsibility as an existential issue means we assume authorship for creating our own life. However, in order to exercise that responsibility, it must go hand in hand with freedom, and that is why Yalom addresses both together. He states: "Unless the individual is free to constitute the world in any number of ways, then the responsibility has no meaning."[12] In other words, life is our canvas, and we must have the freedom to paint any scene we wish, in any colors we choose, and then take responsibility for how that picture turns out.

But many of the world's population are not free to take responsibility for the course of their lives, and even those of us who are blessed to live in a free society may be constrained by physical, mental, economic, or racially prejudiced limitations. However, the challenge of determining to what extent those conditions actually present limitations is each person's responsibility. My cousin Jim, for instance, took responsibility for determining to what extent he would let his physical deficits handicap him from creating a full life.

I frequently work with individuals who perceive that they can't change their lives. When they're surrounded by negative life situations, they lack the hope that those situations can be overcome or improved. Others see themselves as passive victims of certain life events. They take little or no personal responsibility for their problems, when indeed they may have unwittingly had a hand in bringing them about. Each of these viewpoints can detract from seeing potential ways to change life situations when they can be affected.

Brad is a good example of not taking personal responsibility for his problems. It was largely due to his lack of cognitive and emotional insight that he found himself making poor choices, and he maintained his obliviousness by abusing substances.

Others lack the hope that they can change their life situations because they believe they are helpless to bring about that change. This kind of learning can occur when an individual has been subjected to earlier life experiences, where in reality their problems were insurmountable. An example might be a child who was abused or neglected and had no way to change that situation.

There is solid research to support the impact of such early life experiences. Martin Seligman, the psychologist at the University of Pennsylvania who wrote the book mentioned previously titled *Authentic Happiness*, did earlier work on this subject in the late 1960s. It led to developing the theory of *learned helplessness*.[13]

In his research, Seligman gathered three groups of dogs and subjected them to certain conditions. In phase one of the study, all three groups were put in harnesses. After a while, group one was released. Group two and three were put in a cage and subjected to a mild (though not abusive) shock. Group two dogs, however, were given a way to stop the shock, where group three had no means to do so.

In group two, the dogs discovered that they had a lever in their cage. When pushed, they found that the shock would stop. Because group three was not provided a lever, they ultimately viewed the shock as unstoppable, and when it eventually did cease, they learned its termination was random and out of their control.

In phase two of the study, all three groups of dogs were put in another cage. Only this time, *all* the cages had a low back wall that would allow for escape. When each of the three groups were subjected to shocks, the first and second groups of dogs quickly found their way out. Group three just laid on the floor and whined. Due to their earlier experiences, they'd been trained to believe there was no way out. *They learned to be helpless.* They wrongfully believed that their situation could not be changed.

In the advent of more recent brain studies, a few researchers sought to attribute learned helplessness to the effects of neurochemistry or flawed regions of the brain. Interestingly, some of those same researchers found that physical exercise might prevent learned helplessness in humans. In that research, they also discovered that it wasn't how much exercise you do, but that you "just do it!"

Whether it's improving your physical health, or overcoming the helpless belief that you can't change your life, you need to summon your "response ability"—*the ability to respond*—taking the necessary actions to find solutions and achieve goals.

But beyond having the freedom and responsibility to bring about change in your life, another critical ingredient is required. That ingredient is the *will* to change.

For example, the will to change is central to effectively utilizing and benefiting from therapy. One of the most outspoken voices on the importance of the employment of will in therapy was Roberto Assagioli, the Italian psychiatrist and pioneer in the fields of humanistic and transpersonal psychology.

Assagioli was a contemporary of Freud and Jung. While he favored Jungian theories, he ultimately developed his own school of thought called *Psychosynthesis*.[14] His approach to helping people was comprehensive. He viewed man as inherently tending toward harmony and balance within himself and the world. But critical to his theory is the concept of will.

Once asked why he viewed will as so critical in the process of change, Assagioli's response was very much in concert with the major premise of this book. He said: "At some point, perhaps in a *crisis,* when danger threatens, an *awakening* occurs in which the individual discovers his will. The individual sees that he is a living subject, an actor, endowed with the power to choose, to relate, to bring about changes in his own personality, in others, and in circumstances." Assagioli emphasized that "Will is the directing agent in the personality."[15]

In light of Seligman's research, and in full agreement with Assagioli on the importance of the will, I've found that sustaining regular daily activities like exercise and meditation not only produce their own benefits (i.e., physical health and mindfulness), but they strengthen the will. *The will is like a muscle,* the more you exercise it, the stronger it gets.

Determining where you are responsible for your life's events, exercising the freedom you have to change things, not perceiving your situation as helpless when it isn't, not falling prey to a victim's mentality, and harnessing your will to make needed changes are all critical to overcoming crises and leading a successful life.

While it may be a challenge to see situations accurately, and a struggle to exercise your will to change, remember that the butterfly's struggle to free its wings also strengthens them for future flight. Your struggle to change will strengthen you for future crises. Unlike those who learned to be helpless, you'll always recall that since you once found the resources, you *will* be able find them again.

This kind of life lesson wasn't learned by another client who came into my office a number of years ago. Her name was Jackie. She was in an unhappy marriage and saw no way out.

Jackie was a 40-year-old mother of three children who had married early in life. When she sought my help, she was facing both an empty nest and a midlife crisis at the same time. An attractive woman with dark hair, brown eyes, and a Mediterranean background, her husband was ten years her senior. He asked Jackie to be his wife when she was just 17-years-old.

At the start of therapy, Jackie was dealing with excessive anxiety. She was involved in an ongoing affair for more than a year and was afraid that her husband was going to find out. Nevertheless, she didn't want to end the affair.

Jackie came from a very traditional family. She described her father as strict and dominant, and her mother as dutiful and submissive. The oldest of four children, Jackie felt that her father was particularly hard on her. She hated living under his controlling hand. As a way to escape her home life situation, Jackie elected to marry early. Unfortunately, she selected a husband who in her opinion, had similar tendencies as her father. Though she said he wasn't as bad as her dad, she still felt oppressed and controlled by him.

While continuing to work with Jackie, I also recommended that she seek couples counseling, particularly if she wished to save her marriage. She was ambivalent about both. She feared that couples therapy would require she come clean about the affair, and she had largely made up her mind that she wanted to leave the marriage. Though she gave couples therapy a shot anyway, she never changed her position, so the process went nowhere.

With her decided goal to leave the marriage, I helped her examine the many considerations she held about bringing it to an end.

As we did, I'd often have to point to where she was unwilling to take responsibility for certain aspects of her situation. Though she was a middle-aged woman, she came across as very adolescent. It was as if she had developmentally stopped growing at about the time she got married, and shortly afterward became consumed with the needs of her three children. All were born within five years.

Her unwillingness to take responsibility for her life situation was most evident in two areas. Jackie was reluctant to see where she was complicit in the deterioration of her marriage and minimized her role in starting the affair. She made statements implying that her husband "drove her into the arms of another man," or that this fellow she was in the affair with "hit on her" and before she knew it "had her in bed."

In addition to helping her accept some responsibility for her predicament, Jackie needed to recognize where she was free to change her situation. When she said she was trapped in the marriage because her husband controlled the money, I challenged her beliefs. I suggested she look into her finances by consulting a lawyer who could inform her where she might stand once she got divorced.

Even after she was assured of being able to adequately manage her future finances, Jackie balked at officially filing for a divorce. Though she repeatedly affirmed her desire to leave the marriage, she continued to procrastinate. It became clear, however, that it wasn't about the money, nor was it about any of the other surmountable logistical problems. In my opinion, she was blocked by the largely unconscious and unrecognized fear of being alone.

She knew that the fellow with whom she was having the affair would not leave his marriage. He'd made that clear. He also said that he felt safe continuing their affair *because* they were both married. It was not lost on Jackie that when she left the marriage, he would likely exit her life. That likelihood was frightening to her. She'd never experienced living alone before, particularly being emotionally separated and unattached to anyone nearby.

Jackie was a very emotionally dependent person. She'd always been plugged into someone at all times. It was as though she had this emotional umbilical cord, and when she unplugged it from her mother, she plugged it into her husband. When their relationship became distant, she plugged it into her children. And when she was separated from her kids and her marriage continued to deteriorate, she plugged it into the man with whom she was having the affair.

In order for her to terminate her marriage and take a step toward independence, Jackie had to confront another existential concern. It's one that Yalom identifies as *Isolation*.

He defines three types of isolation; in*ter*personal, in*tra*personal, and existential. Jackie's growth needed primarily to come in the area of interpersonal isolation. It's the kind of isolation you can experience when you're separated from other individuals, and it can be the kind of separation that leads you to feel lonely. But that feeling of loneliness can be overcome.

Take living on your own, for instance. Living alone does not have to be bleak and lonely. When you've actually had the experience of successfully living and thriving on your own, you can discover your physical, emotional, and financial self-sufficiency. That can have an exhilarating and even an empowering effect. Paradoxically, it also can be of benefit when choosing a life partner.

When you've truly mastered living life alone and wish to seek someone to share your life with, you're in the best position to select a partner. Your hand is not forced. You've discovered that your self-sufficiency and happiness can be achieved separately. Therefore, your intention for seeking a partner will be to *enhance* what you've already found. Your lack of urgency will enable you to determine if a given person is the right choice for you.

Alternatively, if living in the world alone feels as if you're drowning in the sea of life, then you've not mastered the elements. You need to become a good swimmer, take responsibility for your physical health and learn how to emotionally stay buoyant. You'll also need to learn how to generate income and manage finances so you can secure and captain your own ship.

Once you've gained that kind of independence, it's up to you to determine where you want to go with your life. You need to devise a plan and figure out how to get there—define how to navigate your course and set sail in your desired direction.

When you have the confidence that you can make it alone, know where you're heading, and know how to get there, you won't be inclined to fool yourself into believing that the next person that comes along looking for a relationship is your dreamboat when that's not the case.

Jackie recognized that it would not be advisable for her to jump into yet another relationship, and while she initially struggled with her first experience of being alone, she discovered that she did not fall into pieces and die of loneliness. She gained the needed self-sufficiency to live life independently. She found the will and the way to exercise her freedom and took full responsibility for making her life what she wanted it to be. When our therapy ended, she was still considering which direction she wanted to sail, but she no longer felt anchored and constrained by the fear of being alone.

Clark Moustakas, the American psychologist and leader in the field of Humanistic and Clinical psychology, states in his book *Loneliness,* "There is no solution to loneliness but to accept it, face it, live with it, and let it be. It is a significant experience, one of the few in life where man communes with himself. But with that communion, man comes to grips with his own being. He discovers life, who he is, what he really wants, and the meaning of his existence."[16]

To not make this discovery can lead to a second form of isolation defined by Yalom as *Intrapersonal Isolation.* This is the kind of isolation you can experience when you feel separated off from aspects of yourself. It's like when people say, "I've lived my whole life according to other people's 'shoulds' and 'oughts' and along the way I feel I somehow lost who I am."

The last of the three forms of isolation that Yalom lists is *existential Isolation.* He states that "despite the most gratifying engagement with other individuals, and despite consummate self-knowledge and integration, existential isolation is even more fundamental. It's a separation between the individual and the world."[17] In my mind, this is the kind of isolation we feel when we experience ourselves as being *in* this world, but not *of* this world.

Your existential growth may require coming to terms with any of these three forms of isolation. It may also necessitate an increased understanding of how accepting your inevitable death—and the extent to which you are responsible for your life—can influence how you live. But in addition to these three areas, there remains yet another existential concern that can demand attention.

CHAPTER 11

Got Meaning? Existential Crisis, Continued

If you were on your death bed reflecting back on life, would you say there was any meaning in the ways you chose to live it? Would you be able to identify the purposes your life had served? Meaning and purpose in life are foundational to our existence. Like the other existential concerns about death, responsibility, and isolation, they can have far ranging implications for how we conduct our lives.

Leading a life filled with meaning and purpose can greatly contribute to your level of happiness. But as Victor Frankl points out in *The Will to Meaning*, happiness is not likely to be found by pursuing it; it must ensue.[1] And it's most likely to ensue when you make meaning fulfilment your goal. In other words, happiness is an outgrowth of engaging in activities that feel meaningful.

If you're questioning whether your life has meaning, Frankl also advises that rather than search for some broad and abstract "meaning of life," focus on finding meaning in what you're doing at any given time. He believes that "Everyone has his own specific vocation or mission in life to carry out a concrete assignment which demands fulfillment."[2] Yet when that concrete purpose or meaning are missing, and you find yourself forging on in their absence, that's when a sense of meaninglessness can set in.

Meaninglessness is the last of the four areas of existential concern that Yalom addresses. It can become a clinical problem even if it doesn't accompany a significant level of depression or anxiety. Feeling a lack of meaning or purpose in life can often underlie other problems that prompt people to seek psychotherapy.

For instance, due to the somewhat elusive nature of what contributes to a sense of meaninglessness, a client may attribute the lack of spirit and passion in life to more readily identifiable problems. Those commonly blamed are the exhausting demands of work and family, financial pressures, or an unsatisfying relationship. While these concerns also may require attention, meaninglessness as an underlying or central issue can get overlooked.

Take Reggie, for example, who was primarily caught up in a battle with meaninglessness. He admitted to drinking too much and feeling a little depressed. The problem became most evident during the holiday season that preceded our appointment. He had taken some extended time away from the demands of his job so he could be with his wife and children. While he enjoyed their company, his feelings of discontentment became more pronounced, and the extra availability of alcohol around the holidays didn't help.

Functioning as a vice president at a large corporation, Reggie shouldered a lot of responsibility. He rarely had the opportunity for the kind of downtime he had just experienced. But when he stepped off the treadmill of work, he became acutely aware that something was missing in his life. After discussing it with his wife, he made a New Year's resolution to give it attention.

From all outward appearances, you wouldn't think Reggie's life was lacking anything. At 45, he was a handsome man in good health. Despite his busy schedule, he found time in the early morning to exercise and stay in shape. He seemed to have a good deal of self-discipline and came across as someone who liked to get right down to business. Shortly after he took his seat in my office, he said he suspected he was going through some kind of midlife crisis. I told him we could certainly keep that in mind and went about doing my assessment.

Reggie was financially successful and had a very full life. He traveled the world for business and pleasure, had a solid marriage, two healthy children, and all the material benefits that money could buy. The only thing missing was that he just wasn't happy. He felt empty inside.

During my assessment, I asked him if he had any sense of what might be missing. He closed his eyes for a moment and bore down on my question, but he just couldn't say. All he could add was that his feeling of emptiness had recently grown stronger, and for the first time he felt like he was just going through the motions on his job. In a very disheartened tone, he said he wasn't sure he even wanted to do it anymore, and he wondered if it would be best to just quit.

As we explored what was going on, I suggested that he not make any major life decisions. I mentioned how it's frequently the case that when people don't have full awareness of everything that's affecting them, they can prematurely leap into something just to make a change. This is especially the case with take-charge individuals who are accustomed to executing action.

If Reggie's solution to his problem did involve a career change, he was financially well positioned for such a move. He even had the means to retire, if he wished. His considerable investments already assured he would have what he needed for his children's college tuitions, future weddings, and a well-funded retirement. But when he briefly entertained retirement, he said, "If I quit working, then what would I do with myself?"

For the time being he accepted continuing on with his present position, even if it meant tolerating that sense of meaninglessness. He wasn't debilitated by it, but just felt that sub-acute ache that there must be more to life.

As we moved into further sessions, I dug a little deeper to investigate if there were other personal issues contributing to the existential vacuum he felt. I explored his thoughts and feelings about his marriage, his role as a father and husband, his childhood, and his relationships with parents, siblings, friends, and co-workers.

In order not to work at cross purposes while I conducted that search, I suggested that Reggie see if he could stop drinking for thirty days. I was concerned that if I activated feelings about what might be contributing to his problem, his drinking might dull the emotional clues they can provide. Furthermore, if he couldn't stop drinking for that length of time, it would be clinically indicative that the drinking was more of a problem than he realized.

As it turned out, Reggie's instincts were accurate. He *was* in a midlife crisis, yet he felt a little embarrassed to be going through something that he considered so cliché. When he made a few comments to that effect, I mentioned that a midlife crisis may have become cliché simply because it's such a common part of many people's developmental experience. For those who experience a midlife crisis, they discover that though it may sound like some whiny abstract problem of successful bored people in the world, it is very real.

In her book *Awakening at Midlife*,[3] psychotherapist Kathleen Brehony refers to it as a crisis of awakening. When addressing it, she employs the same metaphor I use throughout this book: "The chrysalis is the crucible for growth of the personality and the emergence of the self. The middle passage is an entranceway into the deepest layers of one's soul. The growth and transformation that can often occur at this transition is nothing short of remarkable."[4]

Though Reggie's problem may seem trivial to some, it does bring about its own kind of suffering. Jung viewed the experience of meaninglessness in life as a "suffering of the soul." He considered it a kind of illness. Fortunately, Reggie was motivated to use his midlife crisis as a Chrysalis Crisis, and I trusted that his struggle would result in his existential growth.

But even if the feeling of meaninglessness is recognized, it still can be seen as a symptom of other concerns. When that's the case, it's assumed that if those problems are fixed, the empty feeling that accompanies meaninglessness will go away. Individuals might believe that if they find another relationship, move to another area, or make more money, then all will be well. But if their lives are absent of meaning and purpose, when those changes are made that sense of meaninglessness still will prevail.

Often the lack of meaning in life can be most evident when other areas of life are fine. That's when people will come into therapy and say they *should* be happy, and are boggled when they're not.

Whether a sense of meaninglessness in life goes undetected, and its accompanying emptiness and suffering gets misattributed to other concerns, or its absence is recognized as the problem, there are a couple of ways people will deal with it. Some will surrender to it, believing that the absence of meaning is just an inevitable part of living. They may embrace the view of Jean-Paul Sartre, the philosopher who professed that life *is* meaningless.

Others will not accept such a dismal view. They may have once felt a sense of meaning in life but have now lost it. They'll frequently recall an earlier time when they pursued activities that felt purposeful and cite the reasons they got abandoned. They know such a life is possible but don't know how to get it back.

Finally, there are those who experience a sense of meaninglessness and will admit that they never gave a life of purpose any thought. While they may agree that a meaningful life is ideal, they feel it's too late for them.

For all these individuals, however, there's hope. Erik Erickson revealed in his research that not only can meaning in life be found, but it can be lost, changed, or rediscovered. It's a fluid process. It's a lot like how one's identity can change throughout the life cycle. So even if you never found meaning or purpose in your life, had it once and lost it, or want to fill its void in later years, discovering it just requires summoning your will to make the search.

In order to look in the right places, though, you might want to first ask yourself a few of the following questions: Is there any particular meaning behind what I do with my days? Is there something I feel passionate about that I wish I were doing? Do I feel stuck, empty, bored, or just going through the motions? Am I directionless, rudderless, or feel like I'm just meandering through life? In my darkest hours, where do I find meaning for carrying on? Have I ever considered a purpose for being in my life?

James Hollis, a highly respected Jungian scholar, suggests that when people feel a sense of meaninglessness during that midlife middle passage, they ask themselves this question: "Who am I apart from my history and the roles I have played in my life?"[5] I would add that people also ask themselves: do I wish to continue playing those roles, or are there others I'd like to pursue?

Maybe you were once happy just to find any job so you could pay the bills. Maybe when it came time to select a course in life, you chose the road *most* traveled because that's where everyone else was heading. For example, maybe you went to college because it seemed like the next thing to do, or you got married because that's what your friends or family members did at your age. Or worse yet, maybe you just followed the prompts of others, never even checking your internal GPS for what direction was personally meaningful.

If you recognize that you've been struggling with meaning-lessness and wish to seek a more meaningful and purposeful life, I encourage you make the effort. But that effort begins with an internal search and some additional self-examination. Keep in mind that what you ultimately determine to be meaningful or purposeful will be a very individual decision. It will reflect your priorities and values. Only you can really say what feels right.

Making this kind of decision harkens back to the issue raised in the last chapter about responsibility and aloneness. It's your responsibility to make this determination. It belongs to you alone. While people can assist you in your search, no one can make it for you. As Frankl emphasizes, "meaning cannot be given, it must be found."[6]

When seeking meaning and purpose in your life, broaden your perspective. Widen the lens when viewing your life. Examine the "forest" of your overall activities, so you don't get lost in the "trees" of your present daily involvements. So don't just focus on work.

There are many ways to fill the need for meaningful activity. Yalom shares a number of examples. You can invest your time in loving relationships, undertake altruistic activities where you help others, dedicate yourself to a cause that you feel is important, engage in creative involvements like art or music, or just live life to its fullest so you can enjoy the pleasures it holds.

Some of you may find meaning in the pursuit of self-actual-ization. That would entail undertaking activities that will help you develop your potential as a human being. Abraham Maslow, the father of Humanistic Psychology, was a strong advocate of this pursuit, viewing self-actualization as *the* purpose in life.

There's also nothing to say you have to choose just one. There are numerous options. Actually, you might find it most meaningful and interesting to engage in a variety of activities. If you can maintain a healthy balance between those you select, your overall life experience may be that much more enjoyable.

If you're unable to find meaning or purpose in any activities, and you continue to feel a sense of meaninglessness, then depending on how long the feeling persists or how deeply it affects you, it can take its toll in a couple of ways. Frankl suggests there are two stages of meaninglessness: The Existential Vacuum stage, and the Existential Neurosis stage.

Being in an existential vacuum is more common and less severe. When you're caught up in this stage, you feel boredom, apathy, and emptiness; you question if what you're doing with your life has any purpose; you feel directionless; or you just feel cynical about life in general.

An existential neurosis can be more severe. It can manifest in problems such as alcoholism, depression, or various obsessions. When that's the case, it makes sense to seek professional help. This was the case with Reggie.

Finding meaning for how and why we live is not just some luxurious philosophical exercise. It can also be lifesaving. That's how it was experienced and viewed by Frankl. He arrived at that conclusion during a life experience that few of us could imagine.

Frankl was a long-term prisoner in the concentration camps of World War II. There he lost his mother, father, and wife to the gas chambers. Other than his sister, his whole family perished. Despite those devastating losses, the harshness of his living conditions, and the ongoing suffering, Frankl made some important observations. He noticed that prisoners who maintained the will to live were more likely to survive because they held onto a meaning and purpose for their continued existence.

Ironically, Frankl found much of his meaning for surviving those camps by making a study of how others did or didn't find theirs. He kept a record of his observations and insights on notes that he stashed away. He hoped that someday he would be able to articulate what he learned after his release.

Once he got through that horrendous ordeal, those insights and notes were developed into a model for conducting psychotherapy. He called it Logotherapy.[7] It's an approach based on the belief that human nature is motivated by the search for a life purpose, and it's the discovery of that meaning and purpose that adds richness to life.

Richness in life wasn't completely missing for Reggie, but he wanted to find meaning and purpose, too. As I got to know him better, it became clear that throughout his life he felt driven to succeed. That drive appeared to have established itself early.

The older of two boys, Reggie was very competitive with his younger brother and peers. He also felt that he had to prove himself in order to win what little attention he could get from his dad. He depicted his father as quiet, disgruntled, competitive, and always comparing himself and their family to others. Reggie felt he never met his father's expectations and had the insight to know that it contributed to what drove him. One area his father specifically considered as the measure of a man was how much money he made. That was a value that also had an obvious influence on Reggie.

Now, however, no matter how large his bank account, Reggie felt bankrupt in other ways. He was also coming to realize that he had more of his mother's nature. She was softer, compassionate, and more loving toward him and his brother. Reggie said she also took great joy in helping others. While she didn't hold a full-time job, she often volunteered at local shelters and hospitals.

Reggie recalled how as a boy he sometimes would accompany his mother to those places. He remembered the appreciation they showed her for what she did. When they'd visit the hospitals, he said that the doctors and nurses were always friendly toward him. For a while, he even entertained the idea of becoming a doctor, but as he moved on in school, he wasn't sure if he could make the grade academically.

When Reggie shared these memories and dreams, he began to consider the idea that he might want to change his career. This time, however, that thought seemed less reactive and driven by defeat, and more the result of an emerging clarity. He began courting the notion of moving into some kind of helping profession. While he felt it was unrealistic to seriously consider becoming a doctor, he started to entertain a career switch to nursing.

Reggie also realized that a career in business might not have been the best choice for him. Once he got on that path, however, his competitiveness drove him to succeed. The benefits of wealth that followed, and the mounting demands of his lifestyle, kept him attached. But now he was experiencing the recognition that Joseph Campbell describes when people come to such a realization: They see that they spent a good part of their life working their way up the ladder, only to discover that the ladder was placed against the wrong building.

After making peace with that recognition, Reggie became more and more enthused that nursing might be a path for him. It was soon obvious that it was more than a passing whim. He decided to look into what such a career shift would entail and found out that he could go back to a nearby community college and be working in the field in two or three years. That excited him, so he passed the idea by his wife. She was fully supportive.

Toward the end of our work together, Reggie already had started taking the prerequisite courses he needed to gain admission into the program. Though his academic skills were rusty and the courses challenging, he managed to do well. We brought his therapy to a close shortly after he started the program.

A few years later I crossed paths with Reggie. At that point he had completed his program and moved into the field. He said the work was demanding, but he found it meaningful and rewarding.

Not all resolutions to midlife crises lead to a change in career. But when you become increasingly more aware that you only have so much shelf-life to your body, you realize that if there is something else that calls you, time is of the essence.

Alternatively, determining what it is that calls you requires patience. Psychotherapist Brehony emphasizes that when we're going through midlife, another layer of the self is trying to emerge. It takes time, she says. It requires a more feminine approach, a receptiveness that allows for gestation. It's as if we're birthing a new self, and you can't rush a pregnancy.

She also says that after we enter and exit the chrysalis of midlife and emotionally renew the flow of psychic energy, "We open ourselves to the dimension of the transpersonal—that is, the parts of our nature that are beyond our ordinary, limited, personal self."[8] These are the areas we will be examining in the next section of the book.

SECTION III

The Key Areas of
Transpersonal Development:
Intuitive and Spiritual Growth

CHAPTER 12

An Abrupt Awakening: Chrysalis Crises and Spiritual Emergencies

My personal experience leads me to agree with Brehony. By opening the flow of emotional and psychic energy from successfully navigating your way through a midlife passage, you can awaken the transpersonal dimension of your being. But you don't have to wait until midlife to achieve the benefits of doing so, and if you are already past midlife, it's not too late. Transpersonal development in the key areas of intuition and spiritual growth can occur throughout the life cycle.

For me, however, the most rapid progress awakening these areas of transpersonal development was during my midlife crisis. But due to the manner in which I went about resolving it, I prompted an abrupt awakening and created yet another crisis.

Rather than navigating that passage in the patient, receptive, feminine manner that Brehony likens to a slow gestation, I took an expedited, active, and vigorous approach. My enthusiasm and commitment to learn all I could about transpersonal development prompted me to undertake too much personal exploration and internal excavation at one time. It was like I did a Roto-Rooter on my psyche and soul. And while I ultimately made some important self-discoveries, I provoked a spiritual emergency along the way.

Stanislav Grof, the Czechoslovakian psychiatrist and "father of transpersonal psychology," defines a spiritual emergency as "a critical and experientially difficult stage of a profound psychological transformation that involves one's entire being. It can take the form of non-ordinary states of consciousness and involve intense emotions, visions, sensory changes, unusual thoughts, and various physical manifestations."[1]

A spiritual emergency can come about in a number of ways. It can result from undergoing a transpersonal experience, where the unfamiliarity and foreignness of its phenomena cause a crisis, or one may be unwittingly induced. In either case, it is my opinion that if you use that spiritual emergency to further awaken keys areas of your development, then it can serve as a Chrysalis Crisis.

The spiritual emergency I went through challenged me to use it as a Chrysalis Crisis, and I'm glad I did. It not only helped me resolve my midlife crises, but it furthered my transpersonal development and prompted me to broaden the focus of my clinical work.

That whole episode began shortly after I turned 44. I had been married for 13 years, had three children, a busy career, an active social life, and was financially secure. My family life was rewarding and my marriage strong, but despite being fully engaged, I had a sense that something was missing. It was a vague feeing that there was something else I intended to do. I just wasn't clear what *it* was.

When I searched for what was missing, I realized I'd lost the passion I once had for my work. Over time, I shifted away from primarily doing individual therapy and became increasingly consumed with other clinical involvements. That work served a needed purpose and was financially rewarding, but I spent the majority of my time providing program development, consultation, and administrative oversight. Those activities were very different from the one-on-one intimate work I once found so captivating when conducting psychotherapy.

While I had the freedom to make a change, I felt like I was attached to a moving train, and it just wasn't so easy to get off. The idea of making a shift in my professional involvements seemed difficult to do without incurring significant consequences. So I stayed the course and hoped that my sub-acute ache and disquieted feelings were primarily symptoms of the stress I was experiencing from juggling so many demands.

In order to manage the stress, I decided to increase exercising. Recalling how sport used to bring joy and distraction into my life, I threw myself into physical conditioning and playing competitive tennis. However, early on in that campaign, it became evident that I'd have to refurbish some damaged body parts. I tore the meniscus in my knee for a second time and had an arthritic shoulder. Both needed repairs, and both repairs required surgery.

I elected to fix them during the same operation—kill two birds with one stone. The results weren't good. While the procedures provided relief from pain, I was told that both joints would eventually need replacement. Tennis was out, and other athletic activities were limited. I was surprised and disappointed by the outcome. But what was even more surprising were the aftereffects of the surgery.

I had a post-operative reaction. In the days that followed, I felt emotionally unraveled. I cycled from feeling fear, to feeling weepy, to feeling agitated. What perplexed me was that I couldn't understand why. When I told my tennis partner the bad news and shared the state I was in, he suggested that it might be a reaction to the anesthesia. As a pharmacist, he wondered if the particular cocktail of drugs they used might have had a bad effect on me.

Later, I came across a *Harvard Review* article which seemed to confirm his suspicion. It said that after a major surgery, feelings of mortality, of loss, and of vulnerability can be profound. While I wouldn't have considered my surgery "major," it gave me more to consider. However, I wasn't sure if I was experiencing a reaction to drugs, the loss of realizing my body wasn't what it used to be, a midlife awakening to my mortality, or something else I had yet to discover. Whatever it was, it lacked clarity, and I wanted to find out.

I assumed that as with everyone else, the answer probably lies within me, so I decided to resume a few activities that had helped me get centered in the past. They entailed doing a daily series of yoga postures followed by a period of meditation. In order to enhance what I was trying to accomplish, I also did some personal journaling and psycho-spiritual readings beforehand.

Starting my day with this ritual helped me get grounded and provided a period for self-examination, but I still struggled to identify what it was that I needed—that something else that felt missing in my life. I realized I had to do some further digging and recognized that I would benefit by getting another person to assist me, so I sought some outside help.

When I considered what kind of help I would choose, I thought I might try working with a counselor who was not practicing conventional psychotherapy. Though I had benefited from that approach before, this time I decided to seek out an individual who affiliated with a psycho-spiritual organization called Pathwork.[2]

I initially became intrigued by the Pathwork organization when I attended one of their weekend retreats a few years earlier. After reading some of their materials, I found their concepts resonated with my leanings. The theory they embraced had a familiar Jungian feel. But I was also intrigued by the way they integrated some of those psychological theories with other non-sectarian spiritual concepts. And finally, I was particularly curious as to how they would integrate those two strands into their counseling process.

One central component of the Pathwork process is called Core Energetics. It's a system of body-oriented psychotherapy that is incorporated into their psychological and spiritual approach. That component was initially developed by a physician named John Pierrakos. His theory and technique are based on three principles: "That each of us is a psychosomatic entity; that the source of healing lies within the self; and that all of existence forms a unity which moves toward creative evolution."[3]

The Core Energetic process grew out of John's collaboration with the renowned Australian psychiatrist Wilhelm Reich, a major force in the field of psychotherapy in the early 20th century. Reich's ideas on how "muscular armor" can create barriers to the healing that lies within the self influenced the development of bodywork techniques, Gestalt therapy, and other therapeutic approaches that emphasize emotional expression.

Since I was aware that both professionally and personally I tended to intellectualize, I wondered if Core Energetics' more physical and emotional emphasis might be just what I needed to free myself from any blocks I unwittingly erected. I hoped that if that were the case removing them might help me get to the bottom of what I needed to discover. So I decided to attend a Core Energetic workshop with John Pierrakos one month after my operation.

During that workshop, I had an interesting experience. On the first night, John had everyone gather in a circle. He then had each of us come up in front of the group, stand before him, and share a little about who we were and what we hoped to gain from the experience. As we did, he walked around us and scanned our bodies. It was a little intimidating to be so exposed before a group of strangers, but we all understood that his technique entailed a willingness to be vulnerable.

When it was my turn, I stood before him and mentioned something about wanting to get back on the path to personal growth. He walked around me while I spoke, and then gave me a rather forcible swat in the back. The gesture stunned me. It didn't hurt as much as it caught me by surprise. Yet it had enough force to send me a step forward to catch my balance. Afterwards, I was asked to rejoin the circle.

I was a little embarrassed, but I didn't sense any ill intent in his gesture. I noted that he didn't do that to any of the other 20 or so participants. I was curious as to why he did it to me, but unfortunately, because I was still recovering from my operation, I had to leave after two days and never got the chance to directly ask. I found the rigors of the Core Energetic technique too demanding on my compromised joints. Nevertheless, I got what I needed while I was there, because my spirit and mood lifted significantly.

After attending that workshop, I shared the incident with one of my therapist officemates. She was also pursuing an integration of spirituality and psychotherapy in her clinical work. When I told her how John slapped me on the back, she said, "Oh, he gave you Shaktipat. It's a spiritual wake–up call."

According to Siddha Yoga, Shaktipat is a spiritual awakening that lies at the heart of the mystical journey. It's an infusion of energy from a spiritual master to the seeker. Shaktipat activates an inner unfolding of awareness that leads to progressively higher states of consciousness. The spiritual power that gets awakened is called Kundalini. It is said to be located at the base of the spine and is conceived of as a coiled-up serpent.

As it turned out, receiving John's Shaktipat did seem to have an impact because it marked a turning point for me. The snake was awake. I became filled with a renewed desire to pursue the interests that initially led me to clinical psychology. They were interests that once held my passion, interests that I hoped I could better understand through my studies in the field. They included mysticism, altered states of consciousness, psychic phenomena, and a host of spiritual experiences common to many of the world's religions.

I became even more motivated to learn how to integrate psychological, spiritual, and transpersonal techniques into doing therapy. And in pursuit of that knowledge, I sought out numerous "alternative" experiences and trainings. In order to fully appreciate what they had to offer, I thought it would be best to directly experience their processes. In that way I could personally attest to their effectiveness.

In addition to working weekly with a Pathwork helper for two years, I attended all their various workshops, including a one-week individual intensive. I began meeting weekly with an energy worker trained in the Barbara Brennan School, and I entered a training program in Past-Life Therapy with a Jungian Analyst in England by the name of Roger Woolger.

Concurrent with these extended programs, I sought out briefer trainings in Shamanic practices in Peru, and learned how to conduct reiki, hypnosis, and neurofeedback here in the states. Along with all of those trainings, I sought out therapeutic experiences with Phoenix Rising Yoga, altered states of consciousness at The Monroe Institute, and took part in various retreats, one combining Jack Kornfield's Vipassana meditation, and Stan Grof's Holotropic Breathwork.

All of these trainings and experiences took place over four years. They proved through my own direct involvement how these alternative and non-conventional forms of treatment can provide physical, psychological, and spiritual healing. It left a lasting impression both professionally and personally. But it wasn't all uplifting and inspiring, because at about two and a half years in I started experiencing some very odd symptoms.

They were similar to those I experienced after my surgery, only this time they were more intense, and they lasted longer. As they persisted, I started feeling vulnerable, shaky, and anxious. I wasn't sure what was happening to me. I even became a little hesitant to venture far from home when it wasn't necessary. I wanted to stay where I felt safe and in control.

When I shared what I was experiencing with my wife, she wisely mentioned that I might possibly be doing *too much* personal experiencing and investigating. She was right because in addition to the emotional uneasiness it was producing, I also started to manifest physical symptoms, and they scared me.

Though I had been regularly exercising and was in excellent health, I began having those episodes of atrial fibrillation. In addition, I started experiencing occasional abdominal pains on my left side. And most bizarre, I began twitching all over my body. When the twitching would occur, my skin would slightly lift, sometimes in a few places at once.

The uneasy feelings and the body symptoms made me feel as if I had excessive energy that I couldn't contain. While I was still of sound mind and had plenty of therapist friends and officemates who could attest to that, I was nevertheless becoming increasingly frightened about what was happening to me.

When the physical symptoms continued, I thought it advisable to seek the help of conventional medical professionals. I've always endorsed the notion that it's best to rule out the physical before seeking a mental, emotional, or in this case, energetic reasons for the physical problems.

For the A-fib, I sought the help of a cardiologist, but he could not determine the cause of its occasional onset and termination. I saw a gastroenterologist, urologist, and a surgeon to explain the abdominal pains, but again they could find nothing. And because my mother had MS, I started to worry that the twitching might be some form of inherited neurological disorder, so I consulted a neurologist. But no cause could be found there either.

I was not one to be a hypochondriac, so I was perplexed as to why I was experiencing all these physical symptoms. Fortunately, I still had that ongoing support of my helper, but we could find no past nor present issues that could explain the emotional uneasiness and the physical symptoms.

It was only after further research and consultation with various transpersonal psychologists that I discovered I was experiencing a spiritual emergency. Apparently, my *excessive* pursuit of all those trainings, workshops, and experiences in such a short period of time brought forth more than I could digest cognitively, emotionally, physically, and spiritually. And until I was able to do so, I suffered the symptoms of overload. In hindsight, I should have curtailed my enthusiasm and conducted my search in a more tempered manner. But once I was finally able to integrate all that I uncovered, and settled back down into a symptom-free state, it ushered in a great deal of personal growth.

Ironically, having that experience contributed to resolving my midlife crisis, too. Like a forest fire, it burnt off the unneeded undergrowth in my psyche. It freed up a lot of energy and allowed new existential directions to emerge in my life. Those new directions led to a shift of purpose and mission in my clinical work, one that increasingly focused on understanding spiritual emergencies. And that emphasis prompted a deeper investigation into the kinds of anomalous phenomena and transpersonal experiences that give rise to them.

In the 20 plus years since I've navigated that passage, I've done a considerable amount of research and therapy with people undergoing various types of spiritual emergencies. That research, my own experiences, and the clinical work I conducted with others have led me to conclude that spiritual emergencies can indeed be used as Chrysalis Crises. How that can be accomplished, and what can be gained from the effort is the subject of the next section.

CHAPTER 13

Sit Lightly in the Saddle of Belief

How can a spiritual emergency be used as a Chrysalis Crisis? How can it awaken your intuitive and spiritual growth? And how can the growth of these two keys areas lead to your overall transpersonal development?

Before I move on to answer these questions, we will examine how various types of experiences give rise to spiritual emergencies, and how your response to those experiences either inhibit or enhance their growth producing potentials. As you'll see, a large part of what will affect that outcome is predicated on what you *believe* about their phenomena. This is an example of how your key area of intellectual growth will influence your experience and understanding of other key areas, particularly with regard to the key areas of transpersonal development.

For instance, experiences that I place under the key areas of intuition and spirituality often include psychic or mysterious phenomena. You may question if they're real, or wonder if they're products of an active imagination. Are they signs of delusion and pathology? Are they misperceptions best explained by other psychological or neurological causes? Were they brought about by fraud? Or, because they defy the known workings of the physical world, are they just plain unbelievable? Let me give you an example of one that I heard early in life.

When I was growing up, I was told a story about a strange incident that occurred to a cherished uncle. It took place on the battlefields of the Second World War. At the time of the incident, my uncle was an infantryman serving under General George Patton. His name was Italo, but everyone called him Atles. He was my mother's next oldest sibling and close confidant.

Atles was a stocky young man who stood about five feet nine, had dark wavy hair, a prominent nose, and classic Roman features. Quick to flash a smile, he got along well with folks and was considered a good soldier. Atles was grounded, battle tested, and a natural leader.

On this particular occasion, Atles was scouting for a patrol that had just crossed over into ally territory after spending time behind enemy lines. Shortly thereafter, they looked for a place to settle down for the night. But once a location was chosen, Atles was overcome with a deep sense of dread and foreboding. For some reason, the spot they selected didn't feel right to him.

When he made his concerns known to the others, they asked why he felt that way. He couldn't explain why. He just said he had a strong sense that the place wasn't safe. Since he didn't provide any tangible or logical reason why, the others felt it no longer warranted consideration. But that did not dissuade Atles from continued appeals. He remained apprehensive and insisted the place was wrong.

Atles wasn't the paranoid type, so a few of his buddies began to wonder if he was experiencing the cumulative stress from all they had recently encountered. They thought he might be suffering from some sort of battle fatigue. But when they checked that out with him, it wasn't the case.

Typically, a compliant soldier who followed orders, Atles in this situation resisted settling down. His persistence about the place being wrong began to wear on everybody, and others started to become unnerved. At one point, their leader thought it be best to just go ahead and relocate. That way everyone could get some rest. But there was a problem.

Due to the lay of the land, there were no nearby locations that seemed as secure, so they ended up backtracking and ultimately settled at a spot they passed earlier. Ironically, that spot was just inside enemy lines.

The whole ordeal weighed heavily on Atles. He felt embarrassed about making such a scene. He was introverted by nature, so drawing that much attention to himself was out of character. As he lay down that night trying to get some sleep, his ruminations about the event made it difficult for him to fall asleep. But the greater disturbance to his sleep came from the unrelenting background sounds of mortar fire.

The next morning their patrol rose early and got on their way. When they again reached their first location of choice, they couldn't believe their eyes. Everyone was astonished. The whole area had been devastated by mortar fire. Needless to say, his fellow soldiers were both thankful and boggled. And so was Atles.

That incident made quite an impression on Atles. Questions circled in his mind. How did he know that settling in that place could have led to tragedy? With no tangible or logical reasons to

185

justify his concern, what was it that made him so sure the place was wrong? Why had it prompted such a strong emotional reaction in him? Was the whole thing just some bizarre coincidence?

Atles brought these questions home from the war, and his desire to find answers led to a life-long search. He became passionate about understanding such paranormal experiences. What he discovered early on was that he had had a premonition. According to parapsychologist Daryl Bem, a premonition is an "affective apprehension of a future event that could not otherwise be anticipated through any known inferential process."[1]

When Atles started learning about such phenomena, he shared what he was discovering with those around him who showed an interest. One such person was my mother. She had her own questions about the mysteries of the mind, particularly if her mind played a part in her contracting MS. She was also curious about the other psychic and anomalous experiences Atles explored.

Paranormal experiences are typically considered anomalous. In the book *The Varieties of Anomalous Experience,* an anomalous experience is defined as "an uncommon experience, or one that although it may be experienced by a substantial amount of the population, is believed to deviate from ordinary experience or from the usually accepted explanations of reality."[2]

If you have a paranormal experience and no previous understanding of such phenomena, you might get swamped by a host of confused thoughts and feelings afterwards. Even if you've heard of these anomalies, when they are your experience they can leave you doubting yourself. One of the more confusing features is that their perceptions are revealed to you by your own mind. That can make you wonder if your mind functioning normally or abnormally? In order to answer that question, let's consider a few examples.

Imagine a person who functions at a fairly high level psychologically and slips into a state of reverie. With mind relaxed, unfocused, and free of its usual distractions, certain feelings, thoughts, or images may come into awareness, like the memory or a fantasy of a deceased loved one. At first, what comes to mind may seem unexpected and uncomfortable, but the content of what's realized would certainly be considered "normal." If it surfaces in manageable amounts, it actually can be helpful to a healing process.

Alternatively, imagine another person whose baseline level of psychological functioning is much lower and less stable. In that kind of unfocused state, his mind might produce a host of paranoid delusions or psychotic thinking. For instance, he might become overwrought with fear that someone who recently called on the phone and hung up, realizing it was the wrong number, is someone who is out to kill him. In this case, what came to mind is more likely the symptom of an "abnormal" condition. It may indicate a loss of reality testing and, if such thinking persists, will require psychiatric care.

There are other times, however, when a relatively healthy functioning person will have certain thoughts, feelings, and perceptions that don't fall into either of the above two categories. The perceptions that come forth may not be familiar or easily identified with what is typically thought to be normal, like the symptom of a grieving process in the first example. Yet at times the perceptions can feel alarming, foreign, unreal, and even irrational, but they're not sufficiently dysfunctional to qualify as symptoms of a deteriorating abnormal state.

The state of mind my uncle was in when he was agitated and couldn't settle down was certainly not his normal range of functioning, but neither was he evidencing an abnormal breakdown into a progressively deteriorating condition. In his situation, what was coming to mind was more of a breakthrough than a breakdown. What was breaking into his awareness was the intuitive premonition of a potential disaster.

When the mind registers these kinds of paranormal experiences, they warrant a third categorization, one that is neither normal, nor abnormal. The 19th century researcher Frederick Myers, one of the original founders of the Society for Psychical Research, suggested that these types of experiences can best categorized as *supernormal* functions of the mind.

Dean Radin, a senior scientist at the Institute of Noetic Sciences, notes in his book *Supernormal* that "Myers used this word to refer to natural, lawful phenomena that presage a more advanced, future stage of human evolution." He says that, according to Myer's conception, "as we gain an improved understanding of ourselves, our capacities, and the physical world, the supernormal will become the normal."[3]

In order to further appreciate why some paranormal experiences may be considered supernormal, it might be helpful to examine the origins and definition of the word paranormal. The prefix *para* comes from the Ancient Greek word *Ttapa*, which means "alongside of" and "beside." The *Oxford Dictionary* defines paranormal as "beyond the scope of normal." Consistent with Myers's notion of supernormal functions, it makes sense that we consider certain paranormal experiences as those that lie alongside of, and beyond, the normal. That would put them on a continuum: *Abnormal – Normal – Supernormal.*

Some of the paranormal experiences that fall on the supernormal end of this continuum are referred to as the *psi* functions. According to Bem, "psi denotes anomalous processes of information or energy transfer that are currently unexplained in terms of known physical or biological mechanisms."[4]

Charles Tart, the transpersonal psychologist, identifies what he calls the "big five psi functions." They include *telepathy*, the transfer of information from one person to another without mediation of any known channel of sensory communication; *clairvoyance*, obtaining of information about a place or event by unknown means; *psychokinesis*, (PK) the influence of mind on an object, physical system, or biological system without direct physical interaction; *precognition/ premonition*, cognitive or affective awareness of future events; and *psychic healing*, the use of the mind to effect healing on living organisms.

But have these various psi functions and their anomalous phenomena been sufficiently proven to the extent where we can trust that they are real? William James, the Harvard psychologist who is considered the Father of American Psychology and was co-founder of the Society for Psychical Research once said, "The concrete evidence for most of the psychic phenomena under discussion is good enough to hang a man twenty times."

Other well-respected researchers, like Dean Radin, have repeatedly shown such evidence. As a result, Dean's present position is that "No longer is psi viewed as unthinkable, or as a meaningless anomaly. Instead psi is being regarded as a genuine, albeit poorly understood human facility."[5] The question is no longer *if* these phenomena actually occur, but *how* it is that they come about—what principles of nature are working that we have yet to define?

Psi phenomena can be subtle, and for that reason they don't easily lend themselves to being produced on demand or measured in the primarily physical ways we've come to determine what is valid. But that doesn't mean they don't exist. It's not necessary to physically prove something exists to establish that it's real.

Anyway, there's a difference between reality and actuality. What is considered reality is more often than not that which your culture accepts as real based on shared experiences. Actuality is that which is established as fact, or supported by empirical evidence. At one time, for example, people embraced the *reality* that the earth was flat. We know now, that in *actuality*, that is not the case.

When it comes to establishing the actuality of psi there are very good arguments for both sides. But even if there may be a number of valid alternative explanations for claims made about psi events, as Williams James said, "If you wish to upset the law that all crows are black, it is enough that you prove one is white."

So when client brings in claims that they have experienced their version of a "white crow," if they wish to use the experience as a Chrysalis Crisis, there are two paths I could take.

One path would be to align my approach with the emerging sub-discipline of *Anomalous Psychology*. It operates on the premise that these kinds of experiences are *not actual*, and "attempts to explain paranormal or related beliefs, and ostensibly (alleged) paranormal experiences, in terms of known (or knowable) psychological or physical factors."[6]

Alternatively, I could adopt an approach consistent with the emerging field of *Clinical Parapsychology*.[7] Clinical parapsychologists are equally committed to diagnosing and ruling out all other conventional considerations. *But* when those are sufficiently examined, the individuals' experience is held as plausible. Then, they seek to help clients integrate their experience into an expanding personal or evolving worldview.

It will not surprise you to know that I favor the clinical parapsychology approach. But that wasn't a choice made blindly. I realized long ago that I was influenced by significant others to consider paranormal phenomena as valid. With that recognition, I attempted to counter that early indoctrination by spending the better part of my adult professional life digging into what conventional clinical psychology had to say about such phenomena, and independently investigating these matters from non-conventional sources and personal experiences.

I took this approach because I wanted to assure myself that I was moving forward with as much conscious awareness as possible, and upholding the professional integrity of my trade. I reviewed the research both for and against the legitimacy of psi and transpersonal phenomena; I sought out and established professional and personal friendships with some of the best minds in psi research; and I acquainted myself directly with a number of gifted individuals who have evidenced psi abilities under controlled conditions.

However, the most significant influence that moved me into the camp of clinical parapsychology is the fact that I've personally had a number of my own anomalous experiences. I'll share a few of the relevant ones in the chapters that follow.

But despite these experiences, I continue to challenge myself to sit lightly in the saddle of what I believe, and I encourage you to do the same. That's because the more I learn about this whole transpersonal area, the more I discover the many ways in which one's belief can affect the perception and even influence the effects of what transpires in paranormal phenomena.

Most practically, it's prudent to keep an open mind because the strength of proof in some areas of psi and transpersonal experiences is greater than others. So it behooves us to not just naively believe in everything considered paranormal or anomalous.

On the other hand, there is sufficient evidence to establish the truth for many of these psychic functions and transpersonal experiences. And in light of those discoveries, if you remain entrenched in disbelief, you may never move on to consider what these experiences have to offer for your evolution and growth.

In addition to considering the validity of psi functions, some paranormal anomalies come in the form of transpersonal experiences, like a near-death experience (NDE), a unity experience, or various mystical states. Psychiatrist Roger Walsh and psychologist Frances Vaughn define transpersonal experiences as those "in which the sense of identity of self extends beyond the individual or personal to encompass wider aspects of humankind, life, psyche, and cosmos."[8] Seen in this light, transpersonal phenomena can also be considered manifestations of human potentials. Stan Grof suggests that they, too, are all part of our evolution.

When these anomalous experiences cause distress for people, that's when they can evolve into a spiritual emergency. But, as I contend, if it is used as a Chrysalis Crisis, that effort can lead to increased intuitive and spiritual growth. But like the Chrysalis Crises discussed earlier, there will likely be a struggle before those benefits are realized. That struggle may begin right at the start when it's unclear what is being encountered.

Not understanding the nature of these difficulties can result in their symptoms being wrongfully identified. Grof notes that oftentimes a spiritual emergency may be viewed "as if it were a disease that has a biological cause and necessitates medical treatment."[9] Of course, in light of the distinctions I just made about normal, abnormal, and supernormal functioning, one needs to carefully differentiate which symptoms belong to which category. This can be a challenging diagnosis.

Making an accurate diagnosis can be helped by understanding the variety of ways a spiritual emergency can be brought on. Grof cites a number of ways. One can result from having what he refers to as a *psychic opening*. A "psychic opening can lead to a transpersonal crisis characterized by a striking instance of extrasensory perception (ESP) and other parapsychological manifestations."[10]

Atles's premonition experience is a good example of a psychic opening. It's the kind of psi experience that can evolve into a spiritual emergency because it's difficult to determine at first what is giving rise to all the dread, foreboding, and agitation. In the aftermath, when it becomes clear what it was all related to, it poses a further challenge to understand and integrate an experience that defies what we've come to believe about time, space, and causality.

Another phenomenon that Grof says can trigger a spiritual emergency is the abrupt awakening of *kundalini energy*. In Yogic theory, kundalini energy is considered a primal, feminine energy. When it awakes abruptly, it produces dramatic physical and psychological manifestations. Yogic literature refers to these as *kriyas*. Most striking of these kriya symptoms are powerful sensations of heat and energy streaming up the spine, tremors, spasms, or other shaking movements. Some are less intense and acute, like the kundalini experience I had in the middle of my four-year exploration. However, kundalini energy is not inherently bad, nor should it be avoided. Different spiritual traditions teach safe ways of awakening it where it can lead to enlightenment and states of bliss.

In addition to psychic openings and kundalini prompted kriyas, spiritual emergencies can arise as a result of being in *nonordinary states of consciousness*. Though meditation and other helpful techniques like hypnosis can be safely and positively employed, if someone is ripe for having long repressed and unresolved unconscious memories arise, they can sometimes achieve breakthroughs in those altered states. While they may temporarily lead to a spiritual emergency, if the crisis is effectively resolved, it can provide a needed clearing that is critical to the individual's growth.

Non-ordinary states of consciousness also can be engendered by less familiar methods, like shamanic initiations. They, too, can facilitate the emergence of deep unconscious thoughts, feelings, and transpersonal experiences. If those shamanic practices include taking psychoactive substances like Ayahuasca, a drug mixture that is used in certain South American rituals, the experience can be particularly intense. I've seen a number of clients over the years who unexpectedly triggered spiritual emergencies when recreationally taking drugs like LSD, psilocybin, and mescaline.

Grof also mentioned that certain individuals report having a spiritual emergency following operations in which they were under anesthesia for prolonged periods of time. When I first read that, I found it particularly interesting in light of my post-surgical reaction.

Along with psychic openings, kundalini awakenings, and various types of non-ordinary states of consciousness, a spiritual emergency can arise from what Grof calls "the emergence of a karmic pattern." This is a spontaneous transpersonal experience of what is thought to be a past-life memory. Sometimes a similar experience can arise from undergoing past-life therapy, but whether spontaneous or facilitated, when a karmic pattern emerges, intense dramatic sequences that feel emotionally and physically real break into awareness. While they may initially be unsettling, as Grof says, "They can suddenly seem to throw a new light on various emotional, psychosomatic, and interpersonal problems in a person's present life, which previously were obscure and incomprehensible."[11]

Finally, to further develop what I briefly mentioned earlier, a spiritual emergency also can result from having a near-death experience (NDE). While NDEs have become better known in recent years, what is not fully appreciated is the fact that some are experienced as negative. Not everyone floats out of their body, sees the "light," feels ecstatic love, and comes back to life with renewed meaning and purpose. Nancy Evans Bush notes that after an extensive review of NDE reports from 1975 to 2005, almost one in five were identified as having some distressing elements.[12]

When I consider all these experiences, and how the spiritual emergencies they produce can be used as Chrysalis Crises for growth, I share the view of Yvonne Kason. Yvonne is a medical doctor who underwent her own traumatic NDE. She refers to the positive potentials of paranormal and transpersonal phenomena as *spiritually transformative experiences* (STEs).[13]

Holding a similar view, Roberto Assagioli suggests that these kinds of experiences be considered "spiritual awakenings." He sees them as the "light of the Self that is trying to shine through. However, when that Self is attempting to shine through, it needs to throw off that which darkens the light of its higher states of consciousness. In the past, this was known as purgation and its process can be laborious. It is a basic aspect of a reliable and permanent channel of contact between the individual and his transpersonal or superconscious nature."[14]

This awakening process is followed by personal regeneration, transmutation, and self-realization. Assagioli says, "It is a long and many-sided process... a period of transition where we're passing out of the old condition without firmly reaching the new; an intermediate stage where *one is like a caterpillar undergoing the process of transformation into the winged butterfly. But the individual does not have the protection of a cocoon...*"[15] [emphasis mine]

Assagioli's use of the chrysalis metaphor, and his description of the transformational process that can result from a spiritual emergency, lends further credence to my contention that spiritual emergencies can be used as Chrysalis Crises. They hold potential for transpersonal development, particularly in the two keys areas of intuitive and spiritual growth, human capacities that fall within the supernormal range of consciousness. They will each be given specific focus in the next two chapters.

CHAPTER 14

It's a Mind Field Out There: Intuitive Crisis

I was about three quarters of a mile into a 10k road race when I witnessed an event I'll never forget. It was a beautiful spring morning in the town of Free Union, Virginia. The redbud and dogwood trees were in full bloom, and multicolored azaleas dotted the landscape. About 400 fellow runners and I were taking on a challenging road race through the foothills of the Blue Ridge Mountains.

The starting line was in front of an old white church in the center of the quaint little town. It was surrounded by homes that looked to be dated back a century or more. After the starter's gun fired and the pack slowly got on the move, it took only a few hundred yards of running before we were out of the town's center and into the pastoral settings surrounding the area.

Half mile into the race, the road took a bend to the left and made a long extended dip. From my vantage point, I could see the field of runners beginning to spread out. The fleet footed were pulling away up front, while the rest of us middle-of-the-packers filled the spaces in between. At that point in the race, the total group of runners spread out about a quarter of a mile from front to back.

My adrenalin was pumping, my legs felt fresh, and I was feeling optimistic about reaching my goal. The long downhill stretch added to my confidence. With the assist from gravity, my stride naturally lengthened and I took the opportunity to look around and enjoy the scenery. The rolling green hills to our right were filled with grazing horses and cows, and the mountains in the background added to the beauty. Then it happened. In one moment, all the animals in the field became alert, turned in the direction we were heading, and simultaneously broke into a run right along with us.

It was like a scene on the plains of the Serengeti. The ground vibrated and the sound of all the pounding feet and hooves rang out in the cool morning air. We were all entrained in the act of running, a mass of animal muscle, unified in motion. I got goosebumps on my skin, felt a surge of feelings, and wanted to scream with pleasure. It was awesome.

Though that herd response probably can be explained by instinctive reactions, I draw upon that experience when I reflect on how at more subtle levels, we are all united by one mind.

In his book *One Mind*, the physician Larry Dossey states that the concept of one mind is based on evidence that suggests a "collective, unitary domain of intelligence, of which all individual minds are a part. *We are intimately connected with one another and all sentient life.*"[1] [my emphasis]

This one mind to which we are all connected is part of the overall consciousness that permeates all facets of material and mental reality. According to Dossey, "Individual minds turn out not to be just individual. They are not confined or localized to specific points in space, such as brains or bodies, nor to specific points in time, such as the present. Minds, rather, are *nonlocal* with respect to space and time."[2]

As a result of this underlying unity, we can connect with others or situations in ways that can often surprise, boggle, or even frighten us. In the latter case, when we're unable to make sense of the experience, it can throw us into a crisis. That was the case for my Uncle Atles, and it was the state of mind that Bill was in when he first walked into the counseling center at Michigan State University in 1978.

At the time, I was in the second year of my doctoral program engaged in the practicum phase of clinical training. Taking Bill onto my caseload marked the first time in my career where I was confronted with a client going through a spiritual emergency. I didn't fully understand his case in that light at that time, but I later discovered that Bill had all its hallmarks.

Bill was a 20-year-old senior majoring in engineering who was first seen by one of the center's intake counselors. When our staff of therapists met at its weekly meeting to distribute the cases that needed to be assumed, Bill was initially portrayed as either going through a brief psychotic episode, or possibly evidencing the onset of schizophrenic symptoms. However, when it was also mentioned that he alleged to have had a Near-Death Experience and claimed to have knowledge of an incident before it actually occurred, I became curious and volunteered to pick up his case.

Having recently read Raymond Moody's bestselling book *Life after Life* about NDEs,[3] and holding a longstanding interest in paranormal phenomena, I immediately saw Bill's case as an opportunity to examine such anomalous claims in the context of conducting psychotherapy. I relished the opportunity to work with him.

Initially, however, I was cautious. I wasn't completely sure how my supervisors would work with me on his behalf, particularly in regard to my interests in paranormal phenomena. I wondered if I would have the latitude to consider alternative explanations for some of his perceptions and experiences and not feel compelled to only view them as symptoms of psychopathology.

It became evident early on that my fears were unwarranted. I received excellent supervision on his case, and it helped me in a number of ways. It enabled me to integrate some previous clinical experiences I had prior to entering the doctoral program, when I lived and worked with long-term institutionalized schizophrenics who were being released and reintegrated back into the community of Newark, New Jersey.

The supervision also helped me clinically apply the new knowledge I was gaining from elective coursework in treating schizophrenics. And finally, in another unforeseen way, my individual supervisor was instrumental in choices I made both professionally and personally a few years later.

In order to gain further understanding of Bill, my supervisor alerted me to research being conducted at the University of Virginia in the areas of near-death experiences, reincarnation, and parapsychology. Those areas of research and the university's proximity to other organizations pursuing similar knowledge contributed to a decision I made to migrate to the Charlottesville area after graduation. For nearly 40 years, those organizations have referred numerous clients like Bill to my practice.

Bill's case brought all my interests together: psychotherapy, schizophrenia, and parapsychology. After a few sessions, however, it became apparent that he wasn't psychotic or decompensating into some schizophrenic state. But when he first told me that he feared he was some kind of "angel of death," I could appreciate why he sounded psychotic to the intake therapist. After he explained more about the reasons why he considered such a bizarre possibility, it started making more rational sense.

Bill had had premonitions that a few people he knew were going to die and they did. These premonitions were of two relatives, and not too long after he had them, both suddenly died of natural causes. The premonitions began after he had his NDE.

The NDE occurred during his summer employment where he worked in construction. Bill had an accident that nearly killed him. During that ordeal, he underwent the classic symptoms of an NDE: he experienced himself out of his body as he watched others come to his rescue; he saw a light that appeared at the end of a long tunnel; he underwent a life review; and despite inclinations to the contrary, he recalled being told that he needed to return to his present life.

Despite the popularity of Moody's book, NDEs were still foreign to most people in the mid-1970s. Bill was one of them. I suggested he get the book. But what neither he nor I knew at the time, and what was yet to be discovered in future research, was that people who have NDEs are noted to have other psychic functions emerge in their aftermath. Bill's premonitions were a good example of this increased psychic capacity.

In addition to the premonitions he had of his relative's deaths, Bill had another premonition that was verified by his roommate. This one had to do with a renowned figure whose kidnapping and murder had gained a great deal of media attention at the time. One morning Bill awoke and told his roommate that he had a dream where he heard the whereabouts and condition of the kidnapped ex-minister of Italy by the name of Aldo Moro. When Moro disappeared, he was functioning as the president of the Christian Democratic party of Italy. When Bill had his dream, Moro had been missing for more than 50 days.

During Bill's dream, he became aware that Moro had been murdered and his body had been found in the trunk of a car. No such news to that effect had yet been announced. A few days later, however, that very information became known, and Bill and his roommate were in disbelief that it actually occurred.

Nevertheless, despite its oddity, Bill put that experience behind him and chalked it up to the kind of anomaly he had with his relatives. But what started putting Bill over the top, and prompted his coming into counseling, was that he began having dreams about his girlfriend dying. Bill and this girlfriend were considering marriage after he graduated from MSU, and the thought that he might be gaining information about her death threw him into a panic.

This aspect of Bill's case proved to be even more enlightening in my education. It provided me with the challenge of discerning where Bill's potential capacity for psychic functioning, can get confused with the more conventional ways in which his unconscious mind was operating.

Upon further clinical investigation, I discovered that Bill was very ambivalent about getting married. He had been dating this girl for quite some time, but since his NDE, he had become less committed to remaining in the relationship. In a way, for Bill, the NDE served as an early mid-life crisis. He began questioning if he truly wanted to marry and settle down so soon, and started considering other things he might like to do beforehand. However, after almost losing Bill in the accident, his girlfriend pressed all the more that they marry.

Bill was a gentle young man who was conflict avoidant, and knowing what a disappointment it would be to tell his girlfriend that he had a change of mind, he felt increasing anxiety about their relationship. When he imagined telling her that he didn't want to get married and even end the relationship, he felt guilty.

Like many people who feel conflicted about a given situation they'd rather not confront, his wish to have her out of his life had gotten converted into a fear that something would happen to her. That flip from wish to fear got cross wired with his other precognitive experiences and further muddied the waters of what was real and what wasn't. I approached the situation tactfully, as I would with any client caught up in such an intolerable unconscious wish. But when I revealed my interpretation to Bill, it resonated as true for him. He then relaxed and realized what had happened.

Because the source of some conventional psychological problems and psi impressions can both come into awareness by way of the unconscious, the need to disentangle what is perceived through that avenue requires ongoing attention and maintenance. To the extent I was able at that time, I helped Bill learn ways of differentiating what arises from his unconscious, as well as how to address some basic conventional issues, like how to effectively confront difficult interpersonal interactions, and how to envision his life after graduation.

Bill and I worked for the better part of my practicum year and his experience served as a Chrysalis Crisis for him. Sorting out what impressions he was receiving through his unconscious mind helped him gain further insight into the ways his mind worked. And learning about the normal, abnormal, and supernormal ways our minds have the potential to work contributed to his development in key area of *Intuitive Growth.*

So what exactly do we mean when we talk about intuition, and how can its growth be developed? As you recall, when I discussed Jung's psychological types, he identified intuition as one of the two basic ways we employ perception. The other is sensing. Both contribute in their own manner to how we become aware of what comes to mind. But where sensing employs the five objective senses of seeing, hearing, touching, smelling, and tasting, Jung defined intuition as a mode of becoming aware by a more indirect perception. He said that intuitive impressions come to awareness by way of our unconscious.

The tricky thing about intuitive impressions is that due to their indirect way of coming into awareness, they can be hard to trust. That's because we're tangibly oriented people. We've learned to primarily depend upon our objective senses. So if you have an intuitive thought or impression and can't initially attribute it to anything you objectively perceived, you may doubt its validity, especially if at times it doesn't seem to make logical sense.

Some intuitive thoughts come in the form of hunches or gut reactions. When you have one of those, you might find yourself saying things like: I don't know why I feel or think this might be true, I just do.

In order to be assured of the accuracy of such intuitive impressions or hunches, you may require further verification. However, when you find that a thought, which intuitively popped into your mind, is indeed accurate, and you're not able to account for its source, it may lead you to wonder how it was realized.

I find that when people refer to having intuitive awareness, their employment of intuition can be described in a variety of ways. In order to distinguish that diversity, I come to differentiate four types of intuitively received information, and I place them on a continuum.

On one end of the continuum is *objectively informed intuition*. These types of intuitive impressions are actually being informed by our objective senses but in ways we're not aware. They intuitively come to mind as objectively registered just below the threshold of conscious awareness, in an area referred to as the subliminal unconscious.

An example of an objectively informed intuition is provided in Malcolm Gladwell's book *Blink*.[4] He describes a situation where in the first few seconds of beholding a sculpture allegedly created by a renowned artist, an art critic and procurer for a museum had the impression that it was a fake. Though all immediately discernably features gave the appearance that it was authentic, this person had what Gladwell calls an "intuitive repulsion." She was subliminally picking up on subtly received objective impressions well before investigators undertook the painstaking measures to establish that indeed it was a fake.

Her "intuitive repulsion" was registered by impressions gathered outside her conscious awareness. It arose from what Gladwell suggests is her "adaptive unconscious," a product of what he calls "a giant computer in the brain that quickly and quietly processes a lot of data we need in order to keep functioning as human beings."[5]

This is a marvelous capacity that we all have the potential to employ, but in my opinion, it's important to repeat that these so-called intuitive impressions are still based upon the objective senses.

Next on my intuition continuum is *proficiency-based intuition*. These perceptions are based on past learning or experience. Their impressions can be the result of years of doing the same activity where the store of mastered knowledge gets relegated out of conscious awareness but nevertheless influences present perceptions.

Proficiency based intuitions include those derived from objectively perceived and intellectually informed intuitions, but they are added to by other non-objectively based impressions. These non-objective impressions may arise in the form of certain feelings or images that come into mind.

For example, after a long career of conducting psychotherapy, an astute clinician may accurately intuit the inclinations, symptoms, or even an early diagnosis of a new client well before a formal assessment is complete. Some of what informs that clinician may be a collection of objectively gathered impressions, like the way the client sits, walks, looks, or talks. But other less physically evident impressions may also be perceived. These might be the subtle feelings that get stirred in the therapist in the presence of the client.

There are times, for instance, when the therapists' anxiety or annoyance may get aroused if the client they're sitting with is repressing a lot of unconscious fear or rage, even before it's recognized by the client, consciously experienced, or made objectively evident. In a similar subtle fashion, the therapist may have other intuitive perceptions come into mind when clients disclose their past, like the image of a sad child sitting all alone when the client talks of having two parents consumed with careers having had little time for him.

In each of these first two ways of how intuitive impressions are perceived, the impressions arise from what is presently and objectively perceived (consciously or subliminally), contributed to by past experience, or added to by subtle non-objective impressions. However, as we move further along the continuum and consider other ways information can be intuitively perceived, I define a third type of intuition: *creative intuition.*

Creative intuitions are distinguished from objectively informed and proficiency-based intuitions by the fact that they provide *new* knowledge. It may be new to the perceiver, but knowledge that's already in existence, like when you think of an invention that you've never heard of before, only to find out that it's already been invented. Frederick Meyers refers to these kinds of creative discoveries as "*subliminal uprushes*"—ideas that come to mind by way of our unconscious, but those that had *no conscious origination*.

The new knowledge can intuitively come to mind in the form of a creative flash, or in an epiphany—one of those "ah-ha" moments when you suddenly have a new shift in understanding about a situation, or a new insight into yourself. Unlike the two previous types of intuition, there may not be any subliminally registered objective impressions informing that intuitive perception, nor is it *accurately inferred* based on past experience or subtly registered present impressions.

That is not to say, however, that creative intuitions may not be contributed to by past learning. They may very well come to mind after previous efforts were made in the pursuit of their discovery. A creative intuition might follow a lot of toiling and searching for new information. It's like Thomas Edison's saying that creative discovery is 90 percent perspiration and 10 percent inspiration. In my thinking, those preliminary efforts establish a resonant state of receptivity conducive to bringing creative intuitions to mind.

Finally, at the other end of the continuum is a fourth type of intuition. I give it the name *psychic intuition*. This type of intuitive perception produces a kind of awareness that is less dependent on subliminally perceived objective input, less the product of past learning and non-objective impressions, and less likely to be in the form of a new creative discovery.

Psychic intuitions come to mind via psi or paranormal means and produce information that often can defy what we've come to believe are the conventional workings of time, space, and causality.

These types of intuitions can also include what Paul Marshall refers to as Mystical Intuition: knowledge that comes into awareness when an individual experiences a mystical state.[6] An example of a psychic intuition is the premonition my Uncle Atles had during World War II.

Because psychic intuitions come to mind in these unique ways, both their means and content leave individuals boggled and even questioning their sense of reality. And even when you have a psychic intuition, you may doubt it's real. Though I was raised in a family where such things were considered valid, when I first had my own, I started wondering if what I experienced could be trusted. Just as in my client Bill's experience, my first psychic intuitive experience came in the form of a precognitive dream. It occurred a few nights before my sister's wedding.

The wedding was a significant event for our immediate family. As the four of us anticipated the big day, we all were filled with excitement and a certain amount of anticipatory anxiety. Each of us was tuned into various aspects and details of what would transpire.

My father was particularly concerned about one aspect of the upcoming event. I was one of a few groomsmen in the wedding party, and he wanted me to be the one who escorted my grandmother down the church aisle to her seat. I wasn't sure why this detail so concerned him, but when he brought it up, I assured him that I would. I suspected he felt his 80-year-old petite Italian mother who was barely four-feet-ten-inches tall, might need some special looking over.

Anyway, in my dream, I'm walking up the side aisle of the church working my way to the back, when I look toward the center aisle and notice that one of the other groomsmen is walking my grandmother to her seat. In my dream, I'm aware of feeling disappointed and a little anxious that I failed to meet my father's one simple request. As the dream proceeds, I walk into the back of the church anticipating his dismay, when instead I'm struck with this beatific vision of my sister in full gown. She's standing by herself, encompassed in a bright beam of light as if she were on stage under a spotlight.

These were bizarre details, and the dream was very vivid. I told my mother about it the morning after I awoke. Sharing our dreams with our mother was something my sister and I tended to do since we were kids. After I shared the dream, we chuckled at its oddity and agreed that it was probably just representative of the anxiety I was feeling about the impending event.

On the day of the wedding, however, my dream went beyond mere symptoms of anxiety. While dressing up to go to the church, I made a disturbing discovery: my tuxedo was too tight and the length was too long. I checked the tag and realized I was mistakenly given the tuxedo for my brother-in-law's best man. He was from out of town, so I immediately called him at the hotel where he was staying. He had not yet made the discovery, but because it was getting late we agreed to meet a little earlier at the church to trade tuxes and get dressed there.

We were to rendezvous at the sanctuary in the front of the church, but because he was unfamiliar with the area, he ran late. When he finally showed up, people had already started to arrive.

After I put on my tux, I hurried my way to the back of the church. But it was too late. Just as I had seen in my dream, while I was walking up the side aisle to the rear, I looked and I saw my grandmother being escorted down the aisle by another usher. I was thrown by the exactness of that vision. It was more than a vague *deja vu* experience. After I arrived at the back of the church, I anticipated seeing my father, but again, like in the dream, I beheld the image of my sister. She looked beautiful, and at that moment she was standing in a stream of sunlight beaming into the church.

I understand how more skeptical thinkers might ascribe statistical odds to those occurrences, but in my mind such numbers would be highly improbable. Furthermore, like Bill, I had another person who could attest to the dream in advance. When I shared with my mother what happened afterward, she was amused but not in awe of the anomaly. She basically confirmed that it was probably a precognitive dream and attempted to further normalize my supernormal experience by sharing what information she could.

That precognitive experience did not lead to a crisis, however, nor was it used as a Chrysalis Crisis. The incident did not create a troublesome ordeal in my life. I was raised to remember my dreams. I naturally employ intuition as a preferred mode of perception, and I was able to make the association between the dream and the incident at the time it occurred. And since I had prior knowledge of such phenomena, it gave me the ability to make sense of the event.

But that is not to say that I didn't learn from it because there is nothing like having your own experience. For me, it marked the first time I consciously registered a precognition. I've had a number since, and I can say this: when you have one, it moves the possibility of something like that being in line with reality, to the personal confirmation that it's an actuality.

For most of the clients who seek my help with spiritual emergencies or to address paranormal and psychic events, *their starting point is having an actual experience*. If they are deemed to be of sound mind, not self-delusional, not the victims of fraud, and not confusing the normal if sometimes boggling way perception can sometimes work, then *they are less interested in proving that their anomalous phenomena occurred* and more interested in explanations and under-standings for what it means for them.

In addition to various readings that can provide those explanations, I direct them to a book written by James Carpenter. He's a clinical psychologist who spent years attempting to understand how psychic abilities work. He developed a theory he calls *First Sight*.[7] Basically, Carpenter's theory suggests that psychic impressions are continually taking place at the subliminal level of our unconscious mind. And while they infrequently break into conscious awareness, they still have influence.

For example, you might decide to drive a different way home with no particular reason for doing so. Later, you find out that after you made that choice, there was a multi-car accident on the route you initially planned to take. Statistical odds may be offered to account for that coincidence, but Carpenter's First Sight theory offers an alternative explanation of what might be operating.

First Sight theory, and all that has been discovered in the research on psi, tells us that so much about how our minds work remains to be understood. From what I've been able to discern, it appears that *mind* has one foot in the physical world and one in the world of spirit. In both dimensions, the mind seems to function in ways we are aware, and in ways we've yet to bring to conscious awareness. But I suspect the greater part of mind's potential that has yet to be brought to awareness arises from the dimension of spirit.

The subtlety of spiritual influences, and the ways in which certain spiritual experiences seem to defy the limits of physical reality, is the focus of the next chapter. In it, I will show how certain Chrysalis Crises can lead to increased awareness and development in the *key area of spiritual growth*.

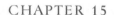

CHAPTER 15

The Eyes to See:
Spiritual Crisis

You may have heard the story of the fellow who was walking down a street one night and saw a man searching the ground around a lamppost. He approached the man and asked him if he lost something. "Yes," the man replied, "I lost my keys." The fellow then offered to help him search, but after a while when nothing was found, he inquired if the man was sure he lost his keys in that location. "No," he replied.

"Then why are you looking here?" the fellow asked.

The man responded: "Because this is the only place where there is light."

In a similar way, when people try to confirm the reality of spirit, they limit their search to those areas that are most evident. For example, they seek verification of the subtle, nontangible dimension of spirit by only looking in the "light" of physicality. But the actual manifestations of spirit can be elusive, so when it evades their detection they wrongfully assume it doesn't exist. As a result, they may reject the whole idea of a spirit dimension to their being, seeing it as irrational, superstitious, or something made up by various religions.

Certainly, concepts about spirit and spirituality have primarily come from the world's religions, and often, because of the negative associations or experiences some people have about organized religion, they turn away from the actuality of spirit. In essence, they throw the baby out with the bath water. But when the existence of spirit and the ways in which it influences human functioning get ignored because of those negative feelings, it undermines people's ability to realize their spiritual potential.

Entangling spirituality with religion is a common occurrence, but the two are becoming increasingly differentiated. According to Harris Friedman, "Religiosity is now frequently seen as pertaining to an organized system of beliefs about the sacred, along with rituals, rules, and other requirements of a belief system endorsed by a group." Spirituality, however, "is increasingly seen as an inner process of connectedness with the sacred, a psychological process internal to the individual."[1]

Deepak Chopra distinguishes the difference between the two by suggesting that religion is the belief in someone else's experience, while spirituality is having your own experience. This view is consistent with that of Stanislav Grof. He sees spirituality as the personal experience of the transcendent or transpersonal states of awareness. And finally, Bruce Greyson, professor emeritus at the University of Virginia, notes that "Spirituality is a quality that goes beyond religious affiliation and involves striving for inspiration, reverence, awe, meaning, and purpose, irrespective of a belief in any God."[2]

In America, it is estimated that between 20 and 35 percent of the population describe themselves as being "spiritual but not religious."[3] So you don't have to be religious to have a spiritual experience. It matters not whether you're an atheist, a religious fanatic, a spirit-denying materialist, a New Age believer, or someone who gives little thought to such matters. Your spirit is as much a part of who you are as your body. It is spirit that infuses your body with life and connects your mind to the subtle dimensions of being. And just as with the other nine keys we've examined, your ability to gain awareness, growth, and mastery of your spirituality is essential to your well-being.

Of course, there are those who won't believe that a spirit dimension in life actually exists until they can verify it with their objective senses. That is why when these individuals have an anomalous spiritual experience, the transpersonal phenomena itself will often throw them into crisis. However, as we've seen with previous crises, if they use that experience as a Chrysalis Crisis, its resolution and understanding can contribute to development of their *key area of spirituality*.

Such was the case for a client named Doug. When we started working together in therapy, he was a 63-year-old engineer who held advanced degrees from some of the best universities in the United States. Doug spent the better part of his professional life teaching, conducting research, and providing consultation. He had come to see me because his wife of 30 years prompted him to do so after he had a cardiac arrest accompanied by a near-death experience.

Doug said he never gave much thought to religion or spirituality, and as far as any consideration about an afterlife, it was his belief that when you die, you die. Poof. Game over. However, that wasn't how it appeared during his NDE. Besides the sobering effect of almost dying, what left him perplexed afterward was that he recalled watching the EMTs attempt to resuscitate him during his experience. He said he clearly witnessed their efforts from a vantage point *outside his body*.

When he shared his experience with me in therapy, it was accompanied by a certain amount of trepidation. He wondered if I would think he'd lost his mind. I assured him that wasn't the case, but in order to help him normalize his anomalous experience, I shared some of the following research about individuals who have had out of body experiences (OBEs) during an NDE.

Pim van Lommel, a Dutch cardiologist, reported that of the individuals he interviewed who had NDEs, 24 percent had OBEs.[4] Ken Ring, the University of Connecticut psychologist and early pioneer in NDE research, found that of the 102 NDE cases he examined, 37 percent experienced separation from their body.[5] And finally, I shared research that I thought Doug might find particularly relevant to his experience. It was conducted by Michael Sabom, a cardiologist from Georgia.

Sabom compared cardiac patients who had been resuscitated from a cardiac arrest but did not report NDEs, to those who had NDEs accompanied by an OBE. When interviewed about their experience afterwards, *all* of the patients in the NDE group accurately described the resuscitation efforts made on their behalf, while more than 80 percent of those who were resuscitated and did not have an NDE made serious errors when attempting to describe what they believed occurred during their resuscitation.[6]

Hearing this research was assuring to Doug, but it still left him with a looming question: If he were to accept his own anomalous experience as real, then what was he to make of the part of him that had awareness and perception outside of his body? Did he indeed have a spirit or soul that existed separately? Was he more than flesh and bones that go poof after death?

Doug began giving attention to these questions, as well as other areas of life he'd been overlooking. When he considered the area of spirituality, however, Doug wasn't sure he wanted to necessarily join a church. I remained neutral while he considered that decision, but I did mention that because he had a significant transpersonal experience, it did not mean that it had to translate into a religious conversion. I referred him to Steve Taylor's book *Out of Darkness*.

Taylor is a transpersonal psychologist and lecturer at Leeds Beckett University in Yorkshire, England. He differentiates a religious conversion from a spiritual awakening, saying that unlike a religious conversion, a spiritual awakening "is not a change in beliefs, but a change in how you experience the world, a shift in being."[7]

Though Doug's Chrysalis Crisis led him to reconsider some of his spiritual beliefs, namely how he viewed the afterlife, he mostly re-prioritized his activities. He shifted what had been his primary focus on work to spending more time with family, taking better care of his health, reading various spiritual writings, and considering what meaningful activities he might like to pursue during his quickly approaching retirement.

For Doug, the most impactful component of his experience was finding himself out of his body yet aware of what was going on around him. But you don't need to be clinically dead to have an OBE. Some people have an out of body experience when it *appears* they're about to undergo a life ending situation, such as realizing their out of control speeding car is about to hit a tree. Others project out of their bodies while undergoing a physical assault, or when subjected to extreme pain.

Having an OBE is not as rare as you might think. Around 10 percent of the population may have experienced an OBE.[8] Locally, in research conducted in 1979, 268 students at the University of Virginia and 354 residents of Charlottesville were questioned about any anomalous or paranormal experiences they may have had. Fourteen percent of townspeople and 25 percent of students reported having at least one OBE.[9]

One of those Charlottesville residents, whose name is Cher, sought my help to address a conflictual marital relationship. During my assessment, she shared that as a young adolescent, she was repeatedly sexually abused by her father. During the abuse she had OBEs and would see herself being violated from a perspective in the upper corner of her bedroom. OBEs are common in women being raped, not due to fear of death, but to get away from the body being attacked.

Seeing your body from an outside perspective like Doug and Cher did is called *autoscopy*. Some researchers suggest that the experience is a defense against the fear of dying, or an attempt to escape from the terror and pain of bodily assault. Others suggest that the individual dissociates from the reality of the physical body and fantasizes being elsewhere. This latter explanation may be true in some cases, but neither Doug nor Cher showed dissociative tendencies, nor any evidence of psychopathology.

But even in the situations where people actually have an OBE, you may ask: What's to be learned from such an experience? What possible benefit can come from having one? Well, many individuals who have an OBE appear to undergo a "shift in being." As a result of their direct experience of a feature of consciousness that allows for awareness independent of the body, they become more open to the actuality of having a spirit. And that has profound implications.

It explains why a significant number of individuals who have NDEs with an OBE component lose their fear of death afterwards. Having an experience where you are still aware of yourself even when you're functionally disconnected from your body underscores what Hindu philosopher Sri Aurobindo said: "When the body fails, spirit prevails."

Loriliai Biernacki, professor of religious studies at the University of Colorado, said the fifth century movement called Tantra "offers a conceptual schema for thinking about a consciousness which integrates mind and body via a third term, namely the idea of a 'subtle body,' a kind of quasi-physical body yet non-material body that links the two."[10]

Tantric thought conceives of mind as dualistic, as having two sides. One is the physical body and ego side, while the other is the spirit or subtle body (astral) side. The Tantric system offers practices to increase self-awareness and teaches individuals how to overcome the limitations of physicality and ego so they can open to the potentials of their spirit.

Many of those potentials of spirit are the *intuitive psychic functions* we examined in the last chapter. In Hindu thought, they're referred to as *siddhis*. In addition to understanding how spirit works through the mind to bring about siddhis or psychic abilities, viewing spirit in this Tantric light provides another important explanation. It accounts for how spirit can survive death even when detached from the side of the mind that works through our physicality and brain.

As John McTaggart argues in *Some Dogmas of Religion*, "Even if the brain is essential to thought while we have bodies, it would not follow that when we cease to have brains, we could not think without them."[11]

The belief that spirit is not exclusively dependent on a physical body for its continued existence is not exclusive to Eastern thought. Western philosophers like Plato also believed that the soul or spirit pre-exists physical embodiment, continues after death, and eventually returns to a physical body.

When you conceive of spirit functioning in this manner, it allows for how it may be capable of moving back and forth across the barrier between incarnate and discarnate existence; how it can maintain continuity over time; how it can become re-incarnated into a new body; how it can infuse that new body with memories of its past lives; and how that new body can become the recipient of its evolving development.

These conceptions of spirit can be difficult to accept. But I'm not here to convince you that you have a spirit, or that after you die your actual spirit continues to exist. Like attempting to prove the actuality of psychic phenomena, at some point direct personal experience needs to play a part in that validation. However, when spirit does evidence itself, the conflict between what is thought to be real and what one is experiencing can result in a crisis.

Billie had this kind of a crisis. She wasn't sure what to make of her strange experiences, and they started to frighten her. At first, she thought her mind was playing games, but when the phenomena continued she feared she might be losing her mind. That's when she reached out for help.

First, she turned to the folks at the University of Virginia's Division of Perceptual Studies, known as DOPS.[12] She heard that their research unit investigated such phenomena. Yet when Billie revealed that her experience was all part of a larger crisis for which she was seeking therapy, she was referred to me.

Billie was petite, attractive, and a bright young woman. She had a spunky, tom-boy quality about her, but it was balanced by a very sensitive feminine nature. When she first sat down with me in therapy and told me why she sought my help, she shared a more complete picture of what she was undergoing. Her story was heartbreaking.

She recently had been on an Island vacation with the love of her life when tragedy struck. Its timing seemed cruel because she and her boyfriend had just decided that they would marry when they got back to the states. After celebrating that decision with a night of cheer and intimacy, everything changed abruptly.

Upon awakening, Billie's fiancé asked if she wanted to go out to the beach and do some walking and snorkeling. Billie elected to sleep in a little more but said she'd come out in an hour or so to join him. When she did, he was nowhere to be found. His towel and bag were on his beach chair, but he was nowhere in sight. Once she started to walk further down the empty beach, however, she saw him floating just offshore among the breakers. He was face down and wasn't moving. When she went out into the water to make contact, Billie was horrified to discover he had drowned.

When Billie shared this with me, she still appeared in shock. The whole experience was traumatic; it had only been a few weeks since it occurred. Her feelings were still very much at the surface, and she knew she had a lot of grieving to do. But what prompted her to seek out the help of DOPS was that Billie began having signs that her fiancé was still in her midst. Though she acknowledged that a part of her wished he were still around, when she actually started having experiences that indicated his continued presence, it scared her.

For example, on a few occasions she saw what appeared to be a grey-like translucent shadow moving across her bedroom. On other occasions, she saw what looked like ripples in the air in an opposite corner. When I asked for further descriptions, she said the ripples looked like the wavy images coming off a road's surface on a hot summer day.

On another occasion, an incident occurred that really frightened her. While she was lying in bed and intensely thinking about her fiancé, her TV changed channels. At the time, the remote channel changer was off to the side of the bed and out of her reach. Yet even more boggling was that the station that came on was directly related to the thoughts she was having of her fiancé at that time. Both the switching of stations and the relevance of the show made her feel that something more than coincidence was occurring.

As she shared all this with me, I maintained an open mind. But I also considered that her intense grief, her desire to maintain connection with her fiancé, and their heightened emotional state just before he died might be responsible for her unconsciously manufacturing what appear to be real experiences. An individual's state of mind can physically affect various surroundings or instruments, and it's been noted to occur particularly as a result of heightened emotionality.

A well-documented emotional exchange between Sigmund Freud and Carl Jung produced just such a psychokinetic (PK) effect. Just as they were engaged in an intense verbal disagreement at a dining room table, a bookcase in the vicinity suddenly cracked. Interestingly, it not only happened once, but twice, and in short succession. However, after the first occasion, the astute Jung, who was familiar with the phenomena, recognized what was occurring and predicted the second occurrence.

Numerous incidents are cited throughout the parapsychology literature where a strong emotional rapport or a strong emotional reaction between two people can bring about such phenomena. The fact that human minds and emotions can affect objects and people around them offered some explanation for Billie's experiences. But the idea that her experience could be the result of an influence from the mind of her deceased fiancé required further explanation.

Billie had experienced two separate NDEs earlier in life. One occurred as a child while she was undergoing a critical operation for a burst appendix; she almost died on the operating table. The other came as a result of a bike accident that nearly killed her.

During the operation, she had visual awareness of looking down upon herself, the large surgical light above her body, and the surgeon performing the procedure. In the mountain biking accident, she fell off the path and tumbled down the side of a ridge into a lake below. There she also had an NDE with an OBE component where she looked down on her body at the edge of the lake.

Having not one but two NDEs strengthened the case that Billie actually had an after-death communication with her fiancé. This is supported by the research. Bruce Greyson, a psychiatrist and past director of DOPS, found that the ability to experience psychic functions increased after individuals have an NDE.[13] That would likely include increased capacity for an individual to behold or have communication with the spirits of the deceased. It's almost as if the individual's tether to the dimension of physicality has been loosened, and those abilities that arise out of spirit consciousness are freer to register.

But as incredible as this may sound, other researchers like Madelaine Lawrence, instructor in the School of Nursing at the University of North Carolina, Wilmington, suggest that after-death communications, or ADCs, are actually rather common. She notes that while as many as 10 to 15 million people in the United States have had NDEs, it is estimated that as many as 50 million have had ADCs.[14] Other studies have shown that anywhere from 67 to 85 percent of the recently bereaved report having ADCs.

Lawrence also adds an upbeat note about their occurrence. She says that "Clinically, these experiences are positive for the friends and family members, bringing joy and happiness, while at the same time decreasing the pain of the grief process."[15] I was hoping that Billie would achieve that same effect because she sought healing *and* understanding of her recent experiences.

While working with Billie, I attempted to balance providing information about her anomalous experiences with conducting therapy in a more conventional way to help her grieve. I knew it would take time for her to move through the many feelings she had yet to sort out and engaging in intellectual discussions about the workings of spirit could derail that process.

When it did seem appropriate to address questions about her anomalous experiences, I had to be clear and grounded. Billie was not some gullible woman pining for evidence of her lost love's continued presence. She was intelligent, assertive, and had a good deal of the skepticism common to a physical scientist.

In addition to beholding the presence or evidence of spirit, there are numerous accounts where individuals exhibit the capacity to *channel* what appear to be the minds of discarnate spirits. According to Jon Klimo, "Channeling is the communication of information to or through a physically embodied human being from a source that is said to exist on some other level of reality other than the physical as we know it ... not from the normal mind (or self) of the channel."[16] Channeled communications are alleged in many spiritual traditions. They serve as one source of their foundational beliefs. Those traditions include Christian, Islamic, Hindu, Buddhist, and Shamanic.

All this research and information helped Billie make sense of her anomalous experiences. That knowledge, combined with my earlier therapeutic support of her grieving process, enabled her to get what she needed. She used her crisis as a Chrysalis Crisis and not only gained additional growth in key areas of her foundational and personal development, but it further awakened her transpersonal development in the key area of spiritual growth.

Near-death experiences, after-death communications, mediumistic contact with the deceased, and channeling all point toward the continuity of spirit and the reality of survival. They give evidence that spirit can function independent of our physical bodies.

Evidence of reincarnation also supports this reality. It not only suggests that your spirit can exist outside your physical embodiment, but that it can return to take on another physical life. Many of the world's religions and cultures profess a belief in reincarnation, as do 24 percent of Americans.[17] There actually exists a sizable amount of empirical research to support its validity. That research suggests that reincarnation is not just some religious or philosophical abstraction, nor some ungrounded conviction embraced by people in denial of death.

Some of the most rigorous and credible research on reincarnation has been conducted at DOPS for more than 50 years. The research was first piloted by Dr. Ian Stevenson, a world-renowned psychiatrist who focused his investigations on the accounts of spontaneous past-life memories in children. This line of research continues to be investigated by Dr. Jim Tucker, a psychiatrist protégé of Stevenson and present director of DOPS.

Of all the people like Billie who reach out to DOPS to make sense of their anomalous experiences, it is the individuals who report having spontaneous past-life memories who bring in experiences that have the greatest therapeutic potential for their overall personal and spiritual development.

Stan Grof shares my intrigue and fascination with reports of the reincarnation type. He referred to them as "the most dramatic and colorful transpersonal episodes."[18] Not only are these cases intriguing, but the implications of what these individuals discover about themselves in their search for understanding and integration bring about dramatic shifts in their lives afterwards.

When I first encountered such a client, I didn't realize how unprepared I was to help. Though I had early exposure to the concept of reincarnation, believing in reincarnation is not enough to help another person understand and psychologically integrate a spontaneous past-life memory.

I have found that after a thorough psychological assessment and the establishment of a strong therapeutic alliance, if the individual shows sufficient ego strength, then using a past-life therapy technique can be an invaluable tool for achieving needed growth and insight. However, it can bring forth strong emotions and even some intense physical reactions that both the individual and practitioner should be prepared to manage and integrate. If either or both are not ready for what comes forth, they may face an experience similar to what I encountered with Joan.

When I first met Joan, she was 34 years old, slightly built, with dark brown eyes, and shortly cropped black hair. She possessed a quiet demeanor, and her gentleness and sweetness seemed well suited for her work as a primary school teacher. At the time, she and I were attending a conference at a nearby retreat center where a host of alternative healing methods were being discussed and practiced.

During the first night's break, Joan allowed herself to be hypnotically regressed by an untrained and unethical practitioner who claimed he knew how to do past-life therapy. He induced Joan into a trance and regressed her into what appeared to be a past-life. However, when she started getting emotionally and physically caught up in her experience, he did not know how to bring her back to the present. Instead, he just walked away and left the conference.

While this was taking place, I was talking with a friend outside the building where they were meeting. Suddenly we heard a blood curdling scream shouting, "No!" Realizing it was coming from inside, we hustled into the building to see what was going on. Joan was flailing and completely consumed in her experience. She looked spasmodic and disabled. People had gathered around, helpless in their ability to calm her. I stepped in and tried to lend a hand.

Standing directly in front of Joan, I attempted to orient her. She was bent over. Her limbs were contorted. Her eyes looked distant, as if her mind was somewhere else. Occasionally, she'd flail her arms like she was trying to throw something off of her. While she flailed, she shouted out with a stutter, "N-N-No, Not Beth! N-N-Not B-Beth!" Whatever she was experiencing, and whoever she thought she was at that time, she clearly didn't want to be that person in that situation.

After making a little headway with calming her down, I decided to escort Joan to an outside deck. A light rain had started to fall. I hoped the fresh air and sensation of water on her skin would invigorate her and get her further grounded to the present surroundings. Others followed behind us. While we stood there, I gently placed my hands on Joan's shoulders, lowered myself to her height, looked directly into her eyes, and repeatedly stated her name and where she was. In time, she came out of her fugue, looked dazed, as if she just awakened from a bad dream.

Joan had been lost in a world in her mind. Someone had called 911, and EMTs arrived to give support. They thought it best to bring her to the hospital just to be assured she was okay and to provide further stabilization if needed.

Joan's ordeal frightened everyone, including me. It looked like she decompensated into some form of psychosis. But to be honest, I wasn't sure what was going on with her. After she was assessed at the hospital, however, they deemed her to be of sound mind, and she was released.

The week after her ordeal, Joan sought me out for additional assistance. Her request challenged me to determine how I would clinically treat what appeared to be the residual trauma of a past-life experience. Stan Grof considered this kind of experience a spiritual emergency, and it was one I wanted to learn how to address. Professionally, it opened a whole new door for me, but it was one that I walked through cautiously.

I was only of limited help to Joan in that early stage of my professional growth. I saw her a few times to be sure that she indeed stabilized and could function as normally as she was capable of before that crisis. Once she appeared to do so, we ended our work. Although I helped her through the crisis, I did not know enough at the time to help her use it as a Chrysalis Crisis.

In addition to not feeling prepared to treat such a problem, I must admit that at that time I was cautious about getting professionally marginalized in a town where I had yet to fully establish myself. It was not lost on me how most clinical psychologists held disdain for the field of parapsychology, and particularly for therapeutic approaches like past-life therapy. But my long-standing curiosity about parapsychology and metaphysics led to a good deal of additional research and included a number of intense personal experiences. As a result, I now hold a more expanded understanding of how psychological, paranormal, and spiritual experiences contribute to our evolution.

I now envision a broad model of human development, one that requires growth and mastery in the ten key areas examined in this book. That growth and mastery enables us to expand our range of consciousness, actualize our human potential, and achieve the spiritual enlightenment that is ours to realize. But such development takes time, and it appears to require more learning experiences than a given life can offer.

CHAPTER 16

Miles to Go Before
I Wake: Spiritual
Growth, Continued

During my undergraduate years, I was a member of the university's track team. When I'd make an occasional visit to the coach's office, I'd always note the poster hanging on the wall behind his desk. It said: "Nothing worthwhile was ever easily attained." Each time I saw those words they reminded me that being successful in track was going to take hard work and extended effort. I've since found that formula is as applicable in life as it was in track. Only in life, the hurdles to be overcome, the weights to be borne, and the distances covered are of a different nature.

In a running event like the marathon, years of effort and physical maturity are required to reach one's potential. Marathoners tend to peak in their late twenties and early thirties. Assuming their training began in high school or younger, that's a lot of years spent pounding the pavement.

In life, extended effort is also required to achieve certain results. Take developing a profession, for example. Years of training and practice are necessary to become a competent artist, a skilled surgeon, an effective lawyer, a fine carpenter, an expert psychologist, or an accomplished musician.

The same can be said for personal development. I trust it's clear from the Chrysalis Crises we've explored that you understand that personal growth requires hard work and extended effort over time. Even without the promptings of crisis, making personal change entails intention, execution, and perseverance.

When you consider the time and effort required to develop and master so many areas of application in life, doesn't it make sense that attaining something as worthwhile as spiritual growth and enlightenment also would require an extended effort? And when you consider the varied life experiences people have on this Earth, and the many possible living conditions that surround them, don't you sometimes wonder how each human being will ever be able to realize his or her inherent potential? Why doesn't each human being appear to get an equal chance at spiritual growth and enlightenment?

With the inequitable distribution of opportunities for people who are born poor, rich, sick, healthy, oppressed, free, or otherwise, how can such a lofty goal like spiritual enlightenment be achieved? How could they ever learn about the many key areas of growth we've covered? Why on this Earth—with a natural environment so much in balance, harmony, interdependence, and the capacity for re-adjustment, healing, and growth—would humans, its highest form of physical expression, not have a built-in mechanism that assures similar outcomes?

Well, that mechanism does seem to exist, and there is evidence and theoretical support for its process. *Envision yourself as a multidimensional being.* Your physicality comprises just one of those dimensions. Spirit is another of those dimensions, and it permeates and contributes to all of who you are.

Even with that said, however, you may still feel unconvinced that you actually possess a spirit. Maybe you view such thinking as the product of religious fairy tales, or just a bunch of hogwash. Maybe you're more like Doug. He didn't think much about a spiritual dimension to his being until he found himself outside his physical body viewing his surroundings from another vantage point.

Trust me, your spirit *is* real. It's what gives your body life. It's a form of energy, and as Einstein says, energy can neither be created nor destroyed—it gets transformed. Yet even if you accept this as true, you may ask: What would be the reason why spirit transforms?

This is an important question, because if you believe there is a greater purpose to your time on this earth than just survival, and that you possess the inherent potential to achieve spiritual enlightenment, then understanding the reason why your spirit transforms will explain how you can acquire the necessary time and experience to attain that goal.

The best explanation I've found that answers this question is that *spirit transforms so it can transition in and out of physical life.* It's similar to the idea put forth by Plato. Your spirit pre-exists its physical body, has the ability to transition into physical embodiment at birth, transitions out of physical embodiment after death, exists in the interim, and transitions back to physical embodiment when needed.

Your spirit serves *as the depository and storehouse of all your previously developed capacities, talents, and accumulated wisdom.* They include the gains you made in the ten key areas of growth addressed in this book. All are recorded and available to be rediscovered, reawakened, and further developed. In this way, your spirit functions like "the cloud" of today's Internet. When the hardware of your body is laid to rest, spirit stores what you've worked so hard to consciously awaken and master.

Your spirit also provides you with a pipeline to an inexhaustible reservoir of infinite wisdom, creativity, joy, happiness, bliss, and love. That reservoir is available to everyone. However—and this is a big HOWEVER—each of our spirits has a reducer valve on that pipeline, and your personal development and spiritual growth will affect the extent to which you are able to open the flow of yours.

When you consider all that your personal and spiritual development has to offer, I trust you'll agree that working to attain those benefits is a worthwhile effort. That development also translates into an expanded understanding of life and death, which diminishes fear and increases peace of mind. It is this kind of expanded understanding that ultimately results in enlightenment.

Enlightenment means "full comprehension." That is why when people describe achieving a state of "spiritual enlightenment" and all the benefits that come from its attainment, it's held as the pinnacle of what we can hope to achieve from our human experience. But when I think of all that needs to be discovered, awakened, and mastered in life in order to actualize that potential, I imagine it to be more of a marathon than a 60-yard dash.

I don't know about you, but as a fallible human being in his seventh decade of life, when I make an honest self-assessment of where I presently stand on all the key areas of growth we've examined, I don't think I'm being unduly pessimistic to assume I won't gain mastery in all those areas during the time I have remaining in this life. And if my full awakening and eventual enlightenment is predicated on achieving a certain level of evolution, I'm not ashamed to admit, I have *miles to go before I wake.*

Yet I don't despair or get discouraged in light of that reality because spiritual enlightenment is a state of being that can be incrementally achieved. Just like most other accomplishments, it's a matter of one step at a time. However, you don't have to wait until you're fully enlightened to derive the benefits. As you make gains, your spiritual reducer valve opens more and more, and as a result, you accrue rewards for your meritorious efforts. While they may not always be immediately evident, they will be realized because as the adage states, "You reap what you sow."

The choice to do the growing, or the sowing, is up to you. Using your life crises as Chrysalis Crises is one way to produce that growth. But how long it takes you to make that choice, or how long you need to forge along your path to attain the necessary growth, will be predicated on having a sufficient variety and number of life experiences. And that brings us back to the issue of time and opportunity.

If, indeed, attaining such a goal is more of a marathon than a sprint, then it raises the question of how we each can be assured we will be provided the necessary opportunities to "go the distance." In my search for an answer to this question, I've found no better explanation than the evident need and actuality of a process like reincarnation.

Sure, giving serious consideration to reincarnation raises all kinds of understandable physicalist questions, like where does the memory reside between lives; if the population on Earth is larger than it's ever been, how can everyone have had a past-life; or why should it take more than one life to reach enlightenment? These and other legitimate questions have been asked by many, and to the extent they can be satisfactorily answered, those answers exist. But because we're dealing with a phenomenon that does not fully lend itself to physicality or logic, coming to accept reincarnation as a plausible reality requires your own independent investigation and contemplation.

For now, I would just ask that you leave the jury out, sit lightly in the saddle of what you believe, and try to intuitively hold reincarnation as a possibility. Reincarnation as an actual process in your soul's evolution is critical to the developmental model I describe in this book, and there does exist a very extensive and impressive body of scientific research that suggests its legitimate occurrence. The bulk of that research is conducted at DOPS. It includes data and details derived from thousands of extraordinary cases of children who claim to remember past lives.

Their cases have been meticulously investigated with extensive follow-up analysis and corroboration. All possible alternative explanations, like fraud or the many ways the mind can produce false memory, are painstakingly examined. In the final analysis, the cases that hold up under such scrutiny are designated as "solved" and considered evidence of reincarnation.

In Jim Tucker's book *Return to life,*[1] he provides an account of one of the most impressive and well documented recent examples of such cases, and while the majority of Ian Stevenson's cases were gathered from children born in cultures that believe in reincarnation, Tucker's case is about an American child.

Briefly, the young individual in this case goes by the name James Leininger. He was born on April 10, 1998, in Lafayette, Louisiana. His father is a human resources executive who was quite resistant to the idea of reincarnation. His mother worked with the American Ballet Theatre. Both parents are Christian, and though James's mother was open to reincarnation, she did not consider it as an explanation for her son's disturbing and perplexing behaviors until eight months after they began.

Apparently, at the age of 22 months, James's father took him to a flight museum where he became fascinated by the planes, particularly those depicted in a World War II exhibit. James repeatedly insisted on returning to that exhibit. Seeing his son's passionate interest in the area, his father bought him a few toy planes.

When James would play with them, he would say, "Airplane crash on fire," as he slammed them into the furniture. Around the same time, he also began having nightmares where he would kick up his legs and scream, "Airplane crash on fire! Little Man can't get out!" These episodes were witnessed by both parents.

In a bedtime talk a few weeks later, he was able to describe his plane by name. He said it was a Corsair plane that he flew off a boat. He also gave the name of the boat as the American ship *Natoma*. Neither parent was familiar with the plane, or the name Natoma, but after his father conducted a search, he found that indeed the Corsair was the type of fighter plane that had been developed in the war effort, and that a ship by the name of the USS *Natoma Bay* had served as an escort carrier in the Pacific during World War II.

Within the next six months, James also was able to name another person who was on the ship with him. It was a friend of his at the time who he said went by the name of Jack Larson. Additionally, during that six-month period, James pointed to an aerial photo in a book that showed Iwo Jima. When seeing it, he said that is where his plane went down.

His father was able to contact a veteran from that ship, and the man remembered a pilot named Jack Larson. A few years later, the father attended a *Natoma Bay* reunion and learned that Larson was still alive. He also learned that only one pilot had been killed from that ship. The name of the deceased pilot was James Huston.

The earlier statements that little James Leininger made closely matched the accounts his father was given about Huston's death on March 3, 1945. In addition, the mother found that Huston had a sister who was still alive.

Jim Tucker's investigation of the Leininger case closely followed the rigorous approach he was taught by Stevenson. In all, James made 58 statements related to Huston's past-life. Forty-two of them were verified. James also was able to correctly provide some other extraneous details. He gave the names and ages of Huston's two sisters relative to his age at the time of Huston's death; an incident which occurred to their father that led to a six-week hospitalization; and he was aware of the fact that in his last life, his mother worked as a maid. All were corroborated by Huston's one living sister.

The Leininger case had many other interesting features and supportive details. I am not aware, however, if any extensive amount of clinical work was conducted to help James and his family integrate his exceptional experience. If it did occur, I would assume it had the effect of a Chrysalis Crisis and imagine that it led to a lot of growth for the whole family.

While there is a good deal of evidence from researchers who investigate past-life memories in children, there is also evidence of reincarnation with adults. Stevenson notes that "under a number of conditions…in the form of vivid (and recurring) dreams, during intoxication with certain drugs like LSD, and during meditation, such past-life images and information can be brought forward."[2]

That was the case with Lisa. When DOPS referred her to me, she was looking for someone who would be willing to conduct a past-life regression so she could explore what she believed were spontaneously recollected past-life memories. Lisa sought help to eliminate the images and feelings that were breaking through during sleep and, more recently, intruding into her daytime hours.

Lisa was in her late 50s at the time, married for over 30 years, and the mother of two adult children. She and her husband traveled a good distance to see me, and we agreed to let him briefly join us in our first meeting. He corroborated much of what Lisa initially told me over the phone. Her husband said that Lisa would awaken at night, initially seem lost in her experience, sometimes be physically agitated, and occasionally speak a foreign language.

Since I had no previous information about Lisa's level of psychological functioning, I told her that I would have to conduct an assessment before doing regressive hypnosis. So after a brief meeting with her husband, we undertook that process.

Lisa was of sound mind. There was no indication of any deception or self-delusion. She sincerely seemed frightened and in crisis because of what was going on. Interestingly, she also didn't believe in reincarnation, and it was only due to the prompting of a friend that she even considered such an explanation. I invited her to return for the first past-life session the next day, and we again agreed to allow her husband to join us for her support.

Once in trance, Lisa went back to what appeared to be a life in an early European culture. She could not specifically identify exactly where, but from details she could provide the life took place many centuries back.

During that life, she said she held a menial role as some kind of house servant. Her days were filled with mundane details. But rather than just gather irrelevant information, I suggested she follow any feelings of discomfort she was aware of and use them as an emotional bridge to where she needed to go.

I knew from my training that memories that surround the form of death, or last thoughts that precede its occurrence, are those that are indelibly impressed on the mind. They are the ones that are most likely to be influential in future incarnations. Therefore, at one point, I progressed her to the end of that life, and as is the case in all this work, once she fully embodied the scene, I just asked, "What's happening now?" and "What happens next?" I strive to not make any leading or suggestive remarks.

Not surprisingly, when she advanced to the end of that life, she described a very traumatic death that came about as the result of an accidental drowning. While she shared the details, many of the residual effects of the trauma were still very charged in her mind and were responsible for much of what was breaking through in her sleep.

Those residual memories needed to be diffused and integrated by engaging the multiple key areas to which they were attached. They were affecting her in this life in all sorts of ways, including physically, intellectually, and emotionally. For example, Lisa needed to let go of the physical memory that caused her to flail during her sleep. Some of those motions mimicked a drowning person trying to stay afloat. She felt intense fear, and after that emotion was expressed, she experienced a deep grief about leaving her children behind. Lisa then slipped into feelings of guilt for not being more careful.

Another interesting feature about Lisa's case was what apparently triggered the spontaneous awakening of that deep memory. Her symptoms began after her friend's child drowned. The thematic similarity of that present life event, and the grief she felt for her friend, seemed to activate this long-buried memory in Lisa's mind.

This insight helped her gain perspective on other issues with which she struggled. For instance, Lisa had excessive concerns about safety and inordinate fears of being around deep water, despite having no present life traumas or incidents that could provide an explanation for these concerns.

But what was most memorable about my work with Lisa was when she started speaking what sounded to be another language. This phenomenon is called xenoglossy. It's an intriguing though rare feature that arises in some past-life cases. The person will just begin to speak the language of the time, one to which there has been no present-life exposure or level of mastery.

What Lisa produced was indiscernible to me and her husband, and since I failed to tape the session, I wasn't able to have it investigated by a language expert. I accepted if for what it was, however, because there are numerous other documented cases of xenoglossy throughout the literature where the validity of the phenomenon has been corroborated and proven.[3]

The crisis that Lisa experienced as a result of those past-life memories, and her willingness to use it as a Chrysalis Crisis, not only brought a halt to the unwanted memories, but it also enabled her to gain insight into how her present life was being affected by their influence. She also gained a good deal of new knowledge that contributed to her continued development in the key area spiritual growth.

Despite some valid criticisms about the ability to scientifically control past-life techniques to establish "reliable experimental evidence" of previous lives, Lisa's case is a good example of how this kind of regressive hypnosis can nevertheless achieve valid therapeutic results.

I've had an experience similar to Lisa's. It also occurred spontaneously and was further explored through a past-life technique. My mind first produced its images, emotions, and physical sensations during sleep and meditation, and it created a crisis at two different times in my life. But it was during the second occurrence that I was able to use it as a Chrysalis Crisis, and as a result I gained needed insight into a long-standing problem.

It happened, it's worth noting, on the day I was supposed to meet Ian Stevenson (after many years of putting it off) and the same day I put my application in the mail to train in past-life therapy with Roger Woolger. A few hours before my appointment with Stevenson, I started experiencing increasing anxiety. Nevertheless, I went about doing my daily meditation, figuring that might help me get calm. But that morning, I was having a lot of trouble containing the underlying anxiety.

While I worked to diminish it, another problem arose. I started experiencing a dry cough. It wasn't something that typically occurred when entering meditation, so it perplexed me as to why it started then. I wasn't sick. But then I started having yet another problem. I began experiencing a prickly, stinging sensation in my hands.

Determined to not let any of these problems distract me, I continued to work at quieting my mind. I finally managed to do so and slipped into a deeper meditative state. Moments later, however, I was suddenly struck with a flash of memory. I recalled something I had completely forgotten. It was a memory that took me back to my early childhood when I was about four years old. It was the first time I had that stinging sensation in my hands.

At that time, the sensations accompanied terrifying experiences that would awaken me in the middle of the night. They'd start off with a feeling like I was slipping off this large sphere, unable to hold on, and then I'd come awake in full panic. I'd jump out of my bed, crying and running around like a deer caught inside a house. And while doing this, I would extend my upturned stinging hands, pleading to be saved from whatever it was that threatened me. But I never knew what it was.

As I meditated and recalled those memories and feelings, I began to cough again, and I also began to have that feeling in my hands. And at one point, I just couldn't take it any longer, so just like when I was a child, I abruptly jumped up. Only this time, I took two quick steps away from my chair and stopped. I stood there with my heart pounding, and thought: What are you running away from?

I realized there was no distance I could run to get away. Whatever it was, it was *inside me*. So, with a certain amount of trepidation, I again returned to my seat and did some slow breathing. As I did, I reminded myself of the advice I once received from my Pathwork therapist: "The only way out, is in and through."

As I slowly re-entered a quiet state, the sensations and feelings again emerged. This time, however, I was determined to see them through. I tried to remain open to whatever would come to mind. And as I did, a very brief but intense series of images and sensations unfolded.

I found myself tied to some kind of post amidst what appeared to be a wood pile around me. Smoke started to rise from below. I realized I was about to be burned. Both in the unfolding story in my mind, and as I sat there in my chair, I started to cough and choke. Again, I felt that stinging sensation in my hands. Only now, I had the awareness that the painful stinging was from flames scorching my hands. I could feel panic with the recognition that there was no way out. As I continued to sit in my chair and let the story unfold, I fought the impulse to physically run away. Then suddenly it ended. The realizations, the images, and the sensations all stopped.

It was a very intense experience that I can easily recall as I write this now. After I first had it, I just sat there trying to be as open and realistic about what occurred. I became aware of other, softer feelings that started to surface. Tears welled up in my eyes as I felt a deep sadness and a sense of loss. But I also felt gratitude for the understanding. It was as if something that resided deep within me, something that had long affected me, had finally been released.

I managed to pull it together over the next few hours and had my meeting with Stevenson. He was every bit the gentleman scholar he was reputed to be. Though he made it clear that he was no fan of past-life therapy, he was nothing but gracious and supportive of my interests. He encouraged me to continue pursuing them, referred people my way, and made himself available for further contact.

In future sessions of past-life therapy with Woolger, I discovered more about the theme that was tied to the life of being burned. It ran like a thread through the tapestry of my present life. It primarily had to do with fears of persecution for embracing and professing controversial beliefs.

Those past-life regressions of persecution did not constitute all that I uncovered during those two years of training. And what I additionally discovered wasn't all that flattering. In other stories, I wasn't always the poor "good guy" who became the persecuted victim. I uncovered other stories where I was the one who persecuted others for their different beliefs and affiliations.

For instance, I had images come forward where I was a soldier who brutally killed others for being a threat toward the powers I was charged to uphold. They were more difficult to accept as "being me." But as Woolger used to say, "Sometimes you're the prayer, and sometimes you're the slayer."[4]

Tucker's research found that there are statistically significant correlations between personality features depicted in the recalled life of the previous personality and those displayed in the individual's present life. When subjected to statistical analysis, he said the odds of that relationship occurring by chance were more than one hundred to one.[5]

Did I, as Tucker speculates, carry tendencies and memories from the past? Did I bring something into this life that informed me and helped shape my development? Do all those memories and lessons learned from lifetimes of experiences and traumas contribute to the growth of some greater Self to which I belong?

"I hope," says Tucker, "that the traumas people suffer are part of a working through process."[6] Me, too. But even if we are working things through, it leaves one to wonder whether the growth that comes about from that working through process is all part of some evolutionary plan. And if so, where is it all leading?

SECTION IV

Evolution, Practice and Synthesis

CHAPTER 17

The Landscape of Spiritual Evolution: Where Are We Going?

Is there a higher purpose for human evolution? Does growth in the key areas of foundational, personal, and transpersonal development have meaning beyond this life? If it's suggested that your growth may occur over multiple lifetimes, what would be the reason for such a long trajectory of development? Some speculate that it contributes to the evolution of a Higher Self. If that's true, where is the evolution heading?

Teilhard de Chardin, a twentieth century Jesuit priest, provided some ideas that have relevance to those questions. He proposed that the ultimate outcome of our personal growth and spiritual evolution takes us to what he called the Omega Point. It's predicated on a spiritual belief that everything in the universe is fated toward divine unification. De Chardin contends that we each have a built-in instinct to return to our source. He calls that instinct a *teleological drive*.

Teleology comes from the Greek words *telos,* meaning "end," and *logos,* for "reason." It refers to our ultimate reason for, and meaning in, life. In my mind, it's a little like the salmon's instinctive drive to swim back upstream. Only in our case, we're heading back to our source.

Another way to understand this drive in human development is the notion that everyone is in the process of *becoming*. Aware of it or not, we're all programmed to eventually achieve that goal of divine unification. It's just that remaining blind to the process, or working at cross purposes with it, prolongs the journey. That leads to innumerable trials and errors and a lot more crises and suffering along the way. However, if we use those crises as Chrysalis Crises, we may better advance ourselves farther up that stream.

But even if you trust that such an inherent drive exists, you may wonder how you will know when you're making headway. Will there be indications along the way to mark your progress? And in light of a monumental undertaking like reunifying with the Divine, the question most critical to making the effort is: What will you actually gain once you get there?

These are important questions, and I'll share what I've learned about their answers. But before I do, I believe it will be more easily understood if it's provided in the context of what that landscape of spiritual evolution may look like, and what constitutes its ground.

As you might suspect, such a landscape will require looking at the big picture—the view of the forest rather than the trees. So, in order to get your arms around what follows, I suggest you employ your intuitive perceptual function. Consider the possibilities. Don't get too hung up on the details. That's because what I will present is a cosmological viewpoint. While it's broad, it can give you an idea of where you're heading, and as Stephen Covey, the author of *First Things First*, suggests, it's helpful to "begin with the end in sight."[1]

This cosmological perspective is not just something I conjured up, however. It's based on scientific, philosophic, and spiritual lines of thought. Looking it over can give you an idea about the route you'll need to take. It's a little like checking the broader map on your GPS before you depart. It enables you to locate yourself relative to your destination. That can be helpful to keep in mind when you get preoccupied with the details of each turn.

Despite keeping the end goal in mind and a view of the route you'll take, the vast majority of us have a long way to go before we achieve the greater heights of spiritual evolution. But not to despair, because enlightened masters, prophets, mystics, and saints who've succeeded in making that climb have left us information about how to scale its course. Fortunately, there appears to be more than one way to reach the goal. As Mahatma Gandhi said, "Truth is one, and paths are many."

I've benefited from many of those paths and combined their knowledge with information from clinical psychology and parapsychology. What I've found is that when I use all of it to treat Chrysalis Crises of a foundational, personal, or transpersonal nature, another more general effect came about, in addition to the growth it fosters in specific key areas. It increasingly raised the level of the individual's self-awareness. And just as life experience combined with knowledge leads to wisdom, increased self-awareness and wisdom lead to the expansion of consciousness—and it is that which ultimately leads to spiritual evolution.

The reason I believe expansion of consciousness leads to spiritual evolution is because consciousness is said to surround, permeate, and give rise to the cosmos and everything within it. So as we expand our range of consciousness, we move closer and closer to that Omega Point. It's consciousness that constitutes the landscape of spiritual evolution.

But before I share a cosmological view of what that overall landscape might look like, let me make a few more points about what I mean when I refer to the word *consciousness*.

I differentiate consciousness from *conscious*. These words are frequently interchanged and often get confused. When I use the word conscious, I mean aware, cognizant, or awake. However, when I use the word consciousness, I'm describing something different. My use of consciousness is informed by the path of Nichiren Buddhism.

Nichiren Buddhism comprises several major schools of Buddhism. It views consciousness as that which "implies a capacity or energy that operates whether we are consciously aware of it, or not."[2] In other words, consciousness exists in or out of our conscious awareness, and it can manifest in us as a capacity, energy, or both. In this light, consciousness can be viewed as a verb and a noun.

It's my contention that *the ten key areas of growth are energies and capacities of consciousness.* Over time, life experience, and learning, we gain increased awareness and mastery of their potentials, and not only do they aid us in life, but by doing so we expand our range of consciousness. As we do, we increasingly awaken to that which is the ground of all being.

Max Planck, the founder of Quantum Theory, was a major proponent of consciousness as the ground of all being. He said, "I regard consciousness as fundamental. I regard matter as derivative from consciousness. We cannot get behind consciousness."[3] What I believe he's saying is that consciousness gives rise to matter. These days, the predominant physicalist view is quite the opposite. It holds that physicality, or the brain, gives rise to consciousness.

But Planck and an increasing number of other Nobel scholars beg to differ. Their position aligns more with the notion that consciousness is the source of all creation. It's the source of the physical universe, the source of energy, spirit, life, mind, knowledge, and the source of love.

When I learned how so many of these brilliant scholars viewed consciousness, I recalled when I first considered such notions. I was twelve years old at the time and studying Catholic theology so I could receive the sacrament of confirmation.

Confirmation is one of three initiations into the Catholic Church. When I reflect back on undertaking its rigorous process of study in order to receive the sacrament, I now view it as my first comprehensive exam in life.

The nuns who taught those classes were very intent on having us master the knowledge of the doctrines, because in addition to meeting the necessary requirements, they also wanted to be assured that when the Bishop showed up at Church to administer the sacrament, everyone would raise their hand when he queried the group with random questions. And it was clear to me that, low and behold, when I raised my hand, if I was called upon and didn't answer correctly, I would need a miracle to save me.

Though my present beliefs are not exclusively aligned with Catholicism, I have to acknowledge that Christian teachings influenced my present understanding of spirituality, and I'll always be thankful for my Catholic education because along with what I learned in my family, it was where those spiritual questions were first raised.

I've since studied other spiritual paths and learned from a number of non-sectarian organizations. All have helped expand my understanding of spirituality, and all contributed to the beliefs I hold today. However, as stated earlier, I try to sit lightly in the saddle of those beliefs; although I have a strong faith that a superior intelligence exists in the universe, it would be less than humble to assert that I know exactly what form or manner that intelligence takes. But when I consider the existence of a creative presence in the universe—that this presence is everywhere, that it gives life, permeates all things, and that it's the infinite source of wisdom, compassion, and love—I arrive at the position that *God is Consciousness.*

Viewing God as Consciousness does not demean nor disrespect God. Neither does it detract from all that is attributed to God. And just as how little we know about God, there is so much we have yet to learn about consciousness. Yet viewing God as consciousness can help operationalize how we can make a conscious connection to our maker. It can be done by mastering the ten key areas of growth, because if you accept them as aspects of consciousness, as we gain their mastery, we expand its range and increasingly establish that connection.

Another benefit that can come from viewing God as Consciousness is that it also provides a bridge between religion and science. For instance, a scientist who's committed to empirical fact does not need to embrace a particular set of religious beliefs to accept the existence of consciousness. Quantum Physics has already proven the reality of its effects. And a devout religious person does not have to forsake a belief in God to accept the scientific evidence of how certain aspects of consciousness have been measured and proven to function in our physical domain. God can still be seen as the infinite source of the universe, only a source that continuously reveals its incredible creative complexity as we deepen our intellectual understanding of its workings.

While viewing God as consciousness may sound radical or even blasphemous to some, the idea that a foundational consciousness creates, underlies, and permeates all of existence is not new. The philosophic worldview that embraces this position is known as *panentheism*. It posits a God or consciousness that interpenetrates every part of nature but is nevertheless fully distinct from nature.[4]

Predicated on this worldview, Michael Murphy, a key figure in the Human Potential Movement, suggests that embracing panentheism can help us understand how our evolution of consciousness is as a progressive process.[5] In my thinking, this kind of evolution suggests a process that increasingly awakens our awareness of that consciousness.

Now that we've examined the evolutionary potential of consciousness, identified some of what contributes to its expansion, and discussed how it serves as the foundational ground in the landscape of spiritual evolution, I'll share the cosmological map I promised. I trust it will help you see the lay of the land and give you a better idea of how you might get to where you're going.

Learning how to get from one place to another has always been an interest of mine. I suspect it's partially attributable to having a father who was a cab dispatcher, and my spending four years driving a cab around New York City while attending college. I also discovered during those years that I had a lot in common with mapmakers. When I took a vocational interest test in my doctoral program, it revealed a strong connection to the profession of cartography, the science of drawing maps.

The map I constructed (see page 257) is labeled *A Panentheistic Map of Consciousness*. It provides a broad representation of the levels within consciousness, and how they align with each other. Its overall structure and composition are based on many of the sources I've previously mentioned. And because I view the ten key areas of growth as energies and capacities of consciousness, I've indicated a place where I believe they belong.

One way to approach this map is to think of consciousness as a Russian Matryoshka Doll. Just as you lift off the outer dolls and find a smaller doll nested inside, the many layers of consciousness are nested within each other. In those layers, the outer doll is the God/Consciousness, and the inner dolls are reflections of the God/Consciousness, similarly comprised of the same elements.

In order for this map to accurately portray a panentheistic worldview, the God/Consciousness is depicted as independently surrounding all other aspects of consciousness, while at the same time permeating all the levels within.

When you refer to the top of the map, however, you'll notice something missing. It's not a typo. The "Con" before "sciousness" in reference to God is removed. This was done for a reason. It's a modification based on the work of William James. He suggests that the prefix *con* implies *with*, and when you add *con* to *consciousness*, the *with* is in regard to a *self*. James believed that since God is the Prime Reality, a "self-brand" is neither needed nor warranted.[6]

The next level in the map returns the con to consciousness. It represents spirit consciousness. While there are likely endless gradations of spirit, I've grouped the whole domain as one vast area. Some mystical texts suggest that at the top of that dimension lies the Christ consciousness.[7] And as Jesus *the* Christ said, it is through Him that we must pass to consciously realize the exalted state of oneness with God. For consistency in this map, I designated spirit consciousness as "GS" to denote its nested and infused relationship with God (sciousness).

I made a similar type of notation on the map's next major level. That is the area occupied by mind consciousness. Since mind is

A PANENTHEISTIC MAP OF CONSCIOUSNESS

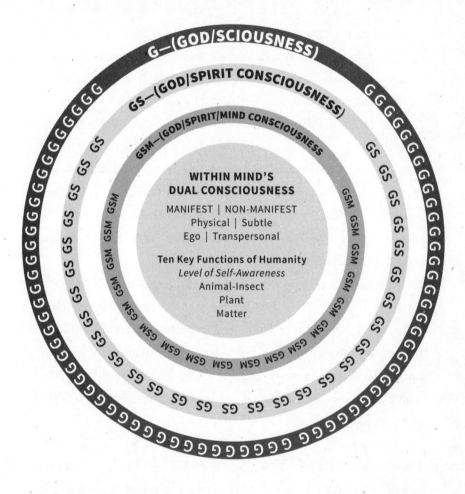

infused by both God (sciousness) and spirit consciousness, it is noted as "GSM." Mind is also represented in a manner consistent with Tantric thought and shown to encompass the dual nature of creation, its manifest: physical/ego side, and its non-manifest: subtle/transpersonal side.

Another important feature of this map has to do with the location of the ten key areas of growth. They're labeled the "Ten Key

Functions of Humanity." Note that they span both sides of mind's dual split. I represented them in that manner because they have the potential to awaken, express, and master mind's manifest (physical/ego) *and* non-manifest (subtle/transpersonal) energies and capacities. I'll say more about how to accomplish this in the next chapter.

Finally, you see a dotted horizontal line below the ten key functions of humanity. This designates the point where there is a significant change in how consciousness functions. Though all of the manifest and non-manifest world is created by God (sciousness) and expressed through spirit and mind, it denotes the level where aspects of mind gain self-awareness. That is not the case with the manifestations of mind that lie below that point. (i.e., animals, insects, plants, and matter).

In regard to making this designation, I draw support from the English philosopher Edward Carpenter. He notes that "The thought of self as 'knower' has not occurred in animals."[8] French philosopher Henri Bergson agrees. He states, "With man, consciousness breaks the chain. In man, and man alone, it sets itself free. The whole history of life until man has been that of the effort of consciousness to raise matter."[9]

In summary, this map represents consciousness in its three nested levels. Mind is depicted at the innermost level and represented in its dual nature. It is shown splitting the physical-ego side and the subtle-transpersonal side. While it remains the *one mind* we all share, at its lower level it manifests consciousness as matter, minerals, plants, and animals. At that stage, mind is in a *state of being*. As mind expands and becomes expressed in our human range of functioning, we gain self-awareness and advance into a *state of becoming*. This proceeds through increased mastery of the ten key areas of growth.

Continued development in the ten key areas of growth progressively awaken our potentials on the manifest side of mind in physicality and ego, and on our non-manifest side in the subtle and transpersonal capacities of spirit. As we continue our spiritual evolution, we increasingly awaken the highest level of expression, God (sciousness). That is the Omega Point, Divine unification, where there is nothing any longer to become. *All is known,* and *All is one.* As described in the words of Sri Nisargadatta Maharaj, *"I am that."*

It's important to be aware you are always in contact with God. Though you may not consciously realize it, that connection can be directly accessed through your mind. Remember, "The Kingdom of God is within you."[10] But in order to access that kingdom, you need to awaken its higher, subtle, and transpersonal nature.

If you wish to do this, set an *intention* to give your *attention* to the personal and spiritual growth that facilitates that awakening. And when you do, be sure to have the necessary tools and knowledge of how to use them, so you can attain that goal. While it may be a long climb up that mountain to Divine unification, it's an achievable undertaking, and one that's worth the effort.

CHAPTER 18

Becoming an Athlete of Consciousness: Climbing that Mountain to Spiritual Awakening

You don't have to become a priest, rabbi, mystic, or monk to achieve unification with the Divine. And you don't have to go through a crisis to prompt the personal and spiritual growth necessary for its attainment. But pursuing that unification will require some of the focused attention a crisis demands, and it will need to be directed toward certain forms of practice. I'll describe those practices in this chapter and explain why they're needed.

These practices have had a long history of being used for this purpose. Their methods and techniques have been around for thousands of years. They've been performed by many of the saints, prophets, and avatars of the various spiritual paths, and have come to be known as the *ascetic practices*.

Asceticism is rooted in the Greek word *asketikos*, which means "to practice strenuously" and "to exercise." The ascetic practices often entailed renouncing material possessions, severely limiting

physical pleasures, seeking isolation to engage in certain meditative and contemplative techniques, and concentrating primarily on
spiritual matters. In early Greece, ascetic practices were also used
for athletic development.

One answer as to why these practices were successful at awakening higher states of consciousness can be found in the Transmission
Theory of William James. It is similar to what was said earlier about
the brain serving as a reducer valve for the expanded potentials of
consciousness. In regard to James's Transmission Theory, philosopher
Michael Grosso states that "the brain does not produce consciousness,
nor does it cause psychic phenomena or supernormal experiences.
The brain transmits. It allows for the movement across thresholds, i.e.,
from the subliminal to the supraliminal mind or awareness."[1]

This is what occurs during states of ecstasy and certain types of
intuitive and spiritual experiences. In other words, these potentials are
already present in the greater mind, and when your brain is in a conducive state of reception, they're *permitted* to arise. That's why "yogis,
mystics, and shamans inflicted harsh discipline on their bodies," says
Grosso. "They were attempting to subdue the distractions, desires,
or attachments that prevent those potentials from crossing over the
threshold to conscious awareness and physical manifestation."

When you're attempting to consciously connect with the energies and capacities of spirit consciousness, you need to quiet the
distractions and preoccupations of physicality, put your brain in a
receptive state, and align your awareness with the spiritual side of
mind. However, you don't have to flog yourself, eliminate physical
pleasure, or deny the material reality of your life. *You can employ a
moderate version of ascetic practices* and conduct them in a manner
that makes sense for our times. Once you make them a regular part
of your daily activities, they'll produce results.

In time, your level of awareness will heighten and it will enable you to expand your range of consciousness. As that occurs, you'll increasingly become attuned to its subtle and transpersonal effects. That will not only confirm the actuality of those effects but produce the kind of peace, security, and happiness that accompany an increasing state of spiritual connection.

Here I intend to show how those same keys can be used to strengthen your connection to spirit consciousness. In general, the more progress you make in developing any of the ten key areas of growth, the more functional and accessible those keys will become when you seek to specifically utilize them for the purposes of awakening your range of spirit consciousness.

It's a little like becoming a skilled pianist who has full access and command over the 88 keys on a piano keyboard. His facility with those keys enables him to use them in whatever octaves are needed to meet the requirements of a given piece of music. Similarly, as you become adept at developing the ten keys areas of human growth, you will be able to employ them to serve a wider range. Only that wider range in this context extends beyond the dimension of physicality and includes the higher "octaves" of spirit.

You may ask, however, how can I utilize the same key area to serve my physical and spiritual needs? I'll give you an example, and since we're specifically addressing the two different sides of mind's duality, I'll use the first key area of physical growth to show you what I mean.

If as a result of your physical growth, you learn to effectively meet your material requirements for food, shelter, and clothing, and care for your body through proper nutrition, exercise, and sleep, you'll have gained a degree of mastery over the physical dimension of your life. That will enable you to marshal your physical and material resources to serve your spiritual needs.

For instance, properly caring for your body would increase the likelihood of having the physical ability to engage in various spiritually enhancing practices like Yoga and Tai Chi, or just sit comfortably in meditation without being limited or distracted by health concerns. Maintaining gainful employment, responsibly managing your money, and living within your means would significantly free you of financial worries. And unless exceptional situations arose, you would be able to avoid having monetary concerns dominate your life. With that mental freedom and time, you could read spiritual material, contemplate what you're learning, gather with others for service, or just have more downtime for solitude and prayer.

This kind of lifestyle obviously requires living in moderation and balance, and unless you drop out of secular life and join a monastery or convent, it's not so easy to set up a living situation that allows for such spiritually enhancing activities. It's also true that not everyone has the blessing of a healthy body, or the ability to acquire adequate income to be free of inordinate financial and material concerns. But the more you can approximate such optimal conditions, the more freedom and resources you will have to direct your conscious attention to the subtle and transpersonal side of mind.

In the same way that a level of mastery in the key area of physical growth can avail its energies and capacities to the expansion of your spirit consciousness, so can the other areas of foundational and personal development be used in that manner. But if those keys areas are lacking, and they cause problems or crises in your life, then not only will they detract from your overall personal development, but they will be less available to serve your spiritual needs.

So gaining a sufficient degree of growth in the foundational and personal areas of development is a must if you wish to fully awaken the subtle and transpersonal side of your mind. You can't just do what Robert Masters calls "a spiritual bypass." That's when people "attempt to use spiritual practices and beliefs to avoid dealing with painful feelings, unresolved wounds, or other developmental needs."[2]

Make no mistake about it: this kind of personal and spiritual development takes a certain amount of commitment and a willingness to give it a degree of priority in your life. And should you wish to undertake a moderate ascetic program to enhance your success, there's something else to be kept in mind. Just as the definition of asceticism implies, it will require *self-discipline, the actual exercise of methods and techniques, and their continued effortful practice.* However, if you stick with the program, then just as the athletes of ancient Greece employed ascetic practices to optimize their physical potentials, so you can optimize your spiritual potentials and become a successful *athlete of consciousness.*

If you wish to undertake a moderate ascetic program, and want to use the ten key areas of growth to serve your higher spiritual potentials, then start by taking an honest inventory of your present state of development. Identify what I call *your personal GPS—your Growth Progression Status.* Determine what needs to be strengthened and be proactive about seeking that growth. Don't wait for a crisis to bring it to your attention.

But also keep in mind that even if there are areas where you determine growth is needed, you don't have to be perfect before you begin the methods and techniques of a practice. They can be started at any time. Actually, their use will help your continued growth and development.

On this note, and in a statement well suited for this book, the transpersonal psychologist and philosopher Ken Wilber says "it's not necessary to become a *decathlete of consciousness,* or a developmental jack-of-all-trades," to achieve increasingly higher states of consciousness. "You don't have to master all lines of development; just be aware of them. This awareness itself will exert a balancing force on your life."[3]

I agree with Wilber, but I would add that at a certain point, while awareness of where development is needed is an important first step, ultimately growth and change will be required. Because the more growth you achieve, the more likely you'll be able to *attain* and *sustain* higher states of consciousness.

The critical point here is not to let your imperfections discourage you. We're all contending with the fallibilities of being human, so try to be self-accepting about where you are. Don't become daunted by the distance you may need to travel to achieve that optimal ideal. Though it may sound cliché, just take one step at a time and know that the higher you climb up that mountain toward unification with the Divine, the better the view and the sweeter the experience.

In addition to maintaining self-acceptance for where your GPS may stand, there's one last point I want to make before we move on. Remember, we're attempting to diminish excessive preoccupations and distractions with the physical/ego side of mind, so we can focus on awakening its subtle and transpersonal energies and capacities. And just as you need to address any inordinate distractions that arise from the dimension of physicality, so you need to confront the limiting effects brought about by its counterpart of *ego.*

Amit Goswami, a theoretical physicist and researcher of the spiritual and scientific understanding of consciousness, says that, "The more we spiritually develop, the more *ego-less* we become."[4]

This is consistent with the position of Steven Taylor, a researcher of transpersonal psychology. He states that when ego is overdeveloped, it "walls us off from nature and our source, contributes to a false sense of duality, and makes the 'I' more important than the 'we.' An inflated ego serves to edit out the experiences we need to get beyond our sense of separateness."[5] And according to Einstein, that sense of separateness is "an optical delusion of consciousness."

But too much ego is not the same as having sufficient ego strength. Sound ego development is necessary for providing a solid foundation in life, for making needed separations so you can become your own person, and for helping you balance life's prohibitions with life's pleasures. A healthy ego combined with humility and a realistic sense of self can help you define achievable goals and take necessary actions for their attainment. And finally, a grounded and secure ego can allow you be comfortable with situations that require surrendering control, remaining passive, and being open to guidance.

The ego can function like a booster rocket that propels a spaceship out of Earth's gravitational pull and lifts it to the heights of outer space. But at a certain point, the initial power and dominance of that rocket is quieted or diminished. Once the spaceship has established sufficient separation from the Earth, further adjustments can be made by less forceful means. Thereafter, the spaceship's original programming can provide the subtler promptings of its internal guidance system and direct it towards its intended destination.

Like that spaceship, you need to be aware of how your ego may get in the way of your growth, and where too much of its continued dominance and thrust may throw you off your spiritual course. If you want to register those subtle and transpersonal influences of spirit consciousness, then your ego has to be sufficiently quieted when needed. The following methods and techniques will help you accomplish that objective, and they will also contribute to your personal and spiritual development.

Some Tools for a Moderate Ascetic Program of Spiritual Development

1. MEDITATION

The best method I know to consciously awaken spirit consciousness is through the practice of meditation. When conducted properly, it will enable you to still your physical senses, quiet your thinking, become more mindful, and extend your awareness beyond the limiting constraints of the ego-self.

There are a number of approaches to meditation, and like choosing a spiritual path, you may prefer to find one that best suits you. But despite the various approaches, I believe there are critical ingredients in meditation that need to be achieved. And because meditation is frequently confused with other related practices, those ingredients can become overlooked or undermined. For instance, people often confuse meditation with prayer, contemplation, and concentration.

While prayer is indeed another powerful and effective spiritual tool, it's not what I believe we're seeking to do when meditating. Neither is entering a process of contemplation, which is also a spiritual tool but has different objectives. And I'm not striving to concentrate when I meditate. Concentrating on spiritual concepts can help advance your store of knowledge, but again, it's not what I'm looking to engage in when meditating.

When I enter into a meditative state of mind, I want to be consciously alert, open-minded, non-directed, and not mentally meandering. In a simple yet clear statement of the state of mind I seek, I provide the following definition of meditation. It was derived from an esoteric essay on the technique. "The object in meditation is not to focus the attention on anything in particular. *In meditation you are endeavoring to change the level of consciousness.* You are attempting to use another state of consciousness, but you do not anticipate what shall manifest."[6]

Meditation is a non-dual state of open awareness. It's one that's accessed by quieting your physical senses and your thinking. When you first attempt to meditate by withdrawing your attention from the outer world, you may become aware of just how many distractions stir below the threshold of your conscious awareness. This experience is called "monkey mind"—where your thoughts jump from tree to tree, and that includes thoughts about whether you're meditating properly.

You might also become distracted by feelings that emerge. These could be feelings related to something that is going on in your life, something that has occurred, or something that may yet happen. All of these thoughts, feelings, and other distracting concerns can compete for your attention. While they can provide indications of where you need to turn your attention at other times, meditation is not the time to entertain them.

These disturbances can make it seem as if your mind just doesn't want to quit its meandering and settle down. When this occurs, you need to learn how to rein it back in. That's part of the process. At first it may feel as if you're herding cats. However, with continued effort, you will get better at the technique. That's why they call it a meditation *practice*.

2. PRAYER

Prayer is another powerful and important spiritual tool. Learning how to effectively employ its many applications can also enhance your life and the lives of others. Evelyn Underhill, the English Anglo-Catholic writer on Christian mysticism, says, "Prayer stretches the tentacles of consciousness." William James defined prayer as "an inward communication or conversation with the power recognized as divine."[7]

I do not have a prescription for how people should or shouldn't pray because there are many ways to engage this process. They are likely influenced by the particular spiritual path or approach to prayer a given individual chooses. It is interesting to note that 90 percent of Americans report that they pray, according to Gallup polls.[8]

Prayers can include asking for intercession on behalf of yourself and others, confessing wrongdoings, adoration, thanksgiving, and engaging in various rituals. It's my opinion that in whatever way you pray, if it's done with humility, respect, and heartfelt authenticity, it *will* "stretch your spiritual tentacles" and attune your mind to spirit consciousness.

3. CONTEMPLATION

The act of contemplation can also help you open to higher levels of consciousness. It can lead to the sort of intuitive insight or spiritual awareness that escapes other forms of discovery and validation. Saint Bonaventure considered contemplation to be one of the three "eyes of the soul," and it's the eye that he believed was most critical in coming to know the reality of God. For example, when questions about the actuality of God or the existence of spirit evade confirmation through objective sensing or logic, the eye of contemplation may prove to be the one that offers the clearest vision.

Ways of Employing the Ten Key Areas of Growth to Serve Their Higher Octave

In addition to meditation, prayer, and contemplation, I include other methods and techniques into this moderate program of ascetic practice. But in an attempt to show how you can utilize the ten key areas of growth to facilitate a stronger connection with spirit consciousness, I present them in association with the key area that they most employ.

PHYSICAL

Since I've already mentioned a few ways you can work with the key area of physicality, I will just share a few other ideas of how to utilize that dimension in your practice. Physical exercises like walking, long distance running, and swimming can also be conducted in ways that serve the subtle and transpersonal side of mind.

I was once introduced to a walking meditation technique taught by Thich Nhat Hanh, the Zen master and global spiritual leader. Its slow and mindful process reminded me of the state I used to achieve when engaging in long distance running. Some people say they achieve the same state from long distance swimming.

I call these and other physical techniques used in this manner *extraverted forms of meditation*. As opposed to sitting still, closing off your senses, and quieting your thinking so you can set your mind free, these activities fully engage the senses with their rhythmic motion. And like meditation, where you might follow your breath to rein in your thinking, the attention you give to the monotony of the recurrent physical motions can serve the same purpose.

While it may be argued that there may still be too much attention directed toward external conditions to fully induce a meditative state, at the very least these activities may engender a state of mind that integrates aspects of meditation and contemplation.

There are other ways the body can be used to enhance spiritual awareness and higher states of consciousness. Fasting, for example, has had a long tradition of serving that purpose, as have certain Tantric sexual practices. Just know that while the physical body may provide spirit with the housing it needs to conduct itself in this tangible domain, it doesn't have to be viewed as its prison. The body can serve as both a vehicle for its learning and an instrument for its release.

INTELLECTUAL

Various forms of Yoga can enhance spiritual states of awareness, and one particular form can specifically be employed in a manner that utilizes the key area of intellectual growth. It's called *Jnana Yoga*. It can be used for the purpose of expanding connection with spirit consciousness.

Jnana means "knowledge" in Sanskrit. Combined with yoga, (to yoke or join together), Jnana Yoga seeks *union through knowledge*.[9] It can be conducted for the purposes of learning more about spiritual growth and development, or it can be undertaken as inspirational spiritual reading. In either case, this activity can be a nice prelude to meditating or contemplating. It's like throwing coals into the furnace of your mind in order to stoke the fires of intuition and spirit.

EMOTIONAL

The key area of emotional growth can also serve the higher purposes of spirit. But even when you have an open and healthy flow of feelings, there are ways you can stimulate them to facilitate a deeper sense of connection. Music is one way to accomplish that goal. It truly does have the power to move emotions. Listening to certain pieces of music can be inspiring, open your heart, and activate the feelings that need to be awakened. And singing, chanting, or performing music can build an emotional bridge to spiritual states.

Having those you love in your midst can keep your heart open, soft, and spiritually accessible. Directing affection towards pets will also have that effect. Engaging in activities that raise your passions keeps your heart stimulated, and performing voluntary service like caring and nurturing activities that make you feel good afterwards can contribute to a deeper connection with spirit.

There are numerous activities that can raise emotions that serve the purposes of spirit, but I believe that no other key area can be more inhibiting or more rewarding in this regard. Because even when a limited connection with spirit bleeds through, toxic emotions can distort what is beheld. And even if you can harness some of spirit's intuitive potentials, how you use them will be affected by your emotional state.

On the contrary, when people report having positive and exceptional spiritual experiences, they often have difficulty describing the joy, happiness, bliss, and love that came from spirit's inexhaustible source.

SOCIAL

The key area of social growth can also serve the higher potentials of spirit. If you attain a certain level of social comfort in groups, you could benefit from taking part in certain spiritual practices with others.

During Vipassana groups, for instance, where meditation is used for self-purification through self-observation, sharing what you're discovering internally with others can be enhanced by their input. There is also an additional effectiveness that comes from praying in groups. And certainly, being a part of a spiritual community that upholds your values and supports your practice can provide a family of kindred spirits.

MORAL

Moral growth can enhance your connection to spirit. Doing what you know is right will strengthen your spiritual muscle, and having a clear conscience will diminish distractions that can disrupt you when you're attempting to meditate, contemplate, or for that matter, sleep. When speaking of meditation, Patanjali, the author of the *Yoga Sutras*—a text on yoga theory and practice—said, "Fulfilling ethical and moral requirements are essential for achieving tangible results. *A mind not strengthened through moral and ethical exercises is easily distracted* by the lure of sense objects."[10]

IDENTITY

While identity growth changes throughout the life cycle to accommodate varying developmental stages, it also needs to be enlarged to accommodate an identification with your Higher Self.

You are more than just your body, your gender, or your nationality. You are more than just your ego-self of this life. You're part of a larger consciousness. Wilber notes: "Human identity can expand to include the All—let's call it Kosmic consciousness, the *unio mystica* ... Individual identity expands to Spirit and thus embraces the Kosmos—transcends all, includes all."[11]

INTIMACY

Similarly, a deeper connection through the key area of intimacy will help you to connect with your Higher and deeper Self. It's an inward journey of discovery. And as Martin Buber suggests, if you are willing to reveal yourself to others by sharing who you are and what you're discovering, both you and they will benefit.

EXISTENTIAL

When you expand your identity and deepen your intimate connection to serve this higher octave, you will also expand your key area of existential growth. Your sense of meaning and purpose in life will widen and deepen. You will awaken what Yalom refers to as a "cosmic meaning," as opposed to a "terrestrial meaning."[12]

Recognizing that your trials and tribulations have far more implications in your development than what they may seem to hold for your present life can help breed tolerance. And as I've said so many times before, if they're used as Chrysalis Crises, the lessons they offer can be seen as opportunities to gain the kind of spiritual growth that will enable you to progressively awaken the energies and capacities of spirit consciousness. That's a perspective that takes meaning and purpose in life to a higher level—the cosmic level of spiritual evolution.

INTUITION AND SPIRITUAL

Finally, as you make progress using the foundational and personal areas of growth at this higher octave, you will begin having increased awareness of the phenomena that arise from the transpersonal side of mind. Since the key areas of intuitive and spiritual growth are more directly connected to the subtle and transpersonal side, you may notice more psychic or spiritual experiences. For that reason, I address them together.

At first, you may doubt yourself when you have intuitive or spiritual experiences. You may discount their occurrences as "mere coincidences" or "figments of your imagination." But part of your extended growth in these two key areas will require interpreting the experiences appropriately. In this regard, Wilber suggests that spiritual intuitions and experiences be "gracefully interpreted." "Well rounded interpretations of spirit," he says, "facilitate Spirit's further descent… (It) facilitates the emergence of that new spiritual depth."[13]

How these experiences get responded to and interpreted will be influenced by the progress you make with the other key areas in regard to spiritual growth. For example, intellectually, you may overlay your interpretations of transpersonal experiences with preconceived beliefs. You may sanctify or demonize them. If fear sets in, you may take a step back and return to blocking them out of awareness. You may lose your sense of humility and misconstrue your identity, undergo what is called "spiritual inflation," thinking you're special because you've had such experiences. There are any number of ways your level of growth in all the key areas will influence how you respond to transpersonal experiences.

But no matter what success you have along the path to spiritual awakening, it's important to remember that as you progress, you bring along your potential for human fallibility, and that is why maintaining humility is so important in the process.

Learning to develop and master the ten key areas of growth in ways that serve both sides of your mind will enable you to bring about a synthesis of functioning that will reveal its underlying unity. Then as you achieve an increased conscious connection to spirit, you will realize more and more what it has to offer. And when you get a taste of its fruits, you will want to permanently reside in the garden that produces them.

CHAPTER 19

Snowflakes and Water

In a cartoon drawing referred to as the Snowman Funeral, six snowmen pallbearers are walking three on a side carrying a platform that holds the remains of their loved one. Each snowman has black dotted eyes, an orange carrot nose, a frowning mouth, and four black buttons down his chest. They're leading a funeral procession followed by a minister snowman in a black hat, a grieving spouse, and a host of family and friends. On top of the platform is the deceased—a bucket of *water*.

I like this cartoon because I believe it exemplifies two points that are worth repeating: While we are each unique as snowflakes, we're all united by the same basic element. And just as ice, water, and humidity are different states of H2O, matter, mind, and spirit are different states of the consciousness that creates, comprises, and surrounds us.

The ten key areas of development we've examined are the primary ways consciousness expresses itself in the range of human functioning. And as you gain increased awareness and mastery of how its capacities and energies function in those ten key areas, rich rewards await you.

But that increased awareness and mastery requires progressive development and growth in those ten key areas. Some of it can result from using your life crises as Chrysalis Crises, and some can be attained by efforts made without the prompting of crisis. But when you achieve that level of development, you truly will have gained conscious possession of the "keys" to the kingdom of happiness.

You may ask, though, what specifically will I behold in that kingdom? What particular rewards will I find when I unlock its door? I will tell you what others have shared and show you what one individual discovered while I was working with her in therapy. She got a taste of those rewards, which as it turns out came from an unforgettable experience.

When Dawn commenced therapy, she was in her late thirties, married to her high school boyfriend, and had three children under the age of ten. Dawn stood about five-feet-six-inches tall, had a slender build, dark curly hair, brown eyes, and a light complexion.

Upon first encountering her, I got the impression that Dawn was very observant, almost to the point of being hypervigilant. During our initial exchanges, I realized that Dawn was verbal, articulate, and direct.

She shared that she'd seen a couple of different therapists over the years, and she soon let on why. Her earlier life had been very difficult. As a child, Dawn suffered continued abuse in her home and, at one point in her adolescence, required a brief hospitalization. Fortunately, she used those ordeals, and the crises that ensued, as Chrysalis Crises, and appeared to have gained a great deal of personal insight and growth as a result.

When I first asked why Dawn sought therapy again, she was less clear. Though she said her marriage had some recent struggles, it had improved significantly after a stretch of couples counseling. While she noted her youngest child prompted some earlier concerns, her special needs were being addressed, and all was well there. And although Dawn said she was thinking about going back to work as an art teacher, she felt no pressing need to do so because her husband's well-paid job enabled her to be a stay-at-home mom for as long as she wished.

Overall, Dawn appeared to be doing well and was certainly not in crisis. She seemed grounded, stable, and highly functioning. So that begged the question: Why enter therapy now? What hurt?

As I continued to pursue those answers, Dawn explained that she wanted to resume a process that she had actively engaged in before she became a mother. It was a process dedicated to her personal and spiritual growth, and it entailed a good deal of reading, self-examination, and time for personal reflection. She knew professional assistance can benefit that process and wondered if I'd be willing to help.

She went on to mention that she sought me out because a friend told her that while I was conventionally trained and experienced, I also incorporate less conventional techniques and methods in my work. She heard that I often recommend adopting various transformational practices like meditation and yoga; I encourage keeping a journal to log dreams and use a Jungian approach when interpreting them; I welcome bringing in art, writing, or music if they might assist the process; and I'm willing to use hypnosis or past-life therapy, if I believe it's warranted.

Dawn emphasized that she wanted to work with me in all those ways. I indicated my willingness to do so, but said I first wanted to complete my assessment to be sure it would be beneficial for her. She understood and, shortly thereafter, revealed something about herself that piqued my interest.

One therapist diagnosed Dawn with a condition called *synesthesia*. It's a condition that was once thought to be rare but is now recognized in one-to-four percent of the population. It's not a form of psychopathology, however. According to neuropsychologist Richard Cytowic, synesthesia is a literal joining of the senses. "Synesthesia," he says, "is an involuntary joining in which the real information of one sense is accompanied by a perception in another sense."[1] The name comes from the Greek word *syn* (union) and *aisthesis* (sensation).

A person with synesthesia might hear colors, taste shapes, or see pain. It comes in numerous forms. For example, one form is called "mirror-touch synesthesia." That's where a synesthete might see another individual being touched on the shoulder and feel that sensation on their own shoulder.

Hearing that Dawn was a synesthete was of interest to me. Although I had limited familiarity with it, a few years earlier I was told that individuals with synesthesia are prone to psychic experiences. Cytowic has noted that "clairvoyant dreams, precognition, and a 'cosmic' world view are reported by individuals with synesthesia more often than one would expect by chance."[2]

Synesthetes are also known to have other highly developed abilities like an inordinate degree of empathy. This was the case with Dawn. She was also told she was an *empath*.

Psychiatrist Judith Orloff states that "Empaths are highly sensitive, finely tuned instruments when it comes to emotions. They feel everything, sometimes to an extreme, and are less apt to intellectualize feelings. Intuition is the filter through which they experience the world."[3]

Upon hearing Dawn was an empath, I asked how her heightened emotional sensitivity had affected her. She said she's affected by the feeling states of those around her. I reflected back on what she told me about the toxic emotional environment she was subjected to in her family of origin. That gave me further appreciation for why her adolescent years were so turbulent. It was like they were the bulls in the China shop of her highly sensitized feelings, at a time when surging hormones were already affecting her moods.

But most of the damaging effects of those earlier years had been resolved. Dawn had navigated through their storms and came away stronger as a result. Now she wanted to move on, utilize her emotional sensitivity, benefit from what her synesthesia could provide, and proceed on her path of personal and spiritual growth.

From what I could determine from my assessment, Dawn was hitting on all cylinders in the key areas of foundational development. With the exception of some resistance to regular exercise and an ongoing effort to not smoke, she generally had the key area of physicality in a good place. She maintained a healthy weight, ate nutritious food, slept well, managed her finances, lived within her means, took care of her home and possessions, and was largely free of preoccupations with her physical and material well-being.

Dawn worked hard at continuing her key area of intellectual growth. In addition to a formal college education, she was quick to read anything that could inform or enhance various needed areas of her life. For instance, she made a study of the complications that were experienced by her youngest child, read books on how to improve her marriage, and did a considerable amount of reading in the areas of personal and spiritual growth.

That latter knowledge was combined with numerous personal insights and modified beliefs that were gained from previous therapy, and it all provided her with a measure of wisdom beyond her years. It was also evident that Dawn was blessed with an above average IQ, which made her quick to grasp new information. And she was curious by nature. She'd read voraciously any new books I'd mention.

Her key area of emotional growth was also highly developed, enhanced by being an empath. Where most people must work to get in touch with their feelings, learn how to express them appropriately, and increase their sensitivity toward the feelings of others, Dawn had the opposite problem. She needed to learn how to protect her emotional sensitivity and be less permeable to the feelings of others. That required she develop healthy defenses so she wouldn't be like emotional Swiss cheese, have too many openings for people's toxic emotions to detrimentally impact her. This was an area that required more work.

Dawn also had a highly developed moral compass. She walked the walk of maintaining good ethics. But sometimes, she struggled with a too rigid adherence to the "shoulds" she believed others "ought" to uphold. Gaining an understanding of what drives people to act in unethical ways, increasing her own self-awareness as to why some particular repulsive behaviors irked her, and finding compassion for both the victims and perpetrators helped soften her reactions.

And though Dawn was more of an introvert by preference, she functioned well socially. Her vigilance and sensitivity to others enabled her to be attuned to social nuances, and her articulateness served her well when she was in groups. She was also willing to go out and engage in social gatherings when necessary, but if the needs of her family were met and she had the choice, she'd rather cozy up with a book or watch a movie at home.

While I helped Dawn do some tweaking in the areas of her foundational development, she was generally solid in all five keys and could positively employ them in her day-to-day life.

Dawn recognized she had greater potentials beyond the key areas of her foundational growth, and while she wasn't a perfectionist, she wanted to gain additional growth in the personal and spiritual areas of her development. Early on in therapy, as part of that intention, she specifically asked if I would help her shed light on any "shadow" aspects of her personality that might need to be transformed.

That request spoke volumes about her level of sophistication with therapy. In Jungian psychology, the shadow refers to the unconscious aspects of the personality that the conscious ego does not identify in itself. They are often unflattering aspects of ourselves that lie in our blind spots. Sometimes they're referred to as our "lower self."

We're usually conflicted about discovering these lower self aspects and particularly hesitant to have others see them, therapists included. However, these are often some of the very attributes that cloud the glass of the higher self and clog the flow of our intuitive and spiritual capacities.

Dawn's willingness to allow me to venture that far into her self-exploration indicated a high level of trust, and it revealed considerable previous development in her key area of intimacy. She wanted to eradicate any unhelpful unconscious aspects of herself that might have gotten incorporated into her identity as a result of earlier life experiences. Dawn sought to achieve the clearest sense of who she truly was, derive a realistic sense of herself, and peel off any inhibiting layers that blocked her from connecting with her higher, truer self.

Our work in this area contributed greatly to her continued development in both of her key areas of identity and intimacy growth. And it also contributed to another area of her personal development—her key area of existential growth.

In essence, what Dawn wanted from therapy was consistent with the priority Abraham Maslow gave the key area of existential growth: She sought further self- actualization. Though she found meaning and purpose raising her children, growing in her marital relationship, and contributing to the community around her, she hungered for more. Dawn wished to continue her existential growth by furthering her other inherent potentials. She was interested in developing her ten key areas of growth at the higher octaves, particularly in the ways they could all serve her transpersonal development.

Consistent with Orloff's description of empaths, and as revealed in her Myers Brigg's inventory of Jung's psychological types, Dawn expressed a strong preference for intuition as her dominant form of perception. Combined with her synesthesia and empathic abilities, Dawn's intuitive capacity provided rich material for her work as an artist, significantly aided her overall creativity, and provided her with dependable gut reactions to situations and people.

But her intuition also functioned in the supernormal range at times. She mentioned that on a few occasions, she had various psychic intuitive impressions, specifically instances of pre-cognitive awareness and telepathy. And she displayed another psychic ability right before me in a session. She showed a capacity for automatic writing.

Automatic writing is also known as psychography. It's thought to be a psychic ability that enables individuals to produce written words without consciously being aware of what is coming through their mind. The words are claimed to arise from a subconscious, spiritual, or supernatural force.

This ability emerged after I asked Dawn to start keeping a journal to monitor her moods and log dreams. After she made a habit of using her journal, she told me that when doing so, she would occasionally go into an altered state where she would lose conscious awareness. After she would return to being alert, she'd discover that she had typed information that she wasn't aware was flowing out of her. I asked if she would let me induce a light trance with her in the office so I could personally witness the phenomenon.

We agreed that I could ask her various questions. While I did, she remained in trance with her eyes closed. After I'd pose a question, nothing would happen for a moment or two, and then she would type on the laptop resting on her knees. When I read what she wrote, the quality of her response, the choice of words, and the level of profundity that came forth seemed to be well beyond her usual range of understanding and articulation. And when we stopped and I brought her out of trance, she had no idea what she had typed until we read it back together.

I also had the sense that Dawn had already achieved considerable development in the key area of spiritual growth. And it was more than just in the form intellectual spiritual development. Through her actions she exhibited a sincere concern for the welfare of those who were less fortunate. She was generous, unselfish, and willing to support activism where needed to bring equality and justice to individuals whose rights were being denied.

And while she was raised in a conservative Christian background, her spirituality had broadened from those early religious influences and become much more non-sectarian and universal. She read books from other spiritual paths and had come to embrace the universal principle of reincarnation, though the belief was not promoted in her Christian upbringing.

As I got to know Dawn better, it became even more evident that her overall level of functioning on all the ten key areas of growth had reached a fairly high level. She was a joy to work with and I looked forward to our time together. I felt like I was a coach who had the good fortune to work with an elite natural athlete. Her combinations of gifts offered me the opportunity to help her improve upon capacities that few others have awakened. But it wasn't until one point in her therapy that we both realized just how far those capacities had the potential to take her. It took place shortly after I conducted some regressive hypnosis.

At the time I decided to employ the technique, Dawn had been struggling with an emerging sense of shame. Considering she had so many positive attributes, that feeling of shame seemed to be out of place. It couldn't be explained by the put downs she received in her family, nor as a result of the embarrassment she experienced for having undergone a brief hospitalization. They had been well addressed by past therapists.

Dawn had been very open about any of her past wrongdoings during the shadow work, and by all accounts she was living a pretty upstanding life at that point. Since there was nothing consciously evident that could explain such feelings, I decided to induce a trance and see if a more direct route to her unconscious might prove helpful. I hoped it might lead to a past situation that had gotten buried and forgotten.

While this process is referred to as regressive hypnosis, I didn't call it "Past-Life Therapy" because I had no idea what we might uncover. If you tell people you're about to do past-life therapy, it can set them up for certain expectations and incline certain individuals to manufacture a story they believe is an actual past-life experience.

Research psychologist Nicholas Spanos refers to these expectations as "demand characteristics" and suggests that the client acts "as if" the vivid images, sensations, and emotions, are a past-life. That is why he is skeptical that what is produced in past-life therapy can provide "proof" of reincarnation.[4] Ian Stevenson would agree.

But when the goal is to use past-life therapy as a healing technique, and the therapist does not lead nor suggest where the story should go, why then, asks Roger Woolger, does the mind produce this particular story, and why now?[5]

Whatever the source of the images and story that emerges, it does appear that the mind has the ability to produce a dramatized story to bring forth whatever insight, sensation, and emotional release is needed. And when I use regressive hypnosis, my goal is to bring about healing and growth, not collect data for the proof of reincarnation.

I can attest to the remarkable results that can often be achieved when using the process in the right way with the right people. And that is what happened with Dawn. It alleviated her feelings of shame and, by clearing them, seemed to unlock her door to that proverbial "kingdom."

We scheduled a double session for the regression so we would have ample time to conduct the process and integrate its findings. The week prior to the session, I asked Dawn to be mindful of any feelings, thoughts, physical sensations, dreams, or images that might come to mind. Sometimes when anticipating the depth work of regressive hypnosis, buried unconscious material starts percolating up into conscious awareness.

At the start of the session, I asked Dawn if anything stood out in the prior week. She said she had a vague sense that something was on her face, something she wanted to take off. When she attempted to describe it, she placed her hands over her face, turned her fingers inward towards her palm, and made the downward motion of scratching off whatever it was. As she did, I asked if the urge to do that was accompanied by a feeling. Disgust came to her mind.

After Dawn shared those impressions, I asked if she could distill the feeling into a statement that could be expressed with words. She thought for a moment and then said with a loathing emotional tone, "Get it off! Get it out of my face!"

I wanted her to amplify the feeling so it could serve as an affective bridge to go where she needed to go, so I had her repeat it a few times. Then I felt we were ready to begin. She lay down on the couch. I pulled up a chair alongside her, and we proceeded with the induction.

When I felt she was sufficiently in a trance, I again asked Dawn to verbally express that feeling statement of disgust. Once she emotionally reinstated that affective bridge, she was ready to cross over. I told her to imagine that she was free to drift toward any situation that would offer insight into those feelings of disgust—to follow them like a beacon and, after my slow count of three, to find herself in a place and time that would provide insight and understanding of their source.

I then asked that she direct her awareness to locating her feet, describe what they look like, what if anything was on them, if she could determine if they were in contact with any surface, or how they were positioned. This is done to ground the person in the scene they're producing. Next, I directed her to pull back her point of perspective as if she were viewing herself from outside, scan her body and describe what she's wearing or how she looks from her feet upward. After that, I expanded my line of questioning by asking her to describe her surroundings, if she had any sense of what she was doing there, or if she had a sense of anything that is going on around her. As I advanced the process and a story began to unfolded, I asked non-leading questions like what's happening now, or what are you feeling, or what happens next?

Generally, Dawn produced a story that placed her far into the past in another life where she lived in a desert region of the world. She described being a young frail man who was discovered to be gay in a culture that was intolerant. For reasons that she couldn't explain, he had been betrayed and exposed by a past lover who had some power and authority, and who feared his own discovery. As a result, this young man was openly humiliated and shamed.

At one point in the story, the young man was held prisoner in a wagon with bars on the side and then openly paraded in front of the community. People scorned, spit, and ridiculed him. Dawn's hands moved to cover her face as she was lying on the couch. I gently placed my hands on hers, and asked: What are you feeling? What are you thinking? Dawn then removed her hands and said in gestures that looked as if she was about to vomit: I hate who I am. *I hate how others see me. I wish I could just rip my face off.*

Much more detail unfolded in that regression. More backstory and other stories about that young man came forth. They all related to a theme of shame. It was like a thread that ran though the tapestry of the many stories we explored. I hoped that by producing "soul dramas," as Woolger called them, Dawn would be able to diffuse their associated feelings, pull up their emotional anchors, and liberate herself from their unwanted influence on her present life.

Once we processed all the feelings, sensations, and insights, I brought her attention back to the room. She removed the patches off her swollen and tear stained eyes, broke a brief smile, and had the "wow" look of someone who just had their first experience wearing virtual reality goggles. But the images, intense feelings, cognitive insights, and physical sensations were produced by her own mind. And after we discussed them, she saw the relevance and understanding they held for now.

It was a very moving experience for Dawn. She felt a great sense of relief afterwards. But the unexpected fruits of that process seemed to precipitate yet another, more memorable experience the weekend after that session. I'll let her describe it to you in her own words, which she wrote down and brought to me.

It was hot. I was wandering around the house, completely in this moment of exquisite but not quite formed clarity: sort of in a happy speechless stupor, taking delight in things like the texture of the dish cloth. Each and every little detail became so telling about humanity. We, people, are so fascinating, so driven to improve upon what we have created. I didn't feel any need to speak or express my experience; just to observe with the knowledge that there had been many, many, many here and nows before and that I was a bit weary of all this now. Slightly impatient, but accepting nonetheless.

I wandered out to the garage where "that man who was my husband this time" (that's how I thought of him) was talking about how he had so much to do and he was overwhelmed. I found myself feeling compassionately toward him. I was sad he didn't know what I knew, that when we lack connection with our essence we remain tethered to small and simple world views. We are pursued by our own obsessions about the hows and whens and whys of our daily lives and our own importance. His love of rationality and evidence (as he incorrectly perceived them) were in terrible error. I also knew that I was supposed to leave him alone with his misconceptions or he wouldn't learn. He wouldn't understand what I meant if I explained things to him. I just needed to let him, and all others, be. So I did.

I didn't linger on that feeling. It was just something I knew and accepted... then moved on. I was able to shed emotional reactions like clothing, but felt them all the same. Then I became AWARE that I was AWARE. I became aware that we all just run around trying so hard, giving our best shot to the simple task of living, and the whole point of living is to get beyond that narrow personal viewpoint that this is all there is. We just keep trying, trying, trying. All this is "busy work." Mastery of simple skills that really don't define us realistically at all. It just keeps us busy until we wake up. This made me feel like laughing. Oh My God, how absolutely hilarious that I haven't seen the forest for the trees until now. How could I have missed it? How could I have ever thought it was any other way? It was so painfully obvious! Ha! The joke was on me! I remember now!

I had a sudden awareness of the convoluted, internal struggle of all humanity on Earth, especially Asia. I was a farmer in a rice field with my ox, with my feet waterlogged and my clothing filthy. At that exact moment as I was standing in my garage watching the paint job on the car glint in the sun, I had an internal vision of what I can only describe as my awareness, (which I learned exists apart from our meager physical form) spilling over and covering the planet Earth like a liquid, on its way to touching all life in the place. All life is pieces of a great "sun." Like rays of light, we bend, and reflect. We relentlessly pursue. We cause shadows to be. We are of the sunshine and are the sunshine at once, buffeted by our own reactions to whatever external stimuli happens upon us or we happen upon.

I knew that linear time is really a human construct. There is no "time" as we have come to know it. There just is. All there is is awareness. We are gentle and unique fingerlings of awareness. We are connected to this awareness that is so much more than we can even begin to realize and far more than the unaware mind can accept. The mysteries must be infinite. I knew this all, in short, because I had known this before. Really, I had always known this. I had just forgotten it while in this form.

As I existed in this awareness, and my husband worked on his car, I experienced a profound sense of relief. I had never experienced this kind of blissful relief and surrender. I was surrendering away my personal paradigm of how life works. POOF! And it was gone! It was that easy! I was suddenly aware I had reached this point of revelation before. This absolute heavenly ease was a familiar feeling. I had somehow, somewhere, sometime, agreed to all of my life's experiences, good and bad, as necessary for growth. My most powerful growth seemed to come from pain. I knew that this awareness that "I" really was, was separate from this body I was inhabiting, and "I" was eternal. What people conceived of as death was merely the end of a short, short, chapter.

At this precise moment, I remember thinking something like, "Oh, Hell. That was a hard one (i.e., the learning curve of my current life up to this point). Damn. Glad that's over with," along with a slight feeling of resentment at the "process" of overcoming this stagnancy again and again during lives. "I" or "IT," wherever this viewpoint was coming from, was an old hand at this waking up thing. There was very little identification with the whole idea of "Dawn." "Dawn" was a simple vehicle that I felt compassionately toward. Sort of like a really old car you loved, but didn't work all the time. Dawn was used to getting to this place, to a certain threshold of alertness. She was only part of the equation.

We had to work as a team. Now, the threshold had been crossed, once again. This was how it was supposed to be. This was the natural state of being. I understood that intellect is simply a tool, and priorities in our culture were unbalanced; that intellect is not really that important. Emotions are all important. That's how everything gets done. And I realized that fear is our most horrific enemy/teacher/motivator. Fear lies sneakily underneath all defeats, whether they be defeats of omission because you never tried, or if you tried and could not succeed, and counted it as a failure. There is very little failure without purpose. Maybe none.

With this knowledge came a beatific and all-encompassing feeling of peace and contentment. It was warm. My body limp with relaxation. Without saying much to my husband, I turned around and went inside to my bedroom. I felt as if every strain, every nagging memory, every physical discomfort, simply….went away. My body was light as air. I was so free. I saw through every misconception I had about the world in one fell blow. Free. Unburdened. My funny little mind was like a background program. I wasn't really associated with that "mind" at all, just aware of the "little me" program running in the somewhere else.

Up to this point, the experience recounted here thus far maybe took 5 minutes linear time. I think I might have said, "oh" in response to my husband a couple of times. Everything took place in my own internal awareness. No one else could have had any idea what I was experiencing. There were no obvious physical signs. This happened all inside the world of me.

Your doorway to who you really are is internal. Don't forget that. It's important. My state of profound peace was a bit like being drunk, but at the same time feeling and knowing that my physical reactions and my mental clarity were enhanced, not hindered in any way. I moved to the bedroom to lie down and submerged myself in this awareness. I was at peace with the thought of death. Wondered how it would end this time. I regarded my children without possessiveness. I saw them as ancient friends, outcroppings of the same awareness. There was a deep compassion toward them as they learned this world. They were not ready, yet, to be awake; too young in this time. Perhaps later in their lives they would have the chance.

I think children are rarely awake, but there are some. I knew they had to learn all the bits and pieces first in order to put the puzzle together. We all do. They had to be taught to feel pain and survive and learn from it. They had to be taught to feel joy, and engage with it completely. They had to be fed a steady diet of compassion, love, and goodwill to continue on their journey. I was supposed to make sure that happened while they were young. I needed to show them a world not hemmed in by religion. Not limited by science. Not constricted by denials of our own experiences. Not strangled by fear. I needed to show them a world fueled by how powerful they can be. How they are master creators of their own life. And then I lay down.

I looked around the room and was awestruck by the creativity of the human race. This dresser. What a great idea! The different weaving pattern on the blankets and sheets—a testament to our desire to create and to continue to improve on our creations. The books, undeniable proof of the need to communicate through symbols and stories… to be heard, somehow, across time and space. I had lived with these signs for years, I have even made these things, but never had I been so appreciative of them than at this moment.

Now I could see it. Now I was aware that I was surrounded by records of creative acts wherever I went. And nature! The mathematical perfection, the cyclical perfection—everywhere. All of it alive with creative energy. And then, for some reason, the phrase, "I am that I am," came to me. I am the great I am. That great conscience. That great aware living force. How his message got lost! How Jesus must have struggled to make himself understood! There was no arrogance or superiority in his words. His answer was as honest as he could make it.

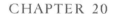

CHAPTER 20

Love Returns

After the Ecstasy, the Laundry. That's the title of a Jack Kornfield book. In it, he describes what Dawn was faced with in the aftermath of her experience—the return to everyday reality. As Jack points out, "Enlightenment experiences can happen," but "They don't last."[1]

Despite this reality, Dawn's world did not shrink back to where it was before. While the expanded state of consciousness contracted, she never forgot what she beheld with her inner vision. The ecstasy that accompanied the enlightenment, the connection she experienced from its sense of unity, and the knowledge she gained from its mystical intuitions, all had a transforming effect.

Yes, Dawn had to resume being a mother and wife, and continue addressing the same day-to-day demands that surrounded her prior to the experience. The Zen proverb states: "Before enlightenment, chop wood, carry water. After enlightenment, chop wood, carry water." But while she had to refocus her mind on the world of physicality and ego, the part of her mind that's in touch with the world of spirit had been significantly awakened. She discovered through direct personal experience that spirit's subtle and transpersonal presence is an actuality. That remained.

But in what practical ways did she benefit from the experience, you might ask? Beyond the confirmation that the transpersonal world is real, how did it change her day–to-day life? In order to get some insight into that question, I asked Dawn if she would fill out a survey that was constructed to assess those outcomes.

After much time had passed, and the glow of Dawn's experience was well behind her, I gave her a self-report instrument that measures potential changes in the lives of people after they undergo what is referred to as an exceptional human experience.

The term "exceptional human experience," or EHE, was first coined by Rhea White in 1990. It includes all types of psychic, mystical, death-related, peak, and other anomalous experiences. One example would be an NDE. According to White, EHEs serve as "a means of moving the experiencer away from a more or less exclusive identification with a self that is bounded by the skin."[2]

Dawn's enlightenment experience certainly qualified as an EHE, so I felt the use of this instrument was appropriate. It specifically addresses 21 different areas of life, like fears about death, feelings of isolation, or the desire to help others. When answering the questions, the person is asked to reflect back on how much a given characteristic or feeling changed as a result of what they've experienced, and to what degree the characteristic or feeling was present before and after the event.

Most prominently, Dawn noted that her fears about the future, her fear of death, her desire to help others, and any passing feelings she might typically have of anxiety, depression, isolation, and loneliness all markedly improved. Generally, she felt happier.

While the "chopping of wood and carrying water" may remain a constant part of your life before and after an enlightenment experience, the change in your state of mind can make all the difference between seeing those tasks as miserable burdens, or doing them with peace, contentment, and maybe even a happy whistle.

But these experiences and aftereffects don't just randomly occur to the lucky few. In my clinical opinion, Dawn's capacity to achieve the conducive state of consciousness that enabled that enlightenment experience to occur, and her ability to positively benefit from it afterward, were directly attributable to her level of personal and spiritual development beforehand.

Some people who haven't made a concerted effort at their personal and spiritual development can still get a sense of what an expanded state of consciousness can provide. For example, they may get a taste of the bliss and contentment from a drug induced state.

It's certainly understandable how enticing that experience can be, especially if it offers relief to the misery or depression they may feel at other times. But there's no spiritual bypass you can take that will enable you to get around the rigors of personal growth and spiritual evolution. And it's my belief that those who seek to avoid that personal work, and opt to utilize other methods to approximate those states, actually set themselves farther back.

If they become dependent upon alternative means to achieve those outcomes, especially if those means lead to addictions, they will have to double back that much farther before they can find the right course to get there naturally. And even if they get a glimpse of what could potentially lie ahead in their evolution, the ability to integrate what they beheld will be limited by their stage of development.

As Sri Aurobindo noted," The spiritual evolution obeys the logic of successive unfolding . . . even if certain minor stages can be swallowed up or leaped over by a rapid and brusque ascension, the consciousness has to turn back to assure itself that the ground passed over is securely annexed to the new condition."[3]

So even if you get a taste of that expanded state, sustaining its effects or increasing the likelihood of incurring it again takes ongoing self-development. It's a gradual evolving process. "Self-mastery must come first," said Gopi Krishna.[4] And as Ralph Metzer noted, "Awakening is not about just getting more information."[5]

There's no app for enlightenment. There's no bypass to its attainment. But it is a worthwhile state toward which to aspire. And keep it mind: as you make progress along the way, you will incrementally derive the benefits. It's a little like climbing a mountain. While the best view may come at the top, you increasingly get better and better views as you ascend. And if your elevated perception translates into increased contentment, joy, and happiness in life, why meander at the bottom of the mountain?

Kornfield said that "When the conditions of the heart are present, the enlightenment experience can happen." So seek those conditions in your heart now—in this life. Determine how those conditions can be developed. If you're facing a crisis, use it as a Chrysalis Crisis. Let it open you to that growth. If you're not in crisis, take the initiative to advance your personal and spiritual development without the promptings of an ordeal. Be "Higher Self-motivated," and as you grow, enjoy the fruits that come from liberating the energies and capacities that are inherently yours.

I'm not suggesting that you have to engage in some constant self-absorbed preoccupation with personal development. Just find a balance between experiencing life and learning from it. Be a human being *and* a human doing. And be realistic about the gains you make as you develop in the ten key areas of growth. You don't have to wait until they usher in some enlightened state before you benefit from their increased development and mastery.

Why not benefit now from mastering your *physical* world? Start with the part that's directly at hand: your physical body. Eat nutritious food, exercise, and eliminate unhealthy habits that you know are compromising your physical wellbeing. Discover the many ways a vital, healthy body can enhance your time on this Earth. If you're facing sickness or physical limitation, seek out ways those problems can least handicap you. Change your thinking, address your feelings, and use your other ten key areas of growth to improve your life despite those physical problems. Remember, your mind has the power to affect your physical world. It can be employed to bring forth healing, reduce pain, or be used to creatively come up with ways to improve your situation.

Manage your body, manage your money, manage your possessions, and respectfully manage the earth you stand upon. To the extent that's possible, free yourself of their concerns so you can use your increased physical energy for other purposes, and derive the happiness that can be achieved as a result.

Seek the knowledge you need to develop all the key areas of your life by expanding your *intellectual* capacity. Find the joy in learning new things about all areas of creation. Cultivate curiosity. Let the information you gain enhance your experience of life. Let it open your eyes to the abundance that surrounds you. Let it teach you how to derive what you need to be content. Learn from others, and teach those who would learn from you.

Recognize that you have the capacity to open your heart to all emotions. You don't have to become some touchy-feely person if that is not in your nature. But you can have an open and available heart. Remember, the *emotional* component in life adds richness. It can be like the difference of watching a black and white TV versus color. Feel intensely. Feel passion. Be able to connect with your feelings and learn to express them appropriately. Share them with others, and use your emotional awareness to empathize and attune to their feelings.

And be a good, *moral* person. Not because everybody tells you to be good. Not because if you're bad, you'll get caught. Because when you do things that are right, you feel better. And when you do things you know are wrong, you darken your light. If you have any level of empathy or conscience, you'll limit your capacity to feel so your wrongdoings don't bother you. If you carry guilt for immoral or unethical actions, you'll imprison yourself and create your own suffering. At some point, your mind will seek its own correction. On a deep psychological and spiritual level, we're all self-cleaning ovens.

Engage in community with others. You don't have to be a social butterfly. Discover what a *social* connection with others can provide. Sure, we are all imperfect humans and can be a handful at times, but if you reach out, you'll find those of us who can be trusted, those who will befriend you. Don't look for reasons to exclude yourself or others. Seek the commonalities we share. We all want to be happy. We all want the best for ourselves and our children. We all want to live in peace. Remember, while we're all unique as snowflakes, we all share the same essence. Connect with that in mind, and drink from the community of humanity. It will replenish your body and spirit.

Try not to get stuck in some outdated *identity* of who you used to be. Give yourself the opportunity to grow and change. Don't feel inadequate because you're not like someone else. Discover who you are and learn to relish who you're becoming. And don't get too attached to that self either. Recall that Erickson said identity changes throughout the life cycle. So get beyond you physical body, your gender, your race, your nation, or even your religion. You're a spirit. You're God in the making.

If you can't fathom that such a grandiose notion is within your potential, dig a little deeper. Be more self-examining and discover the energies and capacities that are inherently yours. Expand your range of *intimacy* with yourself and others. Find the courage to share what you're finding out about yourself, and show an interest in what they're discovering. Share your dreams, confusions, and joys. And share your fears. Sometimes, just revealing them can lessen their intensity, and you may discover the rest of us have the same ones. You'll feel less alone, more connected. We may all be different kinds of snowflakes, but we all think about melting, too.

Find meaning in your life. It can provide a reason why you get out of bed every day. It doesn't have to be some grand objective in life, but it can give a greater purpose to your existence than just being on this side of the grass. It's okay to ask the big questions, like why am I here, or what happens when I die? These are the *existential* questions of life. They're each of ours to answer. Use the wide lens on your life so you can see the forest of your existence, and not myopically get your forehead stuck on the tree in front of you.

When you widen that lens and open to the forest, you'll start registering perceptions beyond those of your objective senses. You'll learn to use and trust your *intuition*. It's just as available as your touch, taste, and hearing. Don't let your uninformed beliefs or fears about psychic intuitions close your mind off to their actuality. Why not employ your "First Sight" to assist what you see with your eyes? Remember, *believing* is seeing. Let yourself have a personal experience that will provide confirmation of your intuitive capacities. Keep the words made famous by Yogi Berra in mind: "If I hadn't believed it, I wouldn't have seen it."

And let your *spiritual* consciousness manifest, too. It also needs to be personally experienced to be affirmed. You already have access to its energies and capacities. No religion has exclusive inroads to its awakening. Spirit is a non-sectarian actuality. Whether you choose to believe it exists or not matters not. You are still a spirit in a body. You're more than your meat and bones. Physical death does not bring an end to your spirit. It only brings about a transition into an alternate state of its manifestation.

Recognizing that your spirit consciousness transforms and does not disappear with the death of your body aligns your thinking with natural law. And knowing that it is on a trajectory of developmental evolution will broaden your perspective on life. Your spirit expands and evolves from direct personal experience over lives of learning. If it's hard for you to believe that because it can't be physically proven or logically deduced, at least open to it as a possibility. What do you have to lose? Doing so will enable you to personally start registering the subtle and transpersonal phenomena that will ultimately verify this truth. Don't close off your perception of those potentials from the restrictions of disbelief.

You are a multidimensional human being who has access to the energies and capacities of the consciousness that created you, comprises you, and surrounds you. Those energies and capacities manifest and are expressed through the ten key areas of growth. Mastering those keys, and having them serve both sides of your mind, will increase your awareness of all the ways that consciousness manifests in the physical, psychological, and spiritual world.

As you gain that awareness and mastery of consciousness, either through Chrysalis Crises or otherwise, you will reap the potential benefits that come from its manifestation. You will awaken your capacities and energies, and experience the enlightenment, bliss, joy, happiness, and peace that it can produce.

But in addition to these potentials, there is another capacity and energy that you will increasingly be able to realize. And it encompasses and surpasses all the others. It's one you're already familiar with. But I'm going to hold off naming it just now, because it's an overused word. Its familiarity, and the preconceived notions of how it's defined, may incline you to dismiss the significant part it plays in consciousness.

So rather than name it, or like many others before me, fail to give it sufficient definition, let me share a personal EHE that further awakened its pervasive, endless, and all-encompassing reality in my life.

This personal experience came about toward the end of the midlife pilgrimage I undertook in my late forties. It occurred during a one-week silent meditation retreat conducted by Jack Kornfield and Stan Grof. The retreat combined Jack's Vipassana approach to meditation with Stan's Holotropic Breathwork technique for achieving a "non-ordinary state of consciousness."

At the time I undertook the retreat, I was experiencing an increasing level of anxiety. It seemed to be related to a theme I had identified years before when I did some work uncovering its source. It had to do with an underlying fear and concern that I would lose people I love. It dated back to my childhood when I would sometimes become fearful that I might suddenly lose my mother to MS, and it was also hypothesized that some of it might be attributed to a vague awareness of being separated from my mother during the first year of my life.

In either case, the feelings of anxiety weren't debilitating or acute during the period leading up to the retreat, but they did seem to percolate back up into my conscious mind more frequently than usual.

Once I got into the week, the combination of Jack's daily meditation periods, the long intervals of silence (which took some effort for an extravert), and Stan's technique worked their magic. On one of the last afternoons, it was my turn to be the recipient of the Breathwork process. As I was lying down on a mat with my eyes covered and in the non-ordinary state of consciousness induced by the process, I was stimulated by the selection of music playing in the background, and my mind started producing this unfolding scene.

I experienced my "self" as some American Indian warrior walking through the woods. I had this sense that I was working my way back home, and that I was exhausted and wounded from having just taken part in some kind of a battle. Upon arriving at my village, I found that many of the women and children were killed. When I first beheld the vivid images of all that carnage, it made me feel sick. And as I lay on the floor of the retreat, a similar sensation came over me.

The images continued to unfold. I felt urgency and panic. I was aware that I left loved ones there, too. When I went to where my tent was located, I saw their mutilated bodies. At first, I was in shock, but then I felt this deep desperation and began to cry inconsolably. And at the retreat center I did the same. While I did, I could feel the touch of my support person's hand on my shoulder.

After a while, I stopped crying, but before I fully gained full awareness of being back in the room, I had the most amazing experience. It was an ecstatic feeling of oneness, peace, and assuredness. It accompanied a deep knowing that *All Is Well*. At a very profound level, I realized there was nothing to fear.

Then I had this sort of intuitive awareness: *We Don't Lose Love!* Realizing that was like remembering something I once knew but had forgotten, like "Oh, that's right, we can't lose love. Love is all around us." Then in a flow of additional awareness I had other insights: that it's our responsibility to realize the existence of love and our potential to experience it fully, and once we learn to open our hearts to its experience, we need to extend it to others in all the ways it can be expressed.

Finally, and most impressionably, I had this clear sense that the love we awaken and share returns. *Love Returns!* Like a beacon, it draws us back to the spirits with whom we've directed it, and leads us towards those who've directed their love to us. Because at the level of spirit consciousness, love never dies. Love unites us.

I felt a little like Dawn felt 20 years later during her experience. I had this sense that my family, my wife, my children, my friends, everyone I loved, and everyone who I've been blessed to have love me are all connected, and we will always be united. It was very liberating and assuring.

Though I know that should any of them give up their body, I'll miss their physical presence. But I'll understand that my work will be in the grieving, accepting, and growing in whatever ways the crisis of their loss can serve as a Chrysalis Crisis. And should a future crisis result from my physical life drawing to a close, I'll pray that I can discover how it can be used to contribute to my continued evolution.

In the meantime, I will aspire to live my life in the way we are all advised: To live life in the now. To allow the past to inform the present when it's needed to enhance the now. And to use present experiences to awaken future potentials.

Should your present experience be met with crisis, once you recover from its initial impact, determine if it can be used as a

Chrysalis Crises. Use the struggle to strengthen the ten key areas of growth that require your development. Let the crisis lead to your transformation. Let it expand your awareness of consciousness, heighten your capacity to love, contribute to your happiness, and enable you to increasingly abide in a state of peace profound.

Acknowledgements

I've been incubating this book for the past three decades. However, it is largely due to the more recent encouragement, support, editorial input, and professional guidance of Patrick Huyghe that I finally got it into your hands. From the outset, Patrick prompted me to express all that I had to say, and he helped me define the path to getting it published.

For accomplishing that latter objective, I am deeply thankful to Jonathan Friedman and the good folks at Rainbow Ridge Books. Jonathan believed in this book and was willing to partner with me to bring it into manifestation.

A deep debt is also owed to Joanne Di Maggio. She served as the book's midwife and helped me birth it. Joanne was the first to read each word, provide needed corrections, and coach me on how to relax into writing my truth.

I will forever be grateful to Bruce Greyson, who provided meticulous editing, and attached his good name to the book's endorsement. And thank you Eben Alexander, Larry Dossey, Dean Radin, Bernard Beitman, and Michael Grosso for your testimonials as well. I am also grateful to my colleagues and friends at The University of Virginia's Division of Perceptual Studies (DOPS)—Jim Tucker,

Edward Kelly, Emily Kelly, Ross Dunseath, Kim Abernathy, and Lori Derr—for supporting my ideas.

I thank my other friends, Steven Sayre, Maggie McIlvaine, Joe Connor, Frank De Marco, Barbara Brownell-Grogan, Cally Olglesby, and my relatives Anthony Perna and Tara Buggy, for reading the manuscript, sharing supportive words, and keeping my spirits up while I sought publication.

A special thanks goes to Kevin Mac Fadden for his earlier tutelage. In his very gentle and wise manner, Kevin sharpened my writing skills by teaching me various forms of poetry and how to compose a novel. From those efforts, I gained the confidence and competence to undertake the writing of this book.

And I would be remiss if I didn't thank my clients for trusting me with their confidences, and for finding the courage to share experiences that I know were difficult to even broach with a therapist. You have all taught me so much.

Finally, in the spirit of saving the best for last, I am deeply grateful to my wife, Jane Pasciuti, for her willingness to support my pursuit of the trainings, experiences, and endless hours required to complete this book. Most cherished is her love, the love of my three children, Renee, Eric, and Michelle, and the love of my extended family. They all provide the anchoring I need to balance my professional activities with that which is most important in my life—all of you.

References

CHAPTER 4

1. Ellis, Albert, Irving M Becker, and Melvin Powers. (1982). *A Guide to Personal Happiness.* North Hollywood, CA: Wilshire

2. Seligman, M.E.P. (2002). *Authentic Happiness: Using the New Positive Psychology to Realize Your Potential for Lasting Fulfillment.* London: Nicholas Brealey

3. Dabrowski, K. (1964). *Positive Disintegration.* Boston: Little, Brown.

CHAPTER 5

1. Goleman, Daniel. (1995). *Emotional Intelligence: Why it Can Matter More Than IQ.* New York: Bantam Books

CHAPTER 6

1. Bazerman, M. H. and Tendunsel, A. E., (2011). *Blind Spots: Why We Fail to Do What's Right and What to do About it.* Princeton University Press

2. Ibid., p. 62

3. Ibid., p. 70

4. Hoffman, Martin. (1981). "Is Altruism Part Of Human Nature?" *Journal of Personality and Social Psychology.* 40, (1. : 121-137

5. Haidt, Jonathan. (2006). *The Happiness Hypothesis: Finding Modern Truth in Ancient Wisdom.* New York: Basic Books

CHAPTER 7

1. Goleman, Daniel. (2006). Social Intelligence. *The New Science of Human Relationships.* New York: Bantam Dell

2. Ibid., p. 84

3. Ibid., p. 91

4. *Myers-Briggs Type Indicator (MBTI).* (2014). CPP. Com, Menlo Park, CA.

5. Jung, C.G. *Psychological Types.* (1976). Bollinger Series XX, The collected Works of C.G. Jung, Volume 6, Princeton University Press

6. See Goleman, *Social intelligence.* p. 319

CHAPTER 8

1. Erickson, Eric. H. (1959). *Identity and the Life Cycle.* International University Press, Inc.

2. Ibid., p. 128

3. Jung, C. G. (1966). *Two Essays on Analytical Psychology.* Princeton University Press

4. Ibarra, Herminia. (2004). *Working Identity. Unconventional Strategies for Reinventing Your Career.* Boston: Harvard Business School Press

5. Ibid., p. xi

6. Singer, June. (1976). *Androgyny. Toward a New Theory of Sexuality.* Anchor Press/Doubleday

7. Erickson, Eric H. (1950). *Childhood and Society.* New York: Norton and Company.

CHAPTER 9

1. Lerner, Harriet. (1990). *The Dance of Intimacy.* Harper and Row Publishers, Inc.

2. Ibid., p. 3

3. Powell, John. (1969). *Why Am I Afraid to Tell You Who I Am?* 1. , Niles, Ill: Argus Communications

4. Ibid., p. 12

5. Jouard, Sidney. (1964). *The Transparent Self.* New York: D. Van Nostrand Company

6. Dossey, Larry. (2012). *One Mind: How Our Individual Mind is Part of a Greater Consciousness and Why it Matters.* Hay House, Inc. p. xix

7. Gottman, John. (1994). *What Predicts Divorce.* Hillsdale. New Jersey: Lawrence Erlbaum Associates, Inc.

8. Gottman, John. (1999). *The Seven Principals for Making a Marriage Work.* New York: Harmony Books

9. Ibid., pp

10. Luft, J. and Ingram, H. (1955). *The Johari Window, A Graphic Model of Interpersonal Awareness.* UCLA, Los Angeles. CA

11. Ercikson, Erik. H. (1959). *Identity and The Life Cycle.* W.W. Norton & Company, Inc.

12. See John Powell. *Why Am I Afraid to Tell You Who I Am?*

CHAPTER 10

1. Yalom, Irvin, D. (1980). *Existential Psychotherapy*. New York: Basic Books, Inc.

2. Ibid., p. 5

3. Ibid., p. 69

4. Hollis, James. (1993). *The Middle Passage: From Misery to Meaning at Midlife*. Toronto: Inner City Books

5. See Yalom. *Existential Psychotherapy*, p. 159

6. Ibid., p. 152

7. Ibid., p. 152

8. Ibid., p. 153

9. Ibid., p. 168

10. Ibid., p. 32

11. Pincus, Lilly. (1976). *Death and the Family: Importance of Mourning*. Faber and Faber

12. See Yalom. *Existential Psychotherapy*, pp 220

13. Seligman, M. E. P. (1975). *Helplessness: On Depression, Development, and Death*. San Francisco: W.H. Freeman

14. Assagilioli, R. (1965). *Psychosynthesis*. New York: The Viking Press.

15. Ibid., pp

16. Moustakas, Clark, E. (1961). *Loneliness*. Prentice Hall, p. 7

17. See Yalom. *Existential Psychotherapy*, pp. 353

CHAPTER 11

1. Frankl, Viktore, E. (1969). *The Will to Meaning*. A Plume Book. New American Library

2. Ibid., p. 34

3. Brehony, Kathleen, A. *Awakening at Midlife*. New York: Riverhead Books

4. Ibid., p. 11

5. Hollis, James. (1993). *The Middle Passage: From Misery to Meaning at Midlife*. Toronto: Inner City Books. p. 7

6. See Frankl, *The Will to Meaning*. p. 35

7. Ibid., p. viii

8. See Brehony, *Awakening at Midlife*. p. 137

CHAPTER 12

1. Grof, Christina., and Grof, Stanislav. (1990). *The Stormy Search for the Self*. New York: Tarcher, p. 31

2. The International Pathwork Foundation. P.O. Box 725 Madison, Virginia 22727

3. Pierrakos, John. C. (1973). *Core Energetics: Developing the Capacity to Love and Heal.* Life Rythem, Mendocino, CA

CHAPTER 13

1. Bem, D. J. (2005). *Precognitive Aversion*. Proceedings of Presented Papers: The Parapsychological Association 48th Annual Convention. Petaluma, CA., pp. 31-35

2. Cardena, E., Lynn, Stephen., & Krippner, S. (2002). *Varieties of Anomalous Experience*. Washington, DC: American Psychological Association. p. 4

3. Radin, D. I. (2013). *Supernormal: Science, Yoga, and the Evidence for Extraordinary Psychic Abilities.* New York: Deepak Chopra Books, p. xix

4. See Bem. *Precognitive Aversion*

5. Radin, D. I. (2006). *Entangled Minds: Extrasensory Experiences in a Quantum Reality.* New York: Paraview Pocket Books, p.79.

6. French, Christopher, C., and Stone, Anna. (2014). *Anomalistic Psychology: Exploring Paranormal Belief & Experience.* New York: Palgave MacMillan, p. 6

7. Kramer, Wim, H., Bauer, E., & Hovelmann, G. H. (2012). *Perspectives of Clinical Parapsychology: An Introductory Reader.* Stichting Het Johan Borgmanfonds. The Netherlands

8. Walsh, R. and Vaughan, F. (1993). "On Transpersonal Definitions," *Journal of Transpersonal Psychology*. 25. pp 199–207.

9. See Grof. *The Stormy Search for the Self*, p. 6

10. Ibid., p. 73

11. Ibid., p. 183

12. Bush, Nancy, E. (2012). *Dancing Past the Dark. Distressing Near-Death Experiences.* Parson's Porch Books

13. Kason, Yvonne. (1994. *Farther Shores: Exploring How Near-Death, Kundalini, and Mystical Experiences Can Transform Ordinary Lives.* Indiana: Author's Choice Press

14. See Grof and Grof. *Spiritual Emergency*, p. 41

15. Ibid., p. 42

CHAPTER 14

1. See Dossey. *One Mind.* P. xxix

2. Ibid., p. xxvi

3. Moody, Raymond. (1975). *Life After Life.* Mockingbird Books.

4. Gladwell, Malcom. (2005). *Blink: The Power of Thinking Without Thinking.* Little, Brown and Company.

5. Ibid., p. 11

6. Marshall, Paul. "Mystical Experiences as Windows on Reality," In *Beyond Physicalism: Toward Reconciliation of Science and Spirituality.* (2015. , pp 39-79. Edited by Edward Kelly, Adam Crabtree, and Paul Marshall. Lanham, MD: Rowman & Littlefield

7. Carpenter, J. C. (2012). *First Sight: ESP and Parapsychology in Everyday Life.* Lanham, MD: Rowman & Littlefield

CHAPTER 15

1. Friedman. H., et al. "Transpersonal and Other Models of Spiritual Development," *Interpersonal Journal of Transpersonal Studies*, 29 (1. , 2010, pp. 79-94

2. Khanna, Surbhi, and Greyson, Bruce. (2014). "Near-death experiences and spiritual well-being," *Journal of Religion and Health*, 53, 1605-1615.

3. Fuller, R. C. (2001., *Spiritual But Not Religious.* New York: Oxford University Press

4. Van Lommel, P. (2006). "Near-death experiences, consciousness, and the brain," *World Futures,* 62, pp. 134-151

5. Ring, K. (1980). *Life at Death: A Scientific Investigation of the Near-Death Experience.* New York: Coward, Mc Cann, & Geoghegan

6. Sabon, M. (1982). *Recollections of Death: A Medical Investigation.* New York: Harper & Row

7. Taylor, Stephen. (2011). *Out of Darkness: From Turmoil to Transformation.* Hay House

8. Palmer, J. (1979). A Community Mail Survey of Psychic Experiences. *Journal of The American Society for Psychical Research*, 73. Pp. 221 -251

9. Ibid., pp. 228.

10. Biernacki, Lorilai. (2015). "Conscious Body: Mind and Body in Abhi-navgupta's Tantra," pp. 349-387 in *Beyond Physicalism*. Edited by Edward Kelly, Adam Crabtree, and Paul Marshall. Lanham MD: Rowman & Little-field

11. Mc Taggart, J. M. E. (1930). *Some Dogmas of Religion*. Bristol: Thoemmes Press

12. The Division of Perceptual Studies. A Research Unit of the Department of Psychiatry and Neurobehavioral Sciences, University of Virginia Health System. 210 10th Street, N.E. Suite 100, Charlottesville, VA. 22902

13. Greyson, Bruce. "Increase in psychic phenomena following near-death experiences," *Theta,*11 (2. , 26-29

14. Lawrence, Madelaine. (2014). *The Death View Revolution*. White Crow Books, p. 147

15. Ibid., p. 148.

16. Klimo, John. (1998. *Channeling. Investigations on Receiving Information from Paranormal Sources*. North Atlantic Books, p. 9

17. Pew Research Center on Religion and Public Life. Dec. 2009

18. See Grof and Grof. *Spiritual Emergency*, p. 89

CHAPTER 16

1. Tucker, J. B. (2013). *Return to Life. Extraordinary Cases of Children Who Remember Past Lives*. New York: St. Martin Press

2. Mills, Antonia., Tucker, J.B. (2015). "Reincarnation; field Studies and Theoretical Issues Today," in *Parapsychology. A Handbook for the 21st Century*. Edited by Etzel Cardena, John Palmer, and David Marcusson-Clavertz. Mc Farland & Company, pp. 314-326

3. Stevenson, Ian. (1974). *Xenoglossy: A Review and Report of a Case*. Charlot-tesville: University Press of Virginia

4. Woolger, Roger, J. Private Correspondence

5. See Tucker, *Return to Life*, p 209

6. Ibid., p. 211.

CHAPTER 17

1. Covey, Stephen, R., and Merrill, Roger, R. (1996). *First Things First*. Franklin Covey Co.

2. Ikeda, Daisaku. (1988). *Unlocking the Mysteries of Birth and Death. A Buddhist View of Life*. Middleway Press, p. 152

3. Planck, Max. (1931). *The Observer*. January.

4. Biernacki, Lorilai, (2014). "Introduction: Panentheism Outside the Box," in *Panentheism Across the World's Traditions*. Oxford University Press, pp. 1-17

5. Murphy, Michael. (2015). "The Emergence of Evolutionary Panentheism," in *Beyond Physicalism*. Edited by Edward Kelly, Adam Crabtree, and Paul Marshall, pp. 553-577

6. Bricklin, Jonathan. Editor. (2006). *Sciousness*. Eirini Press, p. 24

7. Carpenter, Edward. (1920). *Civilization: Its Cause and Cure*

8. Lewis, Spencer, H. (1929). *The Mystical Life of Jesus*. Bloomington, Ill: Pantagraph Press

9. Bergson, Henri. (1911). *Creative Evolution*. Arthur Mitchell, Henry Holt and Company

10. Luke 17:20 -21

CHAPTER 18

1. Grosso, Michael, (2015). "The 'Transmission' Model of Mind and Body: A Brief History," in *Beyond Physicalism*. Edited by Edward Kelly, Adam Crabtree, and Paul Marshall, pp 79-115

2. Masters, Robert Augustus, Robert. (2010). *Spiritual Bypassing. When Spirituality Disconnects Us from What Really Matters*. North Atlantic Books, p. 1

3. Wilber, Ken., et al. (2008). *Integral Life Practice. A 21st Century Blueprint for Physical Health, Emotional Balance, Mental Clarity, and Spiritual Awakening*. Integral Books, p. 86

4. Goswami, Amit, (1993). *The Self-Aware Universe. How Consciousness Creates the Material World*. New York: Penguin Putnam Inc., p. 208

5. See Stephen Taylor, *Out of Darkness*

6. Rosicrucians, A.M.O.R.C. (1970). *Meditation. Its Technique*. Department of Publications. San Jose, CA

7. James, W. (1936). *The Varieties of Religious Experience: A Study in Human Nature*. New York

8. Gallup, G, Jr., & Jones, T. (2000). *The Next American Spirituality: Finding God in the Twenty-First Century.* Colorado Springs, CO: Cook Communications

9. Swami Vivekananda. (1902). *Jnana-Yoga. The Yoga of Knowledge.* Advaith Ashrama Publication department. 5 Deh, Entally Road, Kolkata 700014

10. Carrera, Jacanath, Rev. (2006). *Inside the Yoga Sutras. A Comprehensive Sourcebook for the Study and Practice of Pantanjali's Yoga Sutras.* Buckingham, Virginia: Integral Yoga Publications

11. Wilber, Ken., (2000). *A Brief History of Everything.* Shambhala Publications, Inc., p. 35

12. See Yalom. *Existential Psychotherapy*, p. 422

13. See Wilber, *A Brief History of Everything*, p. 287

CHAPTER 19

1. Cytowic, Richard, E. (1989). *Synesthesia. A Union of the Senses.* Springer-Verlag

2. Ibid., p. 235

3. Orloff, Judith. (1997). *Second Sight.* Grand Central Publishing

4. Spanos, N. P. et al. (1991). "Secondary Identity Enactments During Hypnotic Past-Life Regression," *Journal of Personality and Social Psychology,* 61, pp. 308-320

5. Woolger, Roger. (1987). *Other Lives, Other Selves.* New York: Doubleday

CHAPTER 20

1. Kornfield, Jack. (2002). *After the Ecstasy, the Laundry.* Bantam Books

2. White, R. A. (1993b). *Working Classification of EHE's. Exceptional Human Experience.* Background Papers. 1, 11, pp. 149-150

3. Sri Aurobindo. (1962). *The Future Evolution of Man.* Twin Lakes, WI: Lotus Press

4. Krishna, Gopi. (1974). *Higher Consciousness and Kundalini.* Published by the Kundalini Research Foundation, Ltd.

5. Metzner, Ralph. (1986). *The Unfolding Self.* Ross, California: Pioneer Imprints

About the Author

 FRANK PASCIUTI, Ph.D. is a licensed clinical psychologist and certified hypnotherapist in private practice in Charlottesville, Virginia. He is founder and president of the Associated Clinicians of Virginia, a group that provides psychotherapy and organizational development services to individuals and businesses. Dr. Pasciuti is chairman of the Institutional Review Board (IRB) at The Monroe Institute in Faber, Virginia, and he collaborates on research related to NDEs, psychic phenomena, and the survival of consciousness at the Division of Perceptual Studies, a research unit of the department of Psychiatry and Neurobehavioral Sciences at the University of Virginia School of Medicine.

Rainbow Ridge Books publishes spiritual, metaphysical,
and self-help titles, and is distributed by Square
One Publishers in Garden City Park, New York.

To contact authors and editors, peruse our titles,
and see submission guidelines, please visit
our website at www.rainbowridgebooks.com.

For orders and catalogs, please
call toll-free: (877) 900-BOOK.